Praise for *Old-Fashioned on Purpose*

"This book will inspire you to reconsider how you're spending your days and help you reconnect with what matters most."
—Erin Benzakein, founder of Floret

"Partially a memoir, partially an inspirational primer, partially dispelling the myth of the highly curated Instagrammable homestead, but 100% honest, Jill tells it how it is—chicken poop, cow manure and all. As they say, cream always rises to the top, and Jill is the prime example of this."
—Lisa Steele, creator of *Fresh Eggs Daily*

"In a world where so many of us are craving a life of simplicity and meaning, *Old-Fashioned on Purpose* gives you the roadmap to rediscovering what really matters."
—Hal Elrod, bestselling author of *The Miracle Morning* and *The Miracle Equation*

"An essential must-read resource for anyone whose mind, body, and spirit are craving a healthier way of life."
—Julie Cantrell, bestselling author of *Perennials*

"An important read for anyone who wants to reclaim a richer and more hands-on life today."
—Michael Easter, author of *The Comfort Crisis* and *Scarcity Brain*

"Filled to the brim with inspirational, yet relatable stories, [and] seasoned with homesteading tips throughout."
—Justin Rhodes, YouTuber and author of *The Rooted Life*

Also by Jill Winger

The Prairie Homestead Cookbook

Old-Fashioned
On Purpose

—— A Homesteading Manifesto ——

JILL WINGER

PARK
ROW
BOOKS

PARK
ROW ™
BOOKS™

Recycling programs
for this product may
not exist in your area.

ISBN-13: 978-0-7783-1092-1

Old-Fashioned on Purpose: A Homesteading Manifesto

First published in 2023. This edition published in 2025 with revised text.

Park Row Books
22 Adelaide St. West, 41st Floor
Toronto, Ontario M5H 4E3, Canada
ParkRowBooks.com

Printed in U.S.A.

For those willing to ask bold questions of the world

Old-Fashioned
On Purpose

TABLE OF CONTENTS

FOREWORD

BY RORY FEEK

I've known Jill Winger for a few years now. First, I knew her as the writer of a popular homesteading blog that my wife and I visited often for tips on gardening and cooking. Then, a few years later, she appeared out of thin air in our kitchen—or at least her face did on the cover of *The Prairie Homestead Cookbook*—as she guided us through many wonderful home-cooked recipes and meals. Finally, in the fall of 2019, we met in person at a homesteading conference in Virginia. I listened to her talk in front of thousands of folks who'd traveled from all over the country to learn skills and wisdom that have sadly stopped being passed down generationally, and I walked away inspired.

Over the next couple of years, I visited the Wingers' home a few times on our way to and from Montana. Why she and her husband, Christian, would pick what seems to be the absolute hardest place to homestead in the country, I'm not sure. But my guess is, like most of us, they decided they had found a home and made a go of it. And season by season, year by year, she and her family have coaxed not only vegetables, pasture-raised beef, and an amazing life from the ground they live on, but they've done it publicly—always with a hand stretched out, helping and encouraging others on their homesteading journey.

Eventually, she would make trips to our farm and speak at events that we hosted here, and I've been so blessed not only to get to know Jill and her family on a deeper level, but also to learn much about what comprises the book you are holding in your hands.

This past fall, Jill called and asked if I would write the foreword for *Old-Fashioned on Purpose*. I told her I'd be honored to, and a few weeks later, her manuscript came in the mail. Two hundred and twenty-five pages, printed on white paper, for me to read the old-fashioned way—which was perfect, because I was personally in the middle of a yearlong hiatus from the web.

As I now move into the eighth month of my internet-free year, I have just finished reading the manuscript. From the first page to the last, this book she's written reminds me why I'm taking the break that I'm taking. Not only that, but it challenges me to consider digging even deeper into the good life that I've discovered the last dozen or so years here at our farm.

This book is filled with wisdom and truth from cover to cover. Jill has the spirit and work ethic of a pioneer, but the patience and heart of a teacher. Her passion to do the hard things that make our lives better, and to help others do the same, fills every page.

Old-Fashioned on Purpose is for the homesteader in all of us. Whether you are a newcomer just now discovering the joy of sowing seeds in the soil and baking your first loaf of sourdough bread or have been at it awhile and are questioning everything that the world has told—and sold—us for the last few decades, you are on the path of reclaiming your precious time and attention.

This book also resonated deeply with me on a personal level. Now in my late fifties, I am constantly looking back to see what I can glean from those who came before me. I yearn to seek wisdom from days and people of old, who, though had lived through times much harder than our own, seemed to have more fulfilling lives.

From Part 1—where Jill makes her case for why we need to consider being "old-fashioned on purpose"—to Part 2—where she breaks it down and shows us how to do just that—the information in this book is life-changing. Jill reminds readers that in all of us, no matter where we are in life or in the world, is the power to grow, to cook, to work, to unplug, and to find community. Following this is the peace that comes from striving for something more than "more."

Filled with how-tos and, just as importantly, why-tos, *Old-Fashioned on Purpose* is a life spring of health and hope in a time when what we need most doesn't begin with "insta" or "face," but instead begins with us. It begins with the garden, the kitchen, and the table, and with getting our families to slow down and sit for a while. It begins with not just eating the bounty that God has provided for us, but also knowing that we have taken part in the process ourselves.

It's easy to see that our lives are clearly much easier today than they were a hundred or so years ago, but I don't believe that they are better.

Like Jill, I am unabashedly old-fashioned on purpose, and it has made my life all the richer. This book has given me much to think about and much to put into practice as I step into the new frontier.

—*Rory Feek*

INTRODUCTION

There's something rippling through humanity right now. It's not a trend, but a craving. A longing. A remembering. A sense that we are more capable than we've been led to believe. A whisper that there could be another path—one that's less traveled, but brimming with possibilities that make us feel awake, not sedated. It's not the first time this stirring has visited us—it appears whenever society threatens to lose its moorings. Whenever we become so whipped into a frenzy by fear, panic, or turmoil that we lose our way, this still, small voice taps us on the shoulder and prompts us to pause. To return to the things that matter. To ground ourselves in the rhythms of the earth. To remember from whence we came. It appeared during the Great Depression as financial chaos pushed thousands to the country. It occurred in the 1970s when societal unrest and the Vietnam War spurred the back-to-the-land movement. And it's happening again at this very moment.

I started feeling these tugs as a little girl, but I didn't know what to do with them. After all, the old-fashioned notions that visited my imagination weren't rational. They weren't accepted. And they certainly weren't *normal*. But fourteen years ago, I finally heeded their call. As a result, I now live a peculiar hybrid life. On one hand, I'm probably not much different than any other modern mom of three. A robot vacuums my floors. My online business relies on high-tech apps and software. And I listen to audiobooks while I drive my kids to basketball practice.

Yet… I also dig potatoes for supper from my backyard. My basement is lined with jars of food I've grown and canned myself. I capture wild yeast, ferment cabbage on my kitchen counters, cure hams, and render lard for piecrusts. I also know how to butcher a chicken, ride a horse, tamp a fence post, build a fire, and create my own soap.

These old-fashioned parts of my life would hardly have been worth mentioning a century ago, but in the age of virtual reality, cryptocurrencies, and Uber Eats, they seem wild and revolutionary. I didn't grow up practicing most of these retro skills, but they're second nature to me now. The thought of an existence without farm animals, barn chores, and ever-present kitchen projects rarely crosses my mind.

Each year I take stock of our life and ask myself, *"Should we continue?"*

"Do these vintage ways still serve us?"

"Are these pursuits worth the extra time they take?"

And each year, the answer is a resounding YES. But not for the most obvious reasons. Sure, I love the taste of crisp garden veggies, the scent of freshly cut hay, the sound of roosters in the morning, and the sight of my kids running through the barnyard.

But that's not why I continue. Rather, I persevere in these heritage skills because they're much more than the sum of their parts.

I forge ahead for the rewards that stretch beyond what I can taste, touch, and see. This lifestyle grounds me when the world feels like a whirlwind. It offers meditation during chaos, a healthy dose of adventure, and a quiet confidence born from trusting your abilities. These time-honored practices remind me of what truly matters. And I reach for them whenever I'm craving balance and solace.

Over the decades, this idea of returning to the land and our roots has been given a variety of titles, but I've never loved any of them. I've used the term "homesteading" for years, but believe it or not, it gets muddied by the idea that participants can still find free land (the Homestead Act was repealed in 1976) or that a modern homesteader must live off-grid or own hundreds of acres. None of these assumptions are true. It's time for a better definition.

For me, this is a mindset. It's about stripping away the baggage of our modern lives, recognizing the problems of progress, moving through this world with intention, resisting rampant consumerism, living lightly and consciously, and being rooted in community. If I could give everyone five acres and a milk cow, I would. But that's not possible. And honestly? It's not even necessary. This is a mentality that anyone can adopt, no matter where they live. It has absolutely nothing to do with how much land you own or what types of farm animals you keep.

So what *should* we call it?

I like the term "old-fashioned on purpose" for several reasons. To me, "old-fashioned" doesn't mean out of date or out of touch. Rather, it's a clue that something of value is just under the surface, waiting to be discovered. Our family, and others like us, aren't old-fashioned because we don't know any better…or because it's our only option…or because we resist change…or because a particular social or religious circle has conditioned us to avoid mainstream culture. Instead, this is a conscious choice we've made to reclaim meaningful ideas that have been discarded in the name of progress and restore them to a place of value in our modern day-to-day.

This process will look radically different depending on each person's situation, but regardless of how you make this shift, it has the potential to change your life, just like it has mine.

The homestead remains my greatest teacher. The epiphanies it's granted me continue to shape every part of my perspective. Throughout the following pages, I'll distill down the most impactful lessons I've gleaned so you can make them your own. In Part 1, we'll dissect the past to discover how we got off track as a culture and find clues to help us move forward. In Part 2, we'll weave the past with the present by identifying the eight principles of the old-fashioned on purpose lifestyle that you can adopt no matter where you live. We'll dive into the *how* of growing your own ingredients, cooking from scratch, working with your hands, stepping away from the synthetic, unplugging from technology, caring for the earth, fostering independence in our children, and cultivating community, but more importantly, we'll discuss the *why*. While the technical aspects of these skills are important, it's this deeper intention that will sustain you when challenges arise. The *why* transforms these quaint practices into life-changing propositions. And that's when the magic truly begins. So if you've felt curious about how things used to be, disenchanted with the complexities of modern life, or just strangely drawn to sourdough bread, you're in exactly the right place.

PART 1

The Case for
Old-Fashioned on Purpose

CHAPTER 1

You're Not Alone

Sometimes I think of myself as a "reverse pioneer." Like the original pioneers, I'm headed into the unknown. But while they trekked west in search of opportunities that would usher in the future, I'm going the opposite direction—back to the past.

Like most pioneers, I was met with skepticism when I started my journey. Initially, I didn't know a soul who shared my fascination for churning butter and growing tomatoes. I learned to smile and ignore the comments: *"You're making homemade yogurt? Is that even safe?"*

"Be careful! Canning gives you food poisoning."

"They sell all of that at the store, you know…"

People weren't trying to be negative; they simply couldn't fathom why I'd want to go to all the trouble of reviving these outdated practices. To be fair, I didn't fully grasp the enormity of what I was doing, either. I just knew the gardens and kitchen kept calling to me, so I kept listening. Those early years were exhilarating, yet lonely.

But times have changed.

Over the past few years, backyard chicken coops have become a status symbol of sorts. Real estate listings boast the "homesteading potential" of various properties. "Farm to fork" restaurants are considered fine dining, and consumers are attracted to anything labeled "farm fresh" or "farmhouse chic."

Somehow, I've gone from being the lone pioneer on the fringe to sitting on the front lines of a movement. My inboxes are filled to the brim with people asking for help with their milk cows and compost and garden planning. It's amazing and…shocking.

But it's not hard to figure out why all things farm are experiencing a renaissance, especially right now. Even in a world run by mind-boggling technology, the farm still represents simplicity and security—two things we need more than ever in this complex cultural moment. Some shrug off this renewed interest in old-fashioned living as a passing fad, but I know it's more than that.

When COVID-19 hit in early 2020, this fascination with retro skills reached a fever pitch. During one of the biggest societal upheavals in recent history, people sought a sense of stability by returning to long-lost, age-old traditions. Who would have thought?

Sourdough bread became the hottest new craze as flour flew off supermarket shelves. Pressure cookers and canning lids were back-ordered, and chicks became impossible to find in feed stores as thousands of suburbanites rushed to build backyard coops. Even seed companies sold their entire year's worth of stock in mere weeks as families across the country planted their very first vegetable gardens.

Something inside of us recognized that these time-honored ideas were exactly what we needed during this shaky season. It was as if baking bread and planting seeds brought to the surface longings that had been buried deep within our DNA all along.

And therein lies our first clue to the origins of this old-fashioned revival.

Though years have passed since the first waves of the pandemic, the cracks in society's foundational systems remain exposed. By recognizing the fragility of our modern culture, many people have shifted from asking "How can I perfect my sourdough starter?" to "Is this synthetic lifestyle truly how we're meant to live?"

Perhaps these are the very thoughts and questions that prompted you to pick up this book. Maybe these soul-level yearnings have visited your subconscious through daydreams, as they've whispered intriguing yet improbable ideas in your ear. Maybe you've been fostering a sourdough starter on your counter and have found joy in caring for the spontaneous life that emerges from the unlikely mixture of flour and water. Maybe you've secretly thumbed through the local real estate listings browsing the "farms for sale." Maybe you've even gone as far as to contemplate bringing honeybees or chickens to your suburban backyard. Perhaps your quest for sourdough bread and your questions of life's deeper purpose are more related than you think.

If so, you're far from the only one feeling like this. Most everyone I know is wrestling with modern culture in their own way.

In countless conversations, people have shared with me that they deeply crave stillness and simplicity, but can't seem to grasp them amid frantic schedules.

Others feel disconnected from their relatives, companions, and local communities, even though they have thousands of "friends" on Facebook.

Many of us struggle with chronic disease and unhealthy bodies, but feel helpless to avoid the processed, industrial foods that are making us sicker by the day.

So many parents feel lost in knowing how to steer their children away from screens as they battle their own urge to check their devices constantly.

And many of us secretly wonder…what would it be like to break free and write our own life's story, instead of falling into place as a cog in someone else's machine?

The edges of modernity are beginning to fray, and perhaps it's time to pull on the thread. Not enough to unravel it completely, but enough to expose the treasures that have been buried under the musty layers of industrialism for far too long.

Whether spoken or not, we share a sense that something is off-kilter. Is this modern reality how it was truly meant to be? But making a break from the accepted societal path seems a pipe dream at best. Our conditioning to stay with the herd is strong. We wrestle and reflect at times. But when we glance around and notice that everyone else appears to be content with the status quo, we dismiss our stirrings and march on. Conforming. Following the unspoken rules. Doing what we're expected to do. All the while longing for something different, something simpler, something more meaningful.

There is no shortage of advice to help one create a more "intentional life." The gurus suggest deep breathing to create more mental stillness, time-tracking apps to increase intentionality, gratitude journaling to cultivate more appreciation, meditation to quell a busy mind, taking long walks to connect with nature, and the list goes on and on and on.

All are solid ideas (I could do better with my deep breathing), but none of these has been the answer to my own longings. Instead, I've found stillness amid my garden rows, weeding and primping as the light sinks into the west and the crickets begin their song. I've cultivated intention by plunging my fingers into the compost-rich soil to plant seeds that would grow to nourish my family. I've developed a deep appreciation for ordinary things as I've pondered the way the sun filters through the prairie grasses at dusk or relished how much more delightful food tastes when you make it yourself. I've noticed that when I pause to let the crisp air fill my lungs after a summer rain, my racing mind slows. I've found connection to nature by not shying away from the elements, by embracing the way the air hangs heavy on my skin as a thunderstorm builds or bites at my face when a snow squall blows through the prairie.

> **The more I turned to these old-fashioned practices, the more intensely I was able to connect with what truly matters. It's an awakening to the new and a returning to the old, somehow rolled into one.**

The more I turned to these old-fashioned practices, the more intensely I was able to connect with what truly matters. It's an awakening to the new and a returning to the old, somehow rolled into one. I still can't explain how you can return to something you've never had before, but you'll know it when you feel it. Even though I wasn't born into this lifestyle, it felt like home as soon as I discovered it. And while details of our stories will be different, you'll likely see glimmers of your own path in my journey.

Three Stages of Awakening

If you're reading this book because you're feeling restless with your current life, you're in good company. These stirrings are often a beacon pointing to where you're truly meant to be. Don't shy away from them. This restlessness is a sign that it's time to try something different. Through hundreds of conversations over the years, I've noticed the same three stages of awakening in each of the people I've talked to. In this book, I'll guide you through the first two stages, but then, the third is up to you.

First, there is the **reckoning**. This is when you come to terms with the emptiness you've been feeling—when you allow yourself to say it out loud for the first time. This is the moment when you finally give yourself permission to accept that you want something more— something deeper. This is a pivotal step because most people are never honest or aware enough to admit they're miserable. It feels scary to admit it at first, but we must acknowledge where we are before we can change our path.

Next comes the **research**. You're ready for something different, but what does that mean? Are there alternatives to the standard American lifestyle? Are these old-fashioned ideas even plausible? Are we ridiculous for even considering this?

And finally, the **return**—this is your shaky exodus into the unknown. The return can be small (teaching yourself how to make soap) or big (buying five acres), but regardless, this stage is my favorite. You'll move forward with a sparkle in your eyes and a newfound sense of pride. This phase is full of imperfect yet decisive action. And it will change your life.

My Unlikely Journey to the Homestead

My shift from city girl to prairie woman began in an unassuming neighborhood in the Pacific Northwest, twelve hundred miles away from the wide-open spaces I now call home. Since I was a little girl, I've carried an inexplicable longing for rural life. I suppose that's not too unusual, except for the fact that I grew up on a cul-de-sac in North Idaho and not a farm or ranch. My infatuation with farm life seemed to come out of nowhere— as if it was a remnant imprinted on me from generations past.

While other girls dreamed of Barbie houses, bikes, and party dresses, I fixated on the day I would move to the country and own a piece of land. One aspect of country living captured my imagination more than the others: horses. Many kids go through a horse phase at some point—parents think it's cute for a while, and then they expect the child to move on to other interests. But I couldn't. Since the age of three, I unapologetically nurtured a world-class equine obsession, and I had no desire to give it up. Ever. (Still don't.) It wasn't a great way to make friends, but my obsessions overrode my desire to fit in (a personality trait that would serve me well in years to come).

Despite my sales pitches to move to a property with land for horses to roam, my parents were content living on their sub-division lot. I did the best I could to adapt. I amassed a herd of model horses, drew endless plans of what my farm would look like one day, enrolled in a local 4-H club for members who didn't have horses, and even pushed a wheelbarrow around the yard, pretending I was mucking stalls.

When I turned fourteen, my parents caved to a decade of begging, and *it happened.* With the money I had saved up from my babysitting jobs (plus a little help from my grandfather), I became the proud owner of Jake, a retired hunting horse. He was a gelding in his golden years, with a swayback and frizzy mane, but for me it was love at first sight.

We boarded Jake in a friend's pasture a few miles away from our neighborhood, and I rode him almost every day. I took a job mucking stalls at a local stable and proudly paid for every piece of tack, every vet visit, and every bale of hay myself. I rejoined 4-H (this time in the group for kids *with* horses) and, through the opportunities I was afforded there, realized horses could become my career. After shopping around for the best horse college, I was accepted into an equine studies program at a small community college in Wyoming. At the age of eighteen, I packed everything I owned into the back of my Ford F-150 and set off on my first grand adventure.

In a chance encounter at the college arena one day, I met Christian, an electrician working in the early mornings to wire a new sound system at the facility. As fate would have it, I worked in the arena each morning before class. One of my main jobs was scraping cow manure that had been left behind after roping practice the night before. (Anyone want to turn that into a rom-com meet-cute? Call me.) Christian was impressed that I wasn't afraid to get my hands dirty, and I was impressed that he knew how to build stuff. Construction projects and cow manure. Little did I know it was an indication of life to come. We were married eighteen months later.

While not horse-obsessed like me, Christian had also grown up in the city with a desire for something more. We still didn't know exactly what "more" entailed, but we couldn't stomach the thought of dutifully joining the rat race. Letting our childhood dreams guide us, we decided our first step away from "normal" would be to buy a starter home that included acreage. We committed to living on a shoestring budget to save for a down payment, and waited for the timing to be right.

Two years later, on a Saturday evening in late May 2008, I opened my computer to do a quick real estate search for rural properties. In a matter of minutes, I found a listing located a handful of miles from the home we were renting at the time. I phoned the real estate agent as early as politeness would allow the next morning and begged him to show it to us on a Sunday.

I'll never forget stepping onto that property for the first time. The strangest sensation radiated through my body. I had felt it before, but never this intense. It was the feeling of possibility. Excitement. Inspiration. Knowing.

What sort of amazing property could possibly cause such electric chills?

Picture this: A squatty nine-hundred-square-foot shack covered in yellow plastic siding. (Later, the neighbors would gleefully relay to us that a miniature horse had lived inside the house for a while.) A washing machine in the front yard (with moldy clothes inside). A decaying sheep shed (painted yellow to match the siding color—except it didn't). And broken fence lines as far as the eye could see.

This wasn't a picture-perfect farmstead by any stretch of the imagination. It was unkempt, unloved, and a monument to decades of neglect. But this was *it*. This place, in all its ugly glory, had been waiting for us. I could feel in my gut that it was meant to be a part of our story, even though I didn't yet understand why. Thankfully, Christian felt it, too. We raced home and put in an offer that the seller accepted immediately.

Our eclectic choice of a starter home raised some eyebrows, but Christian and I never doubted it was right for us. We'd taken our first substantial detour off the well-trodden life path, and we were feeling giddy. We had no idea where the rest of this adventure would lead, but it felt good for now.

As we prepared to move into the run-down farmhouse, I was struck with a glimmer of inspiration: *What if* we could make our new purchase productive by growing some food on our land? It was a desperate attempt to rationalize our irrational purchase. But for some reason, the idea stuck, even though the extent of my food knowledge at the time went as far as Cool Whip, Velveeta, and Kraft Mac & Cheese. It didn't matter that we had no idea what we were doing. We looked at those sixty-seven acres and figured we had plenty of room to grow a few vegetables and maybe even raise a steer for beef.

That settled it. Making productive use of the land felt like a logical, "grown-up" way to make the most of our impulse buy. We moved into the ramshackle home, and the school of life commenced.

I have many fond memories from our early days on the property, but there were plenty of hard-earned lessons, too. Our property had potential, but that potential was buried under thousands of pounds of trash. Every fence line needed to be rebuilt. Every building needed a new roof, updated windows, and a fresh coat of paint. A waist-deep sea of junk filled every outbuilding, and rusty metal littered the pasture. By the time we were done trash collecting, the debris filled a total of six (!) construction dumpsters. We sacrificed weekends and vacations to tackle the renovations, and every spare dollar was spent on fencing, painting, roofing, building, landscaping, and cleaning. During these never-ending projects, we quickly realized that no one was coming to do the work for us. When the power went out or a wall of snow blocked the driveway, it was all on us. Our remote location made us low priority for services, so we had to have our own backs.

And so, our little homestead became the ultimate proving ground. Would we have appreciated each small victory as much if we had started with the quintessential farm? I don't think so. There's a unique sort of pride that comes from walking through the fire, the blood, the sweat, and the mud, and knowing you proved yourself worthy of the challenge. Those early years built confidence, resilience, and grit. For that, I will always be grateful.

Little by little, each bit of painstaking progress confirmed we were on the right track. We'd drag ourselves into the house each night exhausted and sore, but deeply satisfied. Our passion for homesteading wasn't dampened by the long hours and tedious projects—it grew, especially as we were able to shift from cleanup mode to building mode.

With the first phase of cleanup done, we could now start on the infrastructure we had been dreaming about. First up? A set of compost bins, which we constructed from old boards we'd salvaged. I'd never composted a thing in my life and was enamored the first time I sifted rich black compost through my fingers. Our humble spark of an idea was igniting into a roaring flame.

One needs a garden to make use of compost, so that was next. Surprisingly, we couldn't find traces of an existing garden plot anywhere on the property, so we started with a blank slate. I selected a rectangular area of prairie grass on the edge of the yard, and Christian borrowed a friend's rototiller to work the soil. We spent weeks extricating the trash that seemed to grow overnight (anyone who owns an old property will relate). Nails, tin cans, wire, and random bits of plastic were our first harvest. Then we covered the soil with our homemade compost, planted seeds, and finally reaped the first edible crop of squash, beans, beets, and carrots a few months later.

Yet as thrilling as it was to build the inaugural compost piles, haul in wheelbarrow-loads of squash from the garden, and drive home from town with baby chicks chirping in a crate, there was one aspect of our new lifestyle that kept me coming back for more. I couldn't ignore the deep satisfaction that would engulf me whenever I learned a new skill. I had never experienced anything like it before.

The first time I made a batch of from-scratch tortillas, I was on top of the world.

The moment I brought in the first eggs from our humble flock of hens? Utter ecstasy.

The evening when we sat down to a meal grown entirely on our property, from the seeds we'd planted and the animals we had raised, I walked on air for at least twenty-four hours afterward.

I had experienced fleeting glimpses of this joy here and there, but it now engulfed me. The world had opened, and I was seeing it in color for the first time. On the one hand, it felt totally illogical—I couldn't understand why adopting a collection of odd, old-fashioned practices was making my heart pound with excitement. But on the other hand, it felt perfectly right.

Okay... I admit I'm painting a pretty romantic picture here, so now allow me to be candid for a moment. Anyone who follows me online knows I like to keep it real. (I once posted a picture of the sticky fly strip hanging from the ceiling in my kitchen on Instagram—I hold nothing back.) Lest you think it was all rainbows and butterflies, I assure you we've experienced plenty of trials, frustrations, and crippling moments of self-doubt along the way. Our budget was tight at the beginning, and for years we struggled to scrape together enough pennies to complete our projects. (Project rationing isn't nearly as fun as it sounds.)

And then there were the heart-wrenching losses. We've lost entire gardens to hailstorms, fought in vain to save newborn calves during raging blizzards, and delivered stillborn baby goats in the middle of the night…not to mention the negativity we've faced along the way from those who don't understand our choice of lifestyle. This path, as wondrous, intoxicating, and satisfying as it is, has rarely been easy. Yet through the hardships, our conviction remains: it's worth it. And we'd choose it all again in a heartbeat. Why? Because the lessons have been priceless—and not just the ones about fences, compost, and livestock.

One of the most pivotal moments in the early days of our homesteading journey happened during a family gathering. I was eight and a half months pregnant with our first child. Christian's extended family was hosting a mini-reunion on a Saturday afternoon, so we decided to make the trek to Colorado one last time before the baby arrived. However, unlike most prospective parents, we brought a trailer-load of goats with us.

I had been obsessively reading homestead books for many months prior and had concluded that dairy goats were the logical next step in our journey toward self-sufficiency. On a mission to eradicate processed foods from our diet, pasteurized, homogenized, store-bought milk would no longer suffice. However, at the time, it was illegal to purchase milk straight from a cow or goat in Wyoming. If I were to possess this highly celebrated raw milk, I'd have to collect it from my own livestock.

We weren't quite ready for the responsibilities of a milk cow (I'd never milked anything in my life), so dairy goats were a natural next choice. It made perfect sense to purchase said goats before our baby arrived. I mean, what new mother doesn't have dairy goats on her baby registry? (Did I mention they were also pregnant and due several days after I was?)

I had found a pair of Nubian goats for sale about an hour from our house. Ever the efficient one, I decided that picking them up the day of the family barbecue was the smartest plan, as it would save us time and gas money (neither of which was ours to spare). Once we arrived at the cookout, we parked our trailer alongside the curb of the neighborhood, leaving our newly ac- quired goats to hang out while we visited with family.

It was in that moment that it became very clear to everyone that we were in deep. They couldn't fathom why we were going to such extreme lengths to grow food. This entire scenario felt incredibly reckless, especially to my former rule-following self, who'd spent my life thus far trying to avoid making waves. Not only was I hauling a pair of screaming goats (Nubians are in- credibly loud) around a well-manicured suburban neighbor- hood, but they were soon to be my source of forbidden fresh milk that the government said I shouldn't drink. I had no idea what was happening to me, but I liked it. Even as some loved ones voiced kind concerns.

It was one of the first times I realized our lives would no longer be "normal." Up to that point, my homesteading activi- ties had been slightly less outlandish, but once you haul preg- nant dairy goats to a barbecue, there's no tucking that absurdity back in.

What I didn't realize at the time is that as I moved further away from the conventional path, I was becoming more authen- tically me. My awakening was in full swing. I would never be the same. That initial goat escapade was an important lesson I would call on again and again: how others see my dreams and aspirations doesn't have to change how I see them. I was taking charge of my own life—the successes, failures, limiting beliefs—Nubian goats and all.

I share this story because it captures the intricacies of what I've learned from homesteading. As we return to our roots through the physical, we also fulfill an intrinsic craving in the human spirit: the need to grow, to produce, to create, to work hard at things that matter, and to be masters of our fate.

As a result, what starts with a reconnection to the external world culminates in humans who are more centered, balanced, and whole on the inside, too. The fresh bread and the colorful eggs hook us, but the deep sense of meaning keeps us coming back for more.

So there I was, a twenty-four-year-old making my own compost, tending chickens, milking goats, and planting a vegetable garden like a Great Depression grandma. My skills expanded and my confidence grew, along with the calluses on my hands, but a deeper transformation was happening as well. As we restored the farmstead, I was experiencing my own *restoration*. For the first time in my life, I possessed a true sense of belonging, both to myself and to this land.

There was just one problem: I couldn't stop talking about it.

I had an insatiable urge to share what I was learning with someone. *Anyone.* I couldn't keep it to myself any longer. These old-fashioned practices aren't meant to happen in a vacuum—they beg to be shared. But no one in my immediate circles cared to hear my ramblings about compost, organic gardening, and raw milk. (And who could blame them, I suppose.)

I may not have had a lot of friends at the time, but I did have a laptop and an internet connection. So I started a blog. I called it *The Prairie Homestead* and typed out my thoughts, revelations, and struggles from my kitchen island while our newborn baby took naps. I had a readership of about ten people back then, but it was cathartic to put words to my passion.

One day I received a message from a friend on Facebook. She said she had been reading my posts and felt so inspired by what we were doing that she hoped to someday follow in our footsteps. Stop. The. Presses. You mean I *wasn't* the only one? There was someone else (under the age of eighty) who wanted chickens and vegetables and dairy goats? I stared at the screen in disbelief. Her confession may not seem all that shocking in the context of today, but this was 2010. Backyard chicken-keeping was hardly commonplace. Shopping for canning jars was an agonizing scavenger hunt, and I didn't know a soul who made sauerkraut or homemade yogurt. I had started to believe I was the only one with such strange interests.

But from that moment on, everything shifted. My writing on the blog became less self-serving and more about bringing others along for the ride as I shared recipes, tutorials, and old-fashioned ideas people could try on their own. I began to attract a community of like-minded people, and my own knowledge grew as we learned from each other and shared our discoveries.

Now I fondly think back to those early years and marvel at how times have changed. Not only has the homesteading movement exploded, but my little website has grown as well. *The Prairie Homestead* (and accompanying podcast, social media, and YouTube channel) now collectively reaches over a million people each month. It's become my family's full-time business and has created more joy and opportunity than I could have ever fathomed back when I was typing out blog posts in the kitchen while my babies slept.

My original blog is still going strong! And I've put together a special set of printable resources just for readers of this book. You can find them here: www.theprairiehomestead.com/oldfashioned.

In that time, these homesteading practices began to feel comfortable and familiar, but my passion for them has deepened as I've witnessed their power firsthand, not only in myself, but also in others who have embarked on their own old-fashioned pilgrimages.

Now It's Your Turn

The age-old principles we're about to explore aren't limited to my family's experiences. I didn't invent them, and they existed long before homesteading became trendy. They are common themes throughout history, science, literature, and even philosophy. In my life (and possibly yours, too), they just happen to show up in a "homesteading" wrapper. But when you start to look, you'll find them everywhere—and they are ripe for the taking, regardless of your age, your income, or your location. When you distill it all down, these practices are simply helping us recapture what we've lost in our rush toward technology, convenience, and modernity.

In a sense, I'm writing this book for the girl I was back in the early days of this journey; the young newlywed standing dreamy-eyed in the middle of a dilapidated property. The one who knew in her gut there was a healthier balance than the typical modern lifestyle, but who didn't yet know how to achieve it. The one who couldn't stand the thought of settling for something less than she knew was possible. The one who was scared to be bold, but felt an old, forgotten path calling to her nonetheless.

This book offers the message I wish I had been given then: "You're on the right track. Keep going."

Sometimes all we need is to know we're not alone. And friend, I can assure you of this—if you're feeling the nudge to step away from the conventional path and build a more meaningful way of life, you are in very good company. But before we pull on our work boots, it's important that we ask some questions to understand how we got here in the first place. Let's take a quick trip back to the past.

CHAPTER 2

Returning to Our Roots

Here in rural Wyoming, the victims of progress punctuate the corners of our remote community. Weathered barns decay in silence, flanked by rusted farm implements and crumbling outbuildings. Stucco houses stare vacantly into the grasslands, their foundations rotting beneath shattered windows. Slabs of concrete and leaning fence posts are swallowed by the earth as the prairie reclaims her territory.

Of course, these empty farmhouses and shrinking agricultural spaces aren't unique to my community. Prior to the Civil War, more than half of the US population lived on farms. Today that number is less than 2 percent. Our agrarian roots have faded into history as our culture shifts from a world anchored on soil and grass to one built on concrete and asphalt.

When I drive by these abandoned farmsteads, I slow my car and take in as many details as possible. At 30 mph, my imagination wanders. Was there joy in that house? Or tragedy? What kind of milk cow did they have? Did their children climb the trees or play in the barn? Did the sweeping expanse of the plains take their breath away like it does mine? Or did they cuss the relentless wind and wish for a different life? My unanswered questions are testaments to an era that is rapidly disappearing from our collective memory.

Of all the skills I've gained from my homesteading journey,

the ability to ask good questions is at the top of the list. Questions lead us down paths we didn't know existed and shake the foundations of what we think is possible. Questions are power. Digging deep used to make me squeamish (What if one of my tightly held beliefs can't hold up to questioning?!), but the truth sets us free. Over the years, my quest for answers has only ever provided me more clarity and confidence, even though the process often makes me uncomfortable at first.

So I keep asking juicy questions—both of myself and of the world around me. And one of my favorite questions is *why*:

"Why did this happen?"

"Why do we do it like this now?"

"Why did we change?"

"Why do I believe this to be true?"

As I fell head over heels for this old-fashioned life, one question in particular kept bugging me: "Why on earth did our ancestors ever leave this way of life behind?"

At first, I thought I knew the answer. After all, every history book and documentary I'd ever consumed had gleefully highlighted the hardships of pre-modern life. "No air-conditioning, running water, cars, or grocery stores... Can you imagine?" they'd proclaim. Perhaps life was so miserable that people couldn't wait to abandon it at the first glimmer of progress.

While it seemed obvious, as I gained more understanding from historical writings, I realized it wasn't that cut-and-dried. Life was certainly harder in the past, but there's ample evidence that people understood the value of what they had. In 1806, one author wrote that crowded cities "may be justly reckoned unnatural" when compared to the pleasures of rural life. Eighteenth-century poets spoke of the noble alchemy of agriculture and how it transformed the earth into gold. And even after the dawn of the twentieth century, while many Americans were flooding into cities, homesteaders out west were celebrating the freedom they found in their rural lifestyle. One wrote, "Out here at civilization's end, they have something which is all their own, which they will mold and manage and make support them; and they are free!" It's evident that many still cherished the "simple life," even as mainstream culture was bidding it farewell.

So my question remained unanswered: If our ancestors once viewed the land as their source of freedom, independence, and security...then why did we ever leave the farm in the first place? What pushed us to transform from a self-sufficient agricultural society to a specialized, industrial, consumer culture? And how did it all happen so fast?

As I dug into the history books, I discovered a handful of factors that led to the flight away from American farms. But at the turn of the century, these factors culminated into a singular force that would change our world in a shockingly short time: industrialization. And this phenomenon just so happened to hold the answers to some of my biggest questions.

Like most children, I learned about the industrial revolution in school. And I couldn't have cared less. I've never been mechanically inclined, so all the talk of steam engines and automobiles and assembly lines was a total snooze-fest. Who cares? Let's move on to something more interesting, *please.*

But despite my personal disinterest, many historians consider the industrial revolution to be the most important event in modern human development. This roughly one-hundred-year period catapulted humankind into a whirlwind of progress that we previously couldn't have imagined. Our newfound fascination with machines was the beginning of the end for quaint, old-fashioned ways. We would never be the same.

The first big shift began in the late eighteenth century with steam-powered engines. Along with advancements in electricity, developments in gas and oil, and the invention of steel, steam engines set the stage for the all-powerful assembly line. The factory model would be the first domino in a line of changes that would ultimately sever our agrarian ties and disconnect us from the natural world. The majority of our current systems, from our patterns of consumption, to public education, to modern agriculture, to our forty-hour workweek, were birthed from this factory mindset.

After America's Civil War, the next wave of advancement focused on transportation. Automobiles hit the scene, followed by the Wright brothers' first manned flight in 1903. But neither of these achievements was as impactful as the ever-expanding railroad. In less than thirty years, the land touched by the railroad was irreversibly transformed. Mountains were blasted to make way for tracks. The once great herds of bison had been replaced with cattle, and the rolling grasslands replaced with corn and wheat. The railroad fed the factories with raw materials and provided a way to ship goods across the nation. As a result, an explosion of new factory jobs lured workers to town, furthering the exodus from the American farm.

> **the solution became clear: the people must be convinced that they need more.**

As factory efficiency increased, so did production of consumer goods. But this created a problem. For the first time ever, there was a surplus. The great minds of industry scratched their heads. If the factories were to maintain their efficiency, demand must increase. But that's a tricky proposition when everyone has what they need. Slowly, the solution became clear: the people must be convinced that they need *more*.

Humans have always consumed things. That's just part of being alive. But the doctrine of consumption ("You need XYZ to be happy. Buy more, more, MORE!") didn't become a substantial force in American society until very recently. Thanks to a freshly minted ability to produce cheaper goods, combined with mail-order catalogs and the novel allure of department stores, consumption was no longer just about survival. For the first time, the idea of buying things to increase happiness and social standing crept into the consciousness of the average citizen. A "new vision of increased consumption" became the rallying cry of marketers across the nation as they worked to help the "vast and wonderful factories of America to keep their wheels moving..." The genesis of the consumer was no accident. It was a carefully coordinated play.

The Great Depression and World Wars slowed the march of consumerism for a while, but it returned with gusto at the end of World War II. As marketing campaigns downplayed the quaintness of rural mindsets and exalted time-saving appliances and shiny new convenience foods, the message was crystal clear: a self-sufficient agrarian life was outdated and backward. Consumption was the only way forward.

And this is the paradigm we're still living within today. It's easy to assume our modern mentality is the norm, but it's a very recent construct. This realization also holds the answer to the question of why we left the farm, or at least part of it. While our ancestors might have recognized the beauty of their agrarian lives, the pull of progress was still too powerful. At least for a time, the grass was much greener on the side of newfangled convenience and comfort.

But I can't say I blame those who came before for the choices they made. As we sit on our modern perches with all the information in front of us, it's easy to judge the choices of generations past. As much as I like to think I would have been one of the holdouts who stayed on the farm to preserve tradition, I can't say for certain. After a lifetime of backbreaking work, the excitement and ease the city offered would have been hard to resist.

Personally, I doubt pioneer mothers thought bumping along the prairie with hordes of children in a four-by-eight-foot wagon box to be nearly as charming as *we* do now. And I'm positive my ancestors would have happily ditched the tedium of hauling buckets in favor of a shiny modern faucet with hot and cold water. Life was extreme for our predecessors, and there's a reason the most inventive minds of the industrial revolution were celebrated for making life easier.

Yet seeing how the story ends is a luxury you never have when you're the one making the tough decisions. And while our forefathers were understandably captivated by progress, the advancements that began during the Gilded Age had unintended consequences that you and I are still dealing with today.

The Modern Paradox

In a sense, the future our ancestors dreamed of is here. We made it. The promises of the industrial revolution have made our lives better than at any other point in history. We no longer must toil in the elements to produce enough food to survive. We don't have to weave fibers to make fabric to sew into clothing. We can choose to make our living in perfectly climate-controlled environments where we are never forced to experience sweat or calluses or sunburn or frostbite.

We can access light, heat, and water with the flip of a switch—three aspects of preindustrial life that drained our ancestors' time and energy. We can fly across the country in a matter of hours—a trip that, not that long ago, took years to complete (with the very real possibility we wouldn't reach our destination alive). Every food we can fathom is available 24/7 in a singular location, wrapped in shiny, sterile packages and displayed under bright fluorescent lights. We can feed ourselves for an entire lifetime without ever touching soil or tending livestock. What a relief!

You would think these advancements would have produced the happiest, most content, and most satisfied group of humans the world has ever seen. But the exact opposite seems to be true. It appears that although we got what we wanted, it's not as great as we thought it would be. Despite our many conveniences, these snazzy, fast-paced lives of ours have failed to provide the satisfaction we long for. In fact, they have left many of us feeling...empty.

> **the easier our lives have gotten, the unhappier we've become.**

While urbanization and industrialization certainly have advantages, they come at a cost. As progress was solving many of our long-held problems, it was simultaneously creating a host of new ones. It would seem the easier our lives have gotten, the unhappier we've become.

It's the first paradox we'll encounter in these pages, but it won't be the last. As we drifted away from our agrarian heritage, we made a concentrated move toward dependence rather than self-reliance. We can be thankful for the inventions that eliminated tedious labor, saved countless lives, and connected the world in faster ways, but we must also be careful not to romanticize the belief that progress always solves our problems. Or that such advances won't create new ones.

In our fervor for convenience and ease, we've accidentally built an artificial existence where we are distanced from nature, our communities, and even ourselves. We've applied the efficiency of the factory to every aspect of our everyday world, but assembly lines don't work for humans like they do manufacturing. And while many of these unnatural conditions now feel normal to us, our bodies are rebelling.

Modern "lifestyle diseases" (the term given to noncommunicable ailments like heart disease, obesity, and type 2 diabetes) are skyrocketing, as are rates of depression and mental illness.

The 2019 World Happiness Report showed that Americans were deeply unhappy, even before the chaos of the pandemic ensued. Despite lower rates of violent crime and unemployment, we're more miserable than ever.

So here we are. Entrenched in modernity. Born into worlds shaped by factories, industrialization, and consumerism. Do we drift along in the current culture and accept our fate, or do we abandon it all and run back to the past?

How about neither?

I believe there's another choice. I'm thankful to be able to enjoy the benefits of progress, as long as we keep them in perspective. One way to do this is to understand the ramifications of what we're leaving behind before exiling it to the history books. In his 1929 book, *The Thing*, G. K. Chesterton describes the importance of being able to explain why a fence was built in the first place before tearing it down. In other words, before we walk away from an old-fashioned skill or tradition, we should consider the long-term side effects of leaving it in the dust.

On the flip side, it's unwise to throw all modern advancements out with the bathwater, too. Lest you think I'm against all factory-made consumer goods, I'm currently typing this chapter on a MacBook while sitting on an ergonomic office chair surrounded by mass-produced water bottles, legal pads, and ink pens. My life is full of the fruits of progress, and I'm thankful for them. I don't wish I'd been born two hundred years ago. While it's tempting to romanticize certain periods of history, that approach is often misguided. Every era had issues. Some people thrived, while others lived in desperation—there is no "golden age" across the board. Despite the rose-colored lenses we sometimes use, there have always been hardships, triumphant moments, dark struggles, beauty, and brutality, just like today. In my quest for a vintage life, it's my desire to carry forward the concepts that have served humanity well, and leave the rest to the past.

So no, modern advancements aren't the enemy. But they aren't the *only* way, either. The old-fashioned mindset invites us to explore *who we were before industrialization told us otherwise.* Asking deep questions of the past gives us something with which to compare the present. This keeps us grounded and shines a light on how we can move forward. We don't have to pit old and new against each other, because they happen to work beautifully in tandem. Over the years, I've found the most joy with the following equation:

Understanding of the past + Using some present advancements = A more balanced future.

This has become my secret formula for creating the most satisfaction around food, health, community, parenting, and so much more.

Mixing Old and New

When I think of this weaving of the past with the future, my windmill comes to mind. Windmills are a common sight out here on the prairie, but I have one *inside* my house. Allow me to explain.

> **Old things are solid and steady. They've withstood the test of time, and they have the scars to show for it. I respect that.**

The process of restoration has always spoken deeply to me. As a young girl, I found more thrill in refurbishing old toys than getting a brand-new one, and to this day, I'll almost always choose something aged over something shiny. Old things are solid and steady. They've withstood the test of time, and they have the scars to show for it. I respect that.

From this childhood passion grew my love of antiques. While some of my current treasures come from local shops, there's nothing I love more than finding a jackpot in unexpected places—like a neighbor's junk pile.

That's exactly what happened in 2015 when Christian and I were contemplating a remodel of our farmhouse. After finally getting the outbuildings to a manageable point, we set our focus on converting our humble abode into a larger home that would accommodate our growing family. I'd never been one who needs a lot of fancy things, but I had one nonnegotiable when it came to our renovations: there must be a wall that could display an honest-to-goodness antique windmill.

I wasn't worried about a luxury bathtub or the size of the closet (I own approximately five pairs of shoes—they don't take up much space), but the windmill? It had to happen. I wouldn't entertain any other options.

Over the years, Christian had become accustomed to my eccentric choices in home decor. From the beat-up chairs and tables I would constantly drag home from yard sales to the re-purposed headboards that adorned our walls, he'd learned to choose his battles. Nevertheless, when I insisted we hang a full-size windmill INSIDE our home, he made several valiant attempts at a reasonable compromise: "Could we get one of those smaller reproductions? What if we hung up half of a windmill? Or a quarter? Or just a few blades?"

His suggestions were valid. But I refused to budge. I didn't know where I'd find said windmill. I didn't know how we'd affix such a monstrosity to the wall. But I was bound and determined there would be a windmill in our newly remodeled home.

After many discussions, rounds of measurements, and conversations with the architect, it was decided. The wall next to the new basement stairwell would be the perfect size to hang a full-size windmill. And the hunt began.

I had heard rumors of a windmill carcass lying dormant in a neighbor's trash pile. I wasn't about to let that lead go. After a brief phone call (and a shameless bribe of homemade cinnamon rolls), Christian made the trek to the back-pasture junk heap to see what he could find. I paced the kitchen the entire hour he was gone, praying that he would find more than just mangled pieces.

An hour or so later, our Ford F-350 rumbled up the driveway. As I peeked over the bed of the truck, chills raced up my spine. There, lying in the back, was a completely intact windmill in all its glory. I was beside myself.

The magic faded as we sorted through the logistics of bringing my prize into the house. Turns out, standard house doors aren't exactly designed to accommodate an eight-foot windmill hub. Thankfully, Christian enjoys a good engineering challenge. After disassembling the entire contraption so we could carry it through the door in chunks, there it was: a legitimate windmill. In. Our. House.

That windmill had weathered record-breaking blizzards, violent high-plains thunderstorms, and hurricane-force winds. It had stood witness as fresh new calves bounded through the soft spring air and prairie grasses shifted from verdant green to dormant brown and back again, year after year.

And in that moment, having been rescued from the trash heap, it was given a second life right there in our home.

Since that day, the windmill has watched our children act out never-ending dramas with their toys in the living room. It has listened to rich conversations shared over homemade soups at the family table. It has observed the stream of loved ones who grace our homestead all year long. The windmill remains a vital part of prairie life, but now it serves inside instead of outside, standing guard over all of us.

My windmill reminds me that old things have something to say. Things like, "There is still value to be found here." And, "Don't forget the lessons you've learned—both good and bad." And, "Don't become so enamored with progress that you forget from where you came."

Every time I walk past its crooked blades, I'm reminded of the importance of restoring old things, and that the things we so often toss aside have lasting value. Like the windmill, the concepts in this book aren't new. Rather, they have been proven to withstand the test of time while providing immense value to anyone who chooses to take hold of them. I'm simply dusting them off and helping them to find fresh purpose in our fast-paced modern lives. And when we master this mix of past and present, our reality becomes just a little bit brighter.

So how do we move forward as disenchanted modern folk grasping for more meaning in life? It's a question with a lot of moving pieces, and I won't pretend to have all the answers. But I can speak to what has served me and countless others who have embarked on a similar journey.

When we look at solving the problems of progress, it's tempting to immediately reach for big, overarching solutions. But I've personally found on-the-ground, grassroots approaches to be more effective than forming committees, writing petitions, or applying for funding. None of those options are wrong per se, but they move slowly and often create too many cooks in the kitchen, increasing the likelihood of things falling apart. In my experience, it's the determined, consistent actions of people like you and me that most often add up to big results. And those are exactly the strategies we'll explore here. The ideas in this book aren't a panacea, but they're a solid start.

So we collectively left the farm, and now, prompted by uncertainty, unrest, and unhappiness, the farm is pulling us back, both literally and figuratively. If we can take matters into our own hands, through small, simple steps, we can find our way home. Our first baby step? We must prepare ourselves to do hard things.

CHAPTER 3

From Cottagecore to Hard Core

Baskets of shiny, multicolored eggs, women wearing crisp white aprons as they hang laundry on the line, and adorable baby goats peering through white picket fences. When we think of an old-fashioned homestead, these images are often the first to pop into our minds.

There's even a modern name for this romantic portrayal of farm life. "Cottagecore" is the official title for the "romanticized farm fashion aesthetic" that's catching like wildfire online. It's no mystery why the crisp, wholesome photos of masterfully arranged garden harvests and farm kitchens brimming with fresh-cut flowers capture so much attention on social media.

But there's just one problem with this farm-based fantasy. Real life on the homestead is rarely curated, staged, or tidy. In fact, most modern homesteaders would agree our lives are the exact opposite. While there's certainly a natural beauty to be found in the barn, the gardens, and the kitchen, it's not nearly as refined as the viral photos would lead us to believe.

The truth is my eggs, while colorful, usually come adorned with poop and feathers. My barn clothes (sweatshirts and jeans, not white linen dresses) are stained from manure and animal slobber. And our goats can be more mischievous than adorable as they constantly escape their pen to snack on my poor prairie trees. Life on our homestead is anything but effortless. In reality, much of the time, it's downright hard. For as many times as I snap an elegant photo of a dreamy-eyed cow or a harvest of colorful veggies, we experience twice as many days when the wind is blowing 60 mph and I'm slogging through mud, trying to coerce an uncooperative animal into the barn. Or afternoons when I'm canning ninety pounds of garden produce and drenched in sweat and tomato guts. Daily homestead life is much more hard-core than cottagecore.

You may be wondering why I'm doing such a poor job of selling you on this lifestyle in the above paragraphs. Isn't the point of this book to encourage you to join me in my old-fashioned ways? As much as I believe in this way of life, I'd be doing you a disservice if I made everything look romantic and shiny all the time. I want you to have the facts right from start—not only so you can be better prepared, but also so you can learn to love the "not so pretty" parts, too.

Herein lies a secret about this vintage lifestyle that many people overlook in their excitement to get to the "good stuff" (aka fresh eggs, vine-ripened tomatoes, and baby chicks). The imperfect moments are just as valuable as the romantic ones. As we lean into the challenges, we're invited to step into our destiny—to grow, to up-level, and to mature into who we are meant to become. But we can only do this when we let go of chasing the picture-perfect fantasy and embrace the whole journey in its gritty, messy glory. In my opinion, that's the real "good stuff" anyway. And one of the first lessons the homestead ever taught me was how to not just tolerate these hard parts, but to *savor* them.

Prairie Blizzards

"Just wait until you see this place when it snows," the neighbor said as he stepped into his truck with a gleam in his eye. I shot him a quizzical glance, trying to decipher what he meant.

Although we were heading into our first winter on our new property, we were no strangers to snow. I had grown up in Northern Idaho, and Christian was a Wyoming native. Surely prairie storms couldn't be that bad, *could they*?

I pushed the conversation out of my mind until several months later. It was a sunny day in February when the radio began to buzz with reports of a substantial storm headed in our direction. As the clouds blew in that afternoon, the skies transformed from cheerful blue to angry gray. The walls of our farmhouse rattled and groaned against the vicious winds that buried the prairie in snow as they passed.

The next morning, I opened our front door and came eyeball to eyeball with a snowdrift. It wasn't one of those cute little piles of snow you can push aside with a plastic shovel. This was a drift of a different category altogether. The nine-foot barricade sealed our front door from top to bottom, with only a tiny sliver of blue sky visible at the top.

So *that's* what the neighbor meant. Noted.

Christian and I stood in stunned silence before grabbing the camera to capture photographic evidence of our predicament. No one would believe this. Our amusement quickly faded as we realized we now had to figure out a way to get *out* of the house. Thankfully, salvation came in the form of the mudroom entrance. While still plastered with snow, as luck (or wind direction) would have it, the pile there was half the size of the drift blocking the front door. We had to climb out of the house that morning, but it beat digging ourselves out with spatulas.

Upon breaking out of our snow prison, it took me a minute to find my bearings in the alien landscape. Our property had become unrecognizable. A towering mountain of snow sealed the main barn door. Fence lines were entombed in five feet of white. A drift in our side yard had formed a ramp that allowed me to touch the top of our full-size juniper tree. It would take days to dig everything out.

And thus began my crash course in the brutality of winter prairie life.

Prairie blizzards can occur any month from September to May. For some reason, Mother's Day has recently attracted some of the most violent storms in a sort of "last hurrah" before summer reluctantly arrives. These weather patterns were shocking to me when I first moved here, but I've since developed a sick fascination with extreme winter weather, especially historic accounts from our area. One particular story from Dr. Bessie Rehwinkel caught my attention. Rehwinkel staked her Wyoming homestead claim in 1907 and recalled a time when a plains blizzard caught her by surprise. "Snow began to fall in shovelfuls, driven over the prairie by a 70-mile gale and roaring past and around me with the thunderous notice of a fast-traveling freight train. [...] It seemed as though the forces of the universe had conspired together to destroy every living thing that happened to be in their path."

If I had read that before I moved here, I would have assumed she took a bit of creative license in her storytelling. But after living on the Great Plains for over a decade, I can attest that every word of her description is accurate. Not much has changed here on the prairie in that regard.

Living in a place with extreme winters makes everything harder, especially when caring for livestock. Over the years, we've adopted proven prairie-dweller strategies to reduce the worst drifts. But while the tree rows, windbreaks, and snow fences have helped, we still experience several storms per year that require our full attention.

There have been moments when sheets of blowing snow prevented me from seeing a cow standing only one hundred feet away. Other times I've found myself heading off in the wrong direction as I walked to the barn. It's almost impossible to open your eyes when violent winds are throwing bits of ice at your face. (The stories about old-time homesteaders tying a rope from the barn to the house are very real.) And more than once, the weather service has clocked the wind in our area at over 100 mph. That's considered a category two hurricane.

All this begs the question—why on earth do we live here?

I am aware that there are places where the air doesn't hurt your face, we wouldn't have to chop ice that's six inches thick (even after the water tank heater has been on all night), and our livestock wouldn't be able to walk over the top of snow-encapsulated fence lines.

Yet here we are, defying all logic and common sense. Why do we stay? Part of it is that after a decade of extreme renovations to make our homestead just right, our roots run deep into this piece of prairie. We've also cultivated some wonderful connections in our little rural community, and we'd hate to leave those friends. But there's one other reason that's taken me a while to admit—*living in a place like this makes us feel a little more alive.* There's something strangely exhilarating about surviving on the rugged edges where every aspect of life isn't micromanaged. The risks are higher, but so are the rewards.

> *Enduring the trials creates an intoxicating cocktail of deep accomplishment, meaningful struggle, and manual labor that matters.*

Feeding hay and chopping ice in below-zero temps makes a crackling fire feel more blissful. Dodging hailstorms and early frosts makes the harvest of a prairie watermelon an extra-sweet victory in more ways than one. Biting into a crisp, sour pickle that took two months to grow and ten days to ferment is far more gratifying than buying a jar at the store. Digging potatoes from the depths of the soil with my own hands makes them taste better than any market potato. And surviving a brutal winter to witness the first shoots of tender grass in an awakening prairie is nothing short of sacred. Enduring the trials creates an intoxicating cocktail of deep accomplishment, meaningful struggle, and manual labor that matters.

Here's what I've learned about things that matter: *they're not always supposed to be easy.* Easy isn't necessarily wrong, but a quest for constant ease will lead us down a path that makes us less healthy and less happy in the long run. Our subconscious even knows this, as evidenced by the tales we all know and love.

A story isn't a story without some sort of conflict. That's why the classics usually explore a trial to overcome, a mountain to scale, or an adversary to outwit. Our favorite tales would be insufferably boring without this sense of adventure.

What if...

Instead of venturing westward in a move that will change their lives forever, Laura Ingalls Wilder's parents decide to remain in Wisconsin. After all, who in their right mind would embark on a cross-country relocation with three kids in a covered wagon? Sounds exhausting. Let's stay home.

Harry Potter goes to Hogwarts, makes some good friends, but never pushes back against the dark forces, because people might think he's a conspiracy theorist and that would really hurt his GPA.

Frodo considers gathering his crew to confront consummate evil and vanquish the ring that threatens to destroy Middle-earth but decides against it. It just feels like a lot with his current schedule. Probably safer to stay on the couch and binge Netflix instead.

As readers (or viewers), we love to root for the rebels, cheer for the risk-takers, and applaud those brave enough to defy the odds. We imagine ourselves in their shoes and assume we'd make the same bold choices. But then we structure our lives to avoid difficulty at all costs. Funny, isn't it?

When I tell my own stories of our epic blizzards, or the awkwardness of hauling goats to a barbecue, people listen with rapt attention, but then promptly say, "I could never live there!" or "I could never do that!" And it makes me want to ask them, "But what if you could?"

That's not to say that moving to blizzard-prone Wyoming or acquiring a haphazard animal farm is the right path for you. But perhaps our collective fascination with these stories is really a subconscious desire for challenge manifesting itself.

It's Okay to Be Cold

"Wear your coat or you'll catch a cold!" is a reprimand we've all heard. While the advice is usually well-meaning, it's not necessarily true. Viruses cause us to get sick—not cold temperatures. Studies show that exposure to cold is actually good for us and may even help us live longer. Cooler temperatures decrease inflammation, help us sleep more soundly, and kick-start our metabolism by turning white fat into healthy brown fat that our bodies use for fuel.

If you're someone who cringes at the thought of being cold, practice makes perfect. The more time you spend in cooler temps, the more acclimated your body will become. (My kids are living proof of this when they race outside in tank tops and shorts as soon as the thermometer inches above 50°F.)

Whether your climate leans toward cold or hot extremes, establishing an intimate connection with your natural environment is a simple, old-fashioned way to boost physical stamina, immunity, and resilience.

Have you ever been around a border collie? These dogs are amazing athletes, but if you don't give them enough to do, they'll start eating the couch. Our brains operate in a similar way. While we might not gnaw on furniture, we come up with other ways to cope with a lack of stimulation. I found one fascinating study that explains some of our modern frustrations perfectly.

In the first round of research, participants were asked to rate photographs of eight hundred faces as "nonthreatening" or "threatening." Some of the facial sketches could clearly be categorized as either friendly or intimidating, while others fell somewhere in the middle. As the session progressed, fewer blatantly threatening faces were included in the lineup. And that's where it gets interesting. When shown fewer threatening images, the participants started to label the more neutral faces as menacing. And a similar phenomenon occurred when participants were asked to label dots in a color range or classify a topic as ethical or nonethical.

So what does this have to do with old-fashioned living? It shows that when true challenges become rare, our brains tend to categorize more things as problems. This perfectly explains much of our modern unhappiness. As our lives get easier, we consider smaller, more trivial things to be troublesome. Therefore, it's up to us to build meaningful challenge into our lives, since day-to-day survival no longer requires it. The good news is that a fulfilling adventure is far more possible than you might think. Adopting an old-fashioned mindset provides plenty of opportunities for you to "slay the dragon," so to speak.

Choosing Your Challenge

When we think of adventure, we might think of extremes like summiting the highest mountains, sailing around the world, or running ultramarathons. However, my escapades, though no less exciting to me, look very different than that. And yours probably will, too.

Any event in my life that I've dubbed as an adventure (either immediately or after the fact) has shared the following traits:

- It's been wildly out of my comfort zone. I'm talking messy beginner mode with all the failures, all the unknowns, and all the *"I have no clue what I'm doing"* moments.

- It has carried an element of risk because nothing great in life comes with guaranteed success. That's what makes it exciting.

- It has required me to dig deep, stretch, and expand my capabilities beyond what I thought possible.

Choosing the harder path has taken many unconventional forms in our family, including:

- Renovating run-down properties that no one else wants

- Owning a restaurant in a town of 175 people

- Choosing to grow vegetables in a region with extremely volatile weather patterns

- Starting a herd of grass-finished beef cattle

Even smaller events, like bringing home an untamed milk cow or driving cross-country with three kids and a puppy in the middle of winter, have provided bursts of adventure. Each of these challenges has forced us to think outside of the box. We've had to push back against what's considered to be rational, endure some raised eyebrows, and overcome many problems along the way. But in the end, we've reaped incredible rewards, every single time.

If you're still scratching your head to think of what your first challenge might be, here's a clue: You know that thing that haunts your dreams and won't go away? That nagging desire you feel for something bigger?

Start with that.

You'll know you're on the right rack when the butterflies start to flutter in your stomach. Your heart will beat just a little faster. You'll feel more awake than you've ever felt. And you'll probably be a little scared. I interpret these signs to mean, "Move forward."

Facing the unknown can be uncomfortable. Unsettling. And downright unnerving. But those moments when we choose to heed the call—butterflies in the stomach and all—define us. Our confidence is bolstered, our resilience is forged, and we begin to trust in our abilities in a whole new way.

When we push ourselves through difficult tasks, we not only reap the results of our work, but we move one step closer to who we're meant to become in the process. And that holds true whether your adventure is running a marathon or planting vegetables for the first time.

And no. Just in case you were wondering—you can't do all the hard things at once. At least not at first. And that's okay.

We can increase our capacity for challenges the same way we build muscle. When we push our body outside of its usual comfort range, we become stronger. Lifting heavy things or jogging longer distances might not feel great at the time, but our endurance expands the longer we stick with it. This principle applies to an old-fashioned on purpose life, too.

When I first started gardening, my tiny plot felt overwhelming. Now I have three sizable growing spaces, and they're (mostly) manageable. By mastering one space at a time, I strengthened my gardening muscle.

Canning used to be a high-stress event for me. The house had to be perfectly quiet, and I'd read the instructions fifteen times before starting. Now? I can process applesauce in the middle of making supper and baking bread with three dogs underfoot. I grew my canning muscle.

Having one person over for supper used to throw me into a tailspin. Now I regularly serve crowds of fifteen-plus without blinking. I expanded my hospitality muscle.

Each aspect of my life, from gardening to cheesemaking to homeschooling to business ownership, came in stages. If I had tried to learn them all at once, I would have crashed and burned in a spectacular way. Start with one thing at a time. Master that. As that process becomes easier, then add in something else. You'll enjoy your old-fashioned skills much more when you learn them in increments versus all at once.

The Hidden Rewards of Responsibility

There's a curious common thread woven through the vintage skills that are calling to us: they each require us to step up and adopt greater measures of responsibility in our lives.

Shouldering more responsibility almost always makes our lives harder (at least for a time), so this is an unexpected development. Are we old-fashioned folk just gluttons for punishment, or is there another force at play? I believe it's the latter. Yet it's a phenomenon I first experienced in the arena, not the homestead.

In my early twenties, I was determined to become a horse trainer. I spent a few years working with horsemen, spending up to ten hours per day in the saddle. I exercised horses for a summer at a guest ranch in Cody, Wyoming, rode cutting horses for a while in Colorado, and spent a year riding colts across the rugged prairies. Although I ended up becoming an entrepreneur instead of a professional horse trainer, the lessons I learned during that period of my life have stuck with me. And one in particular stands above the rest:

Don't blame the horse.

In essence? *Take full ownership of what you can control.*

Your horse reared? You needed to free up the horse's hind-quarters.

Your horse spooked? You needed to direct his feet before that happened.

Your horse bucked you off? Well, maybe next time you'll feel when he's getting tight.

This was a new concept for me, and it didn't come naturally. When something goes awry, it's much easier to point to outside factors, and let's face it—the horse you're riding makes a convenient scapegoat. But I quickly observed that only focusing on the horse's shortcomings didn't work out well. Not only would it produce an unpleasant response from my boss (most horsemen don't mince words), but it never produced any long-term solutions. So instead of off-loading the blame, I learned to take ownership of the problem. Ever so slowly, this approach began to pay off. The more I took responsibility for my own situation, the better my situation became.

My new mindset in the arena leaked into the rest of my life. When I sensed a problem in the world around me, whether that be our unhealthy diets, the culture of consumerism, or environmental issues, instead of placing the blame elsewhere, I started to ask, "How can I take ownership of this?"

> **when we take responsibility for righting things, even in small, unflashy ways, our worlds become alive with meaning and purpose.**

It made my life harder at first, but knowing the buck stopped with me drove me forward. And here's the secret I uncovered: when we take responsibility for righting things, even in small, unflashy ways, our worlds become alive with meaning and purpose.

It's an intoxicating feeling that only appears when we voluntarily shoulder higher levels of ownership. And I believe this is exactly what's driving this old-fashioned on purpose movement—especially in a culture that seeks to off-load responsibility at all costs.

Now an important clarification: Was *every single thing* those horses did always my fault? Not necessarily. And not everything will be in your realm of control, either. Sometimes the horse was young and hadn't had much exposure to the world. Other times, previous riders had made the horse dull and nonresponsive, so I was left dealing with the aftermath. And of course, there were always unpredictable obstacles to overcome, whether a snake in the path, a boom of thunder, or a sudden scare.

But since I had no control over those factors, dwelling on them would have made me nothing more than a passive passenger. That approach is *disempowering*. Therefore, my best bet both then AND now is to focus on what actions I *can* take, regardless of the challenge I'm facing. Over a decade later, this was the mindset that allowed our family to forge the homestead of our dreams from a tumbledown old farmstead. And I continue to reap rewards from these choices daily. No matter what, we can always control how we respond to life. No one can take that away from us. Just be careful not to take it away from yourself.

So on the days when I'm tired and second-guessing myself, I rest in this knowledge. Because even though it'd be easier to let someone else take responsibility for my problems, I know that's where the good stuff lies. So I forge ahead. And it's worth it. Every single time.

How to Take Old-Fashioned Ownership

Living the old-fashioned on purpose life reminds me a lot of the *Choose Your Own Adventure* books I read when I was a kid. Remember those? Readers had no idea if flipping the page would lead to a happy-ever-after resolution or to a death trap in which the main character would be eaten by dinosaurs. Likewise, as we navigated our homestead adventure, we had no idea where each decision would lead. But each of our adventures began with the question of how we could take ownership for our situations. There were always two choices.

Choice #1: We could stay the same. Our pre-homestead life wasn't the dream lifestyle we ultimately wanted, but it was comfortable and safe. Staying in place was tempting because we were happy enough with our situation and had no pressing reason to take the leap. It was easy to make excuses. And at that point in our life, the "if onlys" were pretty compelling:

"*If only* I had someone to teach me these things…"

"*If only* we had been born into ranching families…"

"*If only* we had inherited land…"

"*If only* we had more money in the budget…"

"*If only* raw milk was legal to buy in Wyoming…"

"*If only* I lived in a place more friendly to gardening…"

But just when the excuses threatened to lull me into a state of complacency, an alternative option came into view.

Choice #2: We could do something to improve our situation. Instead of waiting, wishing, and hoping for our dreams to magically materialize, we could take action. The transition might be imperfect and slow, but at least we'd be moving toward our targets.

To be honest, both options felt painful. But as I contemplated, the whispers of the lessons I had learned in the arena came back to me: *Was I going to relinquish responsibility and blame the horse, or would I take it upon myself to improve the situation?* To put it plainly: no one was coming to save us. If Christian and I wanted to build a homestead and create a legacy for our family, we had to be the ones to make it happen.

And this same choice will be offered to you as you move through these pages. Will you simply wish for an old-fashioned life? Or will you take the shaky first steps to make it happen? Excuses are always comfortable and easy, but they'll never take us to where we want to go. So, one step at a time, one project at a time, we chose #2. And in those moments, our "if onlys" began to transform into "if-thens."

If I didn't have someone to teach me these old-fashioned skills, *then* I'd teach myself. (I didn't have YouTube, but I did have a local library.)

If we weren't born into ranching families, *then* we'd start from scratch and create our own rural legacy for our children. (One cow at a time…)

If we wanted land, *then* we'd push aside our dreams of buying a "nice house" and buy a run-down fixer-upper with acreage instead.

If we needed more cash for our projects, *then* we'd pick up whatever odd jobs we could find. (These included casting lead bullets and cleaning toilets.)

If I wanted raw milk, *then* I'd get some goats and milk them myself.

If I wanted to grow vegetables in the arctic (aka the Wyoming prairie), *then* I'd have to learn about season extension and cold-weather crops.

If I wanted to lessen our environmental footprint, *then* I'd have to haul my recycling to town. (We didn't have garbage pickup, let alone curbside recycling.)

If I wanted to work in my garden, *then* I'd have to bring the kids along with me. (Babysitters were few and far between.)

If I wanted to make friends, *then* I'd have to put myself out there. (Waiting for them to show up on my doorstep wasn't going to work.)

And it was through those small, steady mindset shifts that everything changed. As we took ownership of our food, our health, our finances, our habits, our children's education, and our local relationships, our confidence grew. We discovered we were more capable than we had originally thought, and our creativity blossomed. We realized mistakes weren't the end of the world, so our aversion to risk shrank. As a result, our life became unrecognizable, not to mention incredibly exciting.

The Result Road Map

Ideas are cheap—only when we take action do they truly come alive. Yet when you're staring down the barrel of a big mission (like building an old-fashioned on purpose life), it's easy to feel paralyzed. Over the years I've come up with a simple way to help myself get unstuck. The following exercise breaks giant undertakings into small, bite-size steps. As you check these small steps off your list, your brain will reward you with a little bit of dopamine, which will inspire you to take the next step. This process is best done on a big sheet of paper with a crisp new Sharpie, or with a whiteboard and dry-erase markers. There's something about writing it out by hand that makes it stick.

Step One: Brain Dump

When things swirl around in our brains, they tend to feel more formidable than they really are. Therefore, our first objective is to bring all the things into the light. Write down whatever is making you feel overwhelmed or stuck. Don't overthink it—just write. Get it out of your brain and onto the paper. This includes ideas, questions, goals, projects, the things that have to happen before you can start, the phone calls you need to make—all of it.

Step Two: Sort Your List

If your list includes a lot of individual projects, circle up to three to start pushing forward. (The fewer the better, though—multitasking is *never* as effective as we think it is. You can do everything, but not all at once.) If you're having a hard time deciding which ones to choose, assign a date to each item. Then home in on the tasks that are truly urgent versus the ones where urgency is self-imposed. For example, if my list includes outdoor projects and it's springtime, those will take priority since we only have a small window of nice weather. Remodeling the bathroom can wait until it's too cold to play outside.

Step Three: Break It Down

Make a column for each of the projects you circled. Now break each of these into the smallest steps possible, being as specific as you can. Don't worry about the order of the steps. Just think of as many pieces as possible. If one of my columns is "Start a Garden," then my baby steps might be find the sunny parts of my yard, figure out what growing zone I'm in, call around for a source of fertilizer, and order seeds. If one of my columns is "Run a 5K," my baby steps might be get running shoes, print out a training plan, find a local race to enter, and run three times per week. This process transforms a monumental, abstract undertaking ("start a garden") into baby steps that are tangible and attainable ("find my growing zone").

Step Four: Organize

Look at your list of little steps. Which needs to be done first? Number accordingly.

Step Five: Do It!

Now that you have created a path, you can see exactly where to go. If possible, tackle the first baby step *immediately*. Sometimes it's as small as making a phone call or doing a web search. But the sooner you start rolling that snowball of dopamine, the better.

Choosing the harder path, while illogical at first, builds confidence. And little by little, we begin to see ourselves as people we can trust. Our instincts become stronger, and our inner stories shift from "I'm not sure I'm the type of person who can handle this" to "I've overcome challenges before. I have what it takes." By choosing to do hard things, to take responsibility over what we can control, and to seek solutions for problems that may arise, we gain a bone-deep confidence that can only be experienced after putting forth effort and tackling a challenge head-on.

The magic of an old-fashioned on purpose lifestyle is that we don't *have* to do any of it. We live in a world where we are expected to take on as little responsibility as possible. "That's too hard for you," society whispers. "Let someone else worry about it." But these are the exact opportunities that will allow us to become who we were always meant to be.

That's what I love about the people who make up this community. They are the ones who run to pick up the responsibility others have discarded. Instead of waiting for a law, a committee, or a think tank to fix their problems, they put their heads down and do the work. They build their communities, compost their food waste, buy local as much as possible, grow food in their backyards, and push back against an industrialized, consumer culture in a peaceful, pastoral sort of way.

Remember—as you live your own epic tale of adventure, the victories won't always be clear right away. When I was standing next to the moldy washing machine in the front yard of our new house, I couldn't have fathomed that moment would be one of the most pivotal points of our story. At the time, it just felt overwhelming. But since then, it's become a landmark in my life that I fondly remember. A moment when we looked at all the reasons the homesteading leap would be difficult, risky, and scary…and then we dared take the leap anyway.

Wherever you are in your old-fashioned lifestyle journey,

I encourage you to trust the process. Adopt higher levels of ownership when problems arise. Don't shy away from the ugly, the messy, and the hard. One day you'll look back and marvel at how far you've come, and maybe even be thankful for those washing machine moments.

So the next question is, where can we start in taking ownership and doing hard things? Over the years, I've discovered eight distinct traits of an old-fashioned on purpose life. And the foundation of it all begins with eating more responsibly.

PART 2

Becoming Old-Fashioned

CHAPTER 4

Grow Some Ingredients

My family recently got hit with the type of virus every mom dreads—the kind that downs everyone at once except for the six-year-old and the puppy, who are left with complete run of the house. Somehow, we survived. But after a few days of eating nothing but applesauce and crackers, we were ravenous. Only one thing would suffice: chicken noodle soup.

I hadn't been to the grocery store in weeks, so I grabbed a basket and went on a quick "shopping trip" around the homestead. Ten minutes later, a motley crew of ingredients lined the kitchen counter.

The bounty? A whole, defrosted chicken from the batch of meat birds we'd raised the previous summer; a clump of carrots chiseled from the frigid winter garden; a homegrown onion, yellow and crisp; a bulb of garlic with a generous clod of dirt attached; a repurposed jar of broth (stored the previous week); and three brown eggs from the coop.

This was food in its purest form, without the shiny packaging, slick slogans, or barcodes. And it was a beautiful sight—dirt clods, feathers, and all.

I cut the chicken into eight pieces, dicing some for the pot and saving the rest for later in the week. In my trusty Dutch oven, the vegetables mellowed with olive oil before I added herbs and broth, letting the aromas of black pepper, turmeric, thyme, and rosemary warm the house.

Next came the noodles. After a few minutes of kneading, the eggs and a scoop of flour morphed into satiny dough that I sliced into thick strips before dropping into the simmering broth. As I ladled the soup into bowls, I reflected on the alchemy at hand.

I knew this meal, intimately. Long before the ingredients had ever met the pot, I'd been tending them. But while this dish was an offering of the land, it wasn't free. Instead of dollars and cents, we'd paid with sacrifice and sweat. It's a primal transaction that never gets old for me. Rugged and rustic, the major components had been born of our little patch of earth and traveled only a few feet before arriving at our table. The process of growing our own food has been transformative for me, and it's the first foundational principle of an old-fashioned on purpose life: *We grow or source our ingredients.*

Not so long ago, homegrown meals were ordinary. Prior to industrialization, food didn't live in the grocery store. Rather, it was in the backyard, the barnyard, the fields, and on the hoof. But in just one hundred short years, we've become so accustomed to our modern supermarket routine, it now feels strange to eat food that doesn't come encased in crinkly plastic and branded packaging. We think nothing of meals that traveled thousands of miles to reach our table. Other hands besides our own water the vegetables we eat. Unknown faces harvest our fruits. Someone else tends the animals that provide us with milk, eggs, and meat. And while we are conditioned to view this culinary fragmentation as normal, it's a very new concept that's not always good for us.

This contemporary disconnect from our ingredients has created a relationship with food that's tumultuous at best, and toxic at worst. We count calories, chase the latest fad diets, and continually chastise ourselves for falling off the diet wagon. Our hyperfocus on macros, micros, calories, and carbs has created a dynamic where food becomes a source of neurosis rather than nourishment. Our body's intuition has been drowned out by industrial fats, artificial sweeteners, and additives that light up the pleasure sensors in our brain like an arcade game. But all of this is redeemable. As we move further from calorie counts and low-fat gimmicks, food becomes surprisingly simple.

> **Food doesn't have to be the enemy. In its natural form, it can be sustaining, life-giving, and deliciously invigorating.**

For example, instead of weighing food in terms of calories, we can embrace it in terms of nourishment. (I know this cup of warm broth will give my body nutrients it needs. I'm eating this sauerkraut to add more probiotics into my diet.) Studies suggest that a simple move away from the industrialized American diet can add up to thirteen years to your life. Food doesn't have to be the enemy. In its natural form, it can be sustaining, life-giving, and deliciously invigorating.

The food on our plate always has a story, whether we know it or not. The story might be that it was grown on a factory farm, sprayed with pesticides, and harvested by machine. Or that it came from the small farm down the road and was picked by the farmer's children. Or that it was grown just a few steps out your back door. I never thought about these stories until we started homesteading, but they deeply matter. When we can connect the ingredients on our plates to the land, our communities, and ourselves, we have reason to care. This connection sparks critical questions, like: What was this animal fed? Was this vegetable grown sustainably? Was the livestock treated humanely? Did the farmer receive proper compensation? How far did this have to travel to reach my plate? Was the soil nurtured or exploited in the process? What long-term effects will this food have on my health?

While digging into these questions may ultimately lead us to a local farm stand or a garden in the backyard, for most of us (including myself) the journey begins in a more familiar place. The first steps toward repairing our fractured relationship with food can be taken in the aisles of our local grocery stores. I like to think of this journey as a series of three questions we can ask. The first one is, "What's in season?"

Shift to Seasonal Shopping

It wasn't until we started homesteading that I fully understood the seasonality of eating. Thanks to the ever-present variety at grocery stores, it's easy to miss the fact that food is cyclical. But when we honor the seasonal nature of our diets, we develop a deeper appreciation for the meals on our table.

On a homestead, for instance, egg season kicks off in early spring when the lengthening daylight hours stimulate the hens to ramp up production. In response, I cram eggs into as many meals as possible: egg salad, egg sandwiches, puddings, custards, German pancakes, cream puffs, and giant trays of all-you-can-eat deviled eggs. And just when my children begin to threaten mutiny at the sight of another skillet of scrambled eggs, the hens mercifully slow down. I use eggs I tucked away previously (I either freeze them out of the shell or preserve them in a lime/water solution) for baking during the meager months (and I'm not above amending with a carton or two from the store), but for the most part, we enjoy the break. And then, without fail, the anticipation of egg season builds month by month, and we can hardly wait for full nesting boxes in the coming spring.

You'd never know it from the dairy coolers at the super-market, but milk is another seasonal food that changes throughout the year. Most cows freshen (calve) in the spring when the grass is lush. A new calf plus rich spring forage results in the creamiest, most decadent milk of the entire year. Butter from cows eating spring grass contains more beta-carotene, which imparts a golden glow. (This can vary depending on the breed of cow. Older breeds such as Jerseys, Guernseys, and Brown Swiss tend to pass more beta-carotene into their milk when compared to commercial dairy breeds such as the Holstein.) I was blown away the first time I churned my own butter. The creamy spread was almost neon yellow and caught me off guard after a lifetime of eating pale, nearly colorless butter from the store.

"Drowning in milk" is the only way to describe springtime with a milk cow. Since we share milk with the calf, we collect roughly three gallons per day, which is far less than a modern dairy animal would produce but more than enough for a single family. The milk jars turn the refrigerators into a real-life game of *Tetris*. There's homemade yogurt, copious amounts of cream for coffee, curds left over from the batches of hard cheese that are tucked away for later, freshly stretched mozzarella, home-churned butter, ice cream, and all the milk the kids can drink. As the year progresses, the milk supply dwindles until we "dry up" the cow to give her body a rest for a few months before her next calf. Drying up creates a temporary milk famine, but it gives our bodies a break from dairy and makes the milk taste that much better the following spring when the cycle starts once again.

Vegetables are more obviously seasonal, but I didn't realize how short and sometimes volatile their phases were until I started growing them myself. Even though most supermarkets are filled with the same produce year-round, you'll secure the best flavor and prices if you steer toward seasonal items. And of course, you can preserve your seasonal findings for later. Fresh fruits and vegetables can be flash frozen, dehydrated, or canned at home so you can enjoy them year-round. Many of our favorite modern condiments were invented as ways to preserve the bounty for later. Ketchup is a brilliant, space-saving way to condense many tomatoes into a small container, mayonnaise is a semi-shelf-stable way to make use of extra eggs, and relish puts excess garden cucumbers to use at the end of the season when you've made all the pickles you can muster.

Shop by Season

While you might not be able to hold out for spring butter or local tropical fruit, you can begin to sync yourself with the seasons by rethinking how you shop. Just because we can buy strawberries year-round doesn't mean we should. It takes a little discipline, but we'll find the best flavor, nutrition, and prices if we shop by season. Remember: your exact seasonal road map will depend on where you live, so use my plan as a baseline and adjust as needed.

Winter: Think about hearty, belly-filling foods that last well in storage. Squash, onions, potatoes, cabbages, brussels sprouts, carrots, parsnips, and beets. We also eat the most citrus this time of year, since it peaks from December through March. Even though it must be shipped to Wyoming, it's more affordable and tastier during its prime season.

Spring: A welcome, lighter change from the heavier winter foods. Enjoy the more delicate fruits and veggies before the heat of summer whisks them away. Strawberries, spinach, lettuce, radishes, asparagus, mushrooms, rhubarb, peas, and green onions shine this time of year.

Summer: The most abundant season. During the summer months I fill our plates with piles of melons, berries, tomatoes, beans, peppers, sweet corn, grapes, cauliflower, new potatoes, cucumbers, zucchini, and peaches.

Fall: A mixture of the last of the summer bounty and the beginnings of the winter crops. Fall is the time for apples, squash, tomatoes, cabbage, broccoli, turnips, carrots, onions, leeks, potatoes, pears, plums, and of course, pumpkins.

Understanding the cycles of our food helps me feel more at peace not always having everything available. As you shift to shopping by season, remember that it varies depending on your location. For example, tomatoes are a summer fruit for many, but here in Wyoming, we don't have our glut of tomatoes until late September or October. Spending time at your local farmers markets will help you get a feel of what's in season in your location, and then you can supplement the rest with seasonal purchases at the grocery store.

Keep It Local

That brings us to the second question in rethinking how we grocery shop: "How far did my food travel?" Transporting food is nothing new. The spice trade dominated the ancient world for thousands of years, olive oil was exported through trade routes that stretched throughout Europe and Asia, and merchants carried fruits, nuts, and rice across the Silk Road. But none of this can hold a candle to the magnitude of miles our food now travels.

Once again, industrialization has pushed us to the extreme. Cod caught near Scotland is shipped to China for filleting, before it is packaged and sent back to Scotland. In total, the fish end up traveling 10,000 miles. In some parts of the United States, the average fruit or vegetable can travel up to 1,500 miles before it reaches our plate. What's even more shocking is that these world-traveling ingredients are often cheaper than the ones grown in our own communities. These glaring cost differences can be discouraging as we seek a diet inspired by the farm instead of the factory.

However, what these modern equations fail to account for are the hidden costs of this long-distance system, which become painfully apparent when we start to ask better questions. Such as:

What is the *cost in flavor* of produce that has been selectively developed for cross-country treks instead of tastiness?

What is the *cost to our health* from food that has lingered in crates and shelves with nutrients dwindling? Or produce that is irradiated and dowsed with preservatives to ensure it still looks perky after being jostled in a truck for a week?

What is the *cost to our environment* when nearly 20 percent of global emissions can be attributed to transporting food?

And what is the *cost to our national food security* when we're dependent on a food supply not grown within our own borders? As we saw during the COVID-19 outbreak, globalized food systems are more susceptible to shortage and supply chain issues. Buying ingredients from local producers means you don't have to worry about a hurricane in Florida, a ship stuck in the Suez Canal, or a shortage of truck drivers disrupting your supply of food.

It's not about perfection, or never again buying a banana or mango. But rethinking our participation in this relatively new global model is a valuable exercise. As a result, we may just end up with tastier meals that create a positive ripple effect in our health, ecosystems, and communities.

This might surprise you, but when I'm sourcing ingredients from smaller, local producers, I don't always worry about organic certification. It's common to find wonderful farmers who simply can't afford the certification processes. In these cases, I'll always choose small and local over Big Corporate Organic. I tend to care much less about official labels and instead consider the bigger picture: How was the food grown? Was the soil nurtured in the process? How far did it have to travel to reach me? Does this purchase put money directly into my local economy? Contrary to popular belief, certified organic foods could still be sprayed with pesticides that fall into the natural or nonsynthetic category. "Organic" doesn't automatically mean the food contains more nutrients or was grown in a more sustainable way.

And remember: if you're on a tight budget and can't afford food with organic labeling, fresh conventional produce still trumps ultraprocessed junk food.

How does one craft a local food strategy in the city or suburbs? Believe it or not, you can start in your neighborhood grocery store. I've noticed more and more markets including signs in their produce department explaining where each item was sourced. Recently at our local supermarket, I found peaches and sweet corn from our neighboring state of Colorado, which beats ones grown six hundred miles away. While this isn't possible in all stores or with all ingredients, it's a start. If you can't find food grown in your region, perhaps just start with food grown in the USA. Some fruits, veggies, and even meats are shipped internationally, which makes their environmental footprint much heavier. For example, did you know that much of the garlic in our grocery stores is grown in China? That's a long way to ship a crop that can be grown domestically (or in your backyard!). The same goes with beef. A large portion of the grass-fed beef on the market is raised in New Zealand or Australia and shipped to the United States to be split into individual cuts. To me, it makes more sense to find beef that didn't have to be shipped across the ocean, especially if you live in a ranching state like we do.

Growing Your Own Garlic

You, my friend, can grow your very own garlic. If you've never tried it before, buckle up. This information is life changing. And the best part? It's not fussy in the least. Here's the game plan:

1. **Get seed garlic.** It's best to not use grocery store garlic since you don't know if it's been sprayed with anti-sprouting chemicals. Most garden stores stock seed garlic in the fall, or you can order it online. Hardneck varieties have bigger cloves and prefer colder winters. Softneck varieties have smaller cloves and are better at handling warmer winters. I've grown both, but hardneck is my favorite.

2. **Prep your plot.** Garlic likes rich, well-drained soil in full sun. I plant mine in a garden bed that's empty after I harvest my summer crops, but you can plant yours in the corner of your yard or in a flower bed.

3. **Plant.** Most gardeners plant garlic in the fall at the end of their growing season since the bulbs need a period of cold weather to thrive. (I usually sow mine in late September.) If you live in a warmer, southern climate, you can plant later in winter, or use your refrigerator to mimic a cold snap (google "garlic vernalization"). Break the bulbs into their individual cloves and plant the cloves *pointy side up*. (Each clove will produce a whole new plant.) I shoot for a planting depth of six inches with rows that are eight inches apart.

4. **Forget about it!** Cover the cloves with soil and apply a layer of mulch. I water mine for the first few weeks, but once the weather gets really cold, I leave them alone.

5. **Harvest.** In the spring, you'll be greeted by tiny garlic sprouts poking their heads above the soil. Let them grow until midsummer. Your crop is ready to

harvest when the bulbs are full-size (you can dig
below the surface of the soil to check).

From there, branch out into farm stands or farmers markets. Not only are these hubs for regionally grown fruit, vegetables, meats, and honey, they're a perfect place to connect with like-minded people within your local food scene. If there aren't farmers markets nearby, try purchasing pork, beef, chicken, or lamb direct from the producer instead. You may be able to barter with a neighbor who has front yard fruit trees or a backyard coop. Perhaps you can find a local dairy where you can source milk and cheese, or join a community-supported agriculture (CSA) farm share or co-op. Some communities even have gleaning groups that collect surplus food from farms, yards, and markets.

Does grocery shopping the old-fashioned way take longer? You bet. But the added flavor (and nutrition) makes it very worth it.

A Victory Garden Revival

The final question we can ask as we rethink our ingredients is, by far, my favorite. "What can I grow myself?"

At any other point in history, households growing their own food wasn't a farfetched idea. But now that we live in a world with postage-stamp backyards (or no yard at all), it feels downright impossible. Many would say we're too far gone, that we're so accustomed to our modern food paradigm that there's no turning back. But I disagree.

True, most of the population can't move to a homestead or plant an acre of corn in the backyard (although recent shifts to remote-job opportunities are changing that). But never underestimate the cumulative power of small spaces. And the most intuitive place to start is the home garden.

During World War II, more than 40 percent of all fresh produce consumed in the United States was produced in home gardens, commonly called "victory gardens" or "war gardens." In 1939 alone, over $200,000,000 worth of vegetables was grown in home gardens. A US Department of Agriculture (USDA) booklet from 1943 reports that "these 4,800,000 home gardens produced vegetables worth a little more than those grown for sale on 3,000,000 acres." As the saying goes, "Despise not small beginnings," and I would add, "Despise not small gardens."

It's time to resurrect the victory garden, my friend. As we can see from the numbers, if even just a portion of the population began to grow food, it would make a serious impact. Plus, considering the abundant nature of a garden, there's usually plenty to share. (Especially if we're talking zucchini.)

In 2016, researchers gathered data from over thirty home gardens and concluded the yield of the average 253-square-foot plot was enough to supply an adult with the recommended amount of vegetables for nine months. And the best part? This study wasn't conducted in the tropics—these participants lived in Laramie, Wyoming. If a Wyomingite can grow that quantity of food while dealing with high altitude, minimal rain, hailstorms, and the world's shortest growing season, there is hope for anyone, including YOU. I promise. And even if you don't have 253 square feet of growing space, you have lots of options.

Potato Magic

We need to talk about potatoes, because they are magical. And you can grow them in a tiny backyard plot, a trash can, a plastic tub, or a laundry basket. Here's how:

1. Most garden stores sell seed potatoes, but if you can't find them, grocery store potatoes will work in a pinch. If you do go this route, it's crucial to use organic potatoes, since conventional ones are usually

sprayed with an anti-sprouting chemical and won't grow. Plan on planting your potatoes in the spring after the danger of frost has passed. (That means I plant mine mid- to late May, but if you live in a warmer climate, you can plant them much earlier.)

2. If the potatoes are large, cut them into two or three pieces, ensuring there is an "eye" in each chunk. Let the cut potatoes sit out for a day or two so they dry. (This prevents rotting.)

3. Choose a sunny location for your potatoes. If you're planting in the ground, dig a trench six inches deep. Place the potatoes cut-side down in the trench (space them about twelve inches apart), and cover with soil. Potatoes like consistent moisture, so keep the soil damp as the plants grow. Once the leaves of the plant are about eight inches tall, use a hoe to mound more soil around the base of the foliage. Repeat this several times throughout the growing season. If you're growing in a container, add more soil instead of mounding. This will increase your yield, and protect your potatoes from sunlight (which turns them green).

4. The potatoes are ready to harvest once the foliage starts to wither and turn brown. Your exact yield will depend on the variety you planted, the quality of your soil, and how much you mounded the plants, but expect to harvest three to five pounds of potatoes from each plant. Eat your harvest fresh for the most incredible potatoes you've ever tasted, or let them cure for a week or two and then store them in a cool, dark place for up to three months.

I grew up with vegetables in the backyard, but my dad (the primary gardener in our family) tended his plot much differently than I do. He'd built his career as a seed treatment salesman, so his affinity for industrial farm methods came naturally. His

seeds were always dyed pink, indicating they were pretreated
to resist disease and increase germination. (Every ball cap of my
youth was emblazoned with the names of the latest treatment
companies and chemicals: Syngenta, Vitavax, Dividend, and
more.) Like many men of his generation, Roundup remains his
weapon of choice, as he wages chemical warfare on errant this-
tles or dandelions that dare show their faces in his lawn.

In *Second Nature*, Michael Pollan writes that the memories of past gardens live on the fringes of our current growing
spaces. This conventional, chemical-filled garden is the one
that launched my interest in growing. And ironically, it's the
memory that dances on the edges of my minimal-till, generously mulched, compost-fed, organic heirloom vegetable garden.
Gardens have an uncanny way of capturing our imaginations,
even when philosophies differ.

Some are born with a love for gardening. Others (like myself)
come to it later when the pull of a more meaningful life dredges
up fond memories of soil and sun. And so we start to wonder,
"What if I could grow a few things myself?"

For the longest time, I felt alienated from other gardeners.
They always seemed to be bounding through the fields, their
baskets overflowing with pretty, perky produce (which they always posted on Instagram, of course). I couldn't relate to their
fanciful escapades. At. All. In truth, my gardening experience
felt more like an army crawl through two feet of cold mud, with
nothing but measly, slug-eaten tomatoes as a consolation prize.

At first, my garden struggles felt like some sort of moral fail-
ing, but I know better now. Gardening is a highly subjective
pursuit with plenty of moving parts. While some of my obstacles
were related to my slightly impulsive nature, I've since realized
most of my issues were related to location.

I was talking to a friend who spent a year visiting all sorts of
farms and homesteads across the USA. Of all the places he'd
visited, he deemed Wyoming to be one of the most challeng-

ing places to homestead. This declaration left me feeling a little deflated at first, but then...strangely victorious. Because even though I was living in one of the most inhospitable climates in the States, I was growing stuff. And lots of it.

You probably (hopefully) don't live in a climate as brutal as I do, but you will surely face other obstacles. Maybe your challenge is lack of space. Or too much shade. Or restrictive covenants. Or water shortages. Or oppressive heat. Or swarms of aphids, potato beetles, or cabbage moths.

But I stand by my belief that anyone, anywhere, with any amount of space can indeed grow something green and reap the benefits. And nope, there's no such thing as a brown thumb. Your ability to grow (or kill) houseplants is in no way related to your ability to grow food. (Yes, I'm speaking from personal experience.)

Your particular garden may require a bit more effort than your friend's with the perfect sunny plot in the perfect growing zone with the perfectly straight rows. (I don't actually know anyone with the perfect garden spot. And if I did, we probably wouldn't be friends anyway.) But once we step away from the impossible goal of perfection, we can start experiencing the thrill of growing our own food.

Preserving with Powders

As you progress in your old-fashioned adventure, you'll probably start feeling an inexplicable urge to squirrel away food. Don't worry, this is normal. There are endless ways to preserve your harvest, including freezing, canning, dehydrating, salt-curing, or fermenting. However, the following method has become a favorite of mine in recent years since the finished product doesn't take up much space and the flavor is incredible. Vegetable powders can be added to soups for extra flavor, mixed into smoothies for added nutrients, or in the case of tomato powder, reconstituted to make sauce or paste. You will need a dehydrator for this, but you can often find affordable models for under $50, or at garage sales or thrift stores for even cheaper.

1. **Select your veggies.** Tomatoes (my favorite), greens, peppers, garlic, onions, beets, carrots, celery, and mushrooms are all good candidates.

2. **Wash and slice.** We're aiming for consistent slices, although the exact size doesn't matter as much. Keep in mind the thicker the slices, the longer it will take the food to dry. Thinner is better.

3. **Dehydrate.** Load the dehydrator trays in a single layer and turn on the machine. I usually dehydrate veggies at 125°F. Allow the machine to run until the slices are completely dry and brittle (this can take from eight to twenty-four hours).

4. **Condition the slices.** This step is important because it removes remaining moisture. Fill a jar two-thirds full with the dried slices. For the next four to ten days, shake the jar a few times per day. As you do this, any pieces that stick to the jar will need to go back into the dehydrator (or you can eat them).

5. **Grind 'em up.** Pop the conditioned slices into a high-powered blender or food processor. Process in batches until you're left with a fine powder.

6. **(Optional) Stop the caking.** Some powders are more prone to caking. To prevent this (and lengthen the powder's shelf life), complete this final step. Spread the powder on baking sheets and bake it in a 200°F oven for fifteen to twenty minutes. Let it cool, then pour it into glass jars for long-term storage. Your powders will last three to six months on the shelf, and much longer in the freezer.

I'm Ready to Grow... Now What?

Two distinct personalities arise when it comes time to plant a garden.

First up, the researchers. Eliminating mistakes and mapping out the perfect game plan is priority number one, so down the rabbit hole you go. As with most rabbit holes, the more you dig, the more tunnels you find. Soil has a pH? Wait, what's MY soil's pH? Do I have clay or sand? Does my soil have enough nitrogen? Too much nitrogen? What about potash and potassium? Should I build raised beds or just stick these seeds in the ground like an animal? Do I need to buy a rototiller? Wait...this guru says tilling is evil? Compost or fertilizer from the store? And if I DO compost, then should it be sourced from horse, steer, sheep, goat, rabbit, mushroom, chicken, or kitchen scraps? Heirloom or conventional seeds? What about mulch?

Suddenly the produce aisle at the supermarket seems more appealing than ever.

Then there are the fly-by-the-seat-of-their-pants folks. On Friday afternoon, the idea of a garden pops into your head. By Saturday, your garden is planted. The rows may be a little crooked, and you may not remember all the names of the seeds you planted, but hey, it's in. And that's good enough.

Personally, I'm a pants-seat flyer. I've occasionally dipped my toe into ultraresearcher territory, but it left me feeling so tied up in knots that I swore it off completely. Jumping out of the airplane and building my parachute on the way down is more my style. Sometimes that strategy ends poorly, but most of the time, it somehow works.

> **don't overthink it.**

So I will share the advice that has served me well time and time again: don't overthink it.

You need just four simple things to grow vegetables: seeds, soil, sunshine, and water. (I've been sitting here for ten minutes trying to think of a word for water that starts with an *s*. No such luck.)

It's really that easy. No need to complicate things, especially when you're getting started.

Start by buying a couple packets of basic vegetable seeds (save the exotic stuff for later).

Stick with vegetables that can be planted directly into the soil, like beans, squash, or carrots. (Some plants, like tomatoes or peppers, require a longer season, so most people start them indoors and transplant later. It's not difficult, but it does add a layer of complexity. So, I recommend direct planting for brand-new gardeners.)

Find a sunny spot along the edges of your yard and rough up the soil a bit.

Stick the seeds in the soil, cover them up with soil, and spray the area with the hose.

And now you wait.

Within a week or so (maybe sooner, depending on what you planted), you'll see the delicate seedlings make their appearance. It's a miraculous moment, no matter how many gardens I've planted. I dare you to convince me otherwise.

At this point, your job description shifts from cultivator to nurturer. But again, it's not complicated. All you do is water, weed, and watch. Press your finger into the soil every day or so—if it's dry, add more water. If it's still soggy or damp, you can skip watering that day. While you're there, pluck out any volunteer plants that don't match the emerging seedlings because it's best to catch weeds early, before they gain a stronghold.

You might murder a few plants along the way (not intentionally of course—it just happens), but you will have *started* your new life as a home gardener. And that's where the magic takes root.

As with most new pursuits, beginning is the hardest step: the first shovelful of overturned soil, the first batch of biscuits, the first brooder of chicks, the first words on the page, the first brush-strokes on the canvas. Create as much momentum as quickly as possible and ride that wave of excitement as far as it can take you.

Mistakes are to be expected. I've messed stuff up royally over the years. Once I accidentally planted a lawn in my garden, thanks to improperly composted horse manure that was full of grass seed. Another year I poisoned my entire garden with hay mulch that, unbeknownst to me, had been sprayed with a potent herbicide (I'll tell you that whole story in Chapter 9). And I'm still embarrassed by how long it took me to figure out the difference between humus and hummus (one is organic matter produced by decaying organisms, and the other is a tasty bean dip). But all my foibles aside, I've grown many thousands of pounds of vegetables over the last decade, even amid contaminated mulch, an overgrowth of grass, and snowstorms the first week of September. I'm proof that even the most dismal garden disasters are redeemable. So have no fear.

Planting History

If you're hankering for a bit of fanciness without the fuss in your first garden, consider heirloom seeds. An heirloom or heritage vegetable is a variety that has existed for fifty years or more. Because they are open-pollinated, you can save seeds from these plants from year to year and keep the cycle going. Heirlooms are the perfect entry point into the world of unconventional gardening, since they don't cost much more than regular seeds and give credence to long-forgotten or endangered varieties. Besides, who wouldn't want to grow "Magenta Sunset" chard, "Moon and Stars" watermelon, or "Red Cored Chantenay" carrots?

No Land? No Problem.

My primary gardening challenges are early blizzards and hail-storms, but yours might be a complete lack of land. Even if that is your situation, growing food is still within your grasp.

Some of the gardens I find most inspiring are the ones shoe-horned into the most densely populated areas. Their ingenuity and creative use of space make our utilization of sixty-seven acres seem downright sloppy. I've seen folks fill fire escapes with vegetables, turn their apartment balconies into edible jungles, and fill postage-stamp-sized front yards with masterful arrangements of squash, corn, and beans. Sometimes I daydream about what I'd do if I were suddenly dropped in the middle of a big city. My game plan would look something like this:

First, I'd fill my home with green things—even if I lived in a tiny studio apartment. Southern-facing windows are gold, so I'd use them to their maximum potential. *Year-Round Indoor Salad Gardening* by Peter Burke teaches a brilliant method of growing nutrient-packed microgreens or salad greens on a windowsill.

If I didn't have any windows (which feels unlikely, unless one is living in an underground bunker, but I'll roll with it for the sake of the example…) I'd invest in a few grow lights. Sure, the neighbors might think you're gearing up to grow something else, but that's okay. Let them talk. In my indoor grow space, I'd plant herbs, lettuce, spinach, green onions, and peppers in recycled or thrift store containers. In fact, I use a similar method to start seedlings in my basement here on my farm. I hang fluorescent shop lights from an inexpensive baker's rack (one light per shelf). Then I pack a hefty number of growing trays in my shelves of green.

Finally, don't forget the sprouts—they can be grown right on your kitchen counter in a glass jar—no sunlight required.

Homegrown Sprouts in Seven Simple Steps

1. Buy seeds specifically designed for sprouting to ensure they aren't treated with fungicides or other chemicals. Alfalfa, broccoli, radish, pea, mustard, or clover seeds are the most common options.

2. Place one-fourth to one-half cup of sprouting seeds in a clean quart-sized glass jar (a mason jar or old spaghetti sauce jar works great).

3. Cover the seeds with lukewarm water and soak them overnight (or about twelve hours).

4. Drain the water from the seeds—you can buy fancy sprouting lids for this, but I usually just use a small kitchen sieve or strainer.

5. Cover your jar with a towel and keep seeds out of direct sunlight. Rinse the seeds with cool, fresh water two or three times per day, or until they've sprouted (aka developed little tails).

6. When seeds have sprouted, remove from the jar and clean and dry your jar. Then place the sprouts back in the jar and place in indirect sunlight for twelve to twenty-four hours. The sprouts will produce chlorophyll and carotenes and are then ready to be enjoyed.

7. Lay out any sprouts you don't eat right away on a linen towel to air-dry before storing them in the refrigerator, where they should keep for at least four or five days. Homegrown sprouts are delicious on sandwiches, on salads, or straight out of the jar.

From there, I'd annex the balcony (if I had one) and focus on growing bigger veggies in pots. Tomatoes, cucumbers, beans, and even roots like radishes and carrots all thrive in containers with the proper soil. Some people grow dwarf citrus trees in pots and move them in and out of their houses each season. (I once bought a potted lemon tree and moved it, depending on the weather. It grew happily until I forgot to bring it inside during a hailstorm and it died a horrible death. But I'm sure you'd never do that.)

If I had a patio or porch, that'd be even better. I'd line the edges with rectangular growing boxes, squeeze pots among the seating areas, and train the tomatoes, beans, and squash to climb the railings. It would be a patio food forest of sorts—a place to entertain supper guests among the vegetables.

If I had a larger yard, things would get even more exciting. Instead of spending time and money tending to a lawn, I'd fill my grassy areas with vegetables. In the front yard, I'd use creative landscaping and raised beds to keep the growing areas aesthetically pleasing. Instead of landscaping with typical shrubs and bushes around the margins, I'd plant fruit trees and perennial edibles: berry bushes, asparagus, and artichokes, with some annuals thrown in, too. I think a well-kept vegetable plot is just as stunning as the most sophisticated flower garden. (Although I have nothing against flowers—we need them to keep the bees happy.)

For those concerned about the time commitment involved in gardening, keep in mind many of us are already farming in a sense—our crop is the modern American lawn. Lawns cover approximately 40 million acres of the United States, which makes them our largest irrigated crop. Since turf grass isn't native to most states, it takes considerable effort to keep it looking presentable. In fact, the average American spends around seventy hours per year nurturing our outdoor carpets. Perhaps our innate urge to tend to nature is still alive in all of us; we're simply fulfilling it through mowing and fertilizing rather than planting and weeding.

What would happen if we replaced even just a portion of these 40 million acres with home food production instead?

Mulch It

When someone shares with me that they are struggling to keep up with their garden chores, my answer
is MULCH. Mulching saves me countless hours of work
each summer by reducing weeds, conserving water,
and creating soil with soft, crumbly texture and lots of
happy worms. I apply a generous layer of mulch to my
garden several times throughout the growing season
and again when I put my garden to bed in the winter. If
you don't want to use grass clippings, then leaves, old
hay, or straw can also work. The key is to make your
layer thick enough to smother the weeds (I aim for at
least six to eight inches). And make sure that whatever
you use has not been sprayed with herbicides.

If you don't have a yard or lawn to transform, there's ample
potential in borrowed land.

Vacant lots, community gardens, and even industrial rooftops
hold a lot of promise, especially in postindustrial cities. One study
done in Cleveland, Ohio, looked at scenarios where flat roofs and
empty lots could be used to grow 46 to 100 percent of a community's fresh produce and up to 94 percent of their poultry and eggs.

The USDA website estimates 13.5 million people in the
United States reside in a food desert, which is defined as a geo-
graphical area where residents have limited access to grocery
stores—especially ones with healthier options. What if postindustrial cities could become hubs of healthy foods instead of
deserts filled with industrialized junk food? Just the thought
makes me excited.

Maybe that's why, in recent years, like-minded advocates
have been working hard to establish urban farm opportunities,
particularly in underserved areas. The USDA offers grants for
urban farmers, and other organizations like the National Young
Farmers Coalition and regional programs like Urban Harvest in

Houston, Texas, offer support for beginners of all ages. Not only can they help you access training opportunities, but some can even help match you with landowners who allow their property to be used for agricultural purposes at no cost to you. The landowners benefit with tax write-offs, and you get free access to farmland. It's a win-win for all involved.

In recent years, more cities and towns of all sizes are moving toward more sustainable practices. With community gardens, rooftop gardens, vertical gardens, and school gardens, they're striving for more locally sourced foods. Aside from that, some public libraries have begun offering "seed libraries" (in which you can obtain free heirloom seeds and replace them the following year with new ones from your harvest), and many USDA extension offices rent everything from garden tools to apiary equipment, often with an agent willing to show you exactly how to use it all. (Plus, they'll usually provide free soil analysis to help you get those nutrients perfect for high-yield harvests.) Some cities also offer curbside compost services, recycling your food waste and delivering fresh organic compost as needed. Of course, you can always take it a step further and try hydroponics (growing plants without soil) or aquaculture (farming in water), two trendy alternatives for people without a lot of space (or soil). The options are endless—they're just waiting for someone brave enough to give them a go.

The Gift That Keeps Giving

One of the main reasons I love gardening with heirloom or open-pollinated seeds is that I can save seeds from year to year. Seed saving is an ancient practice that has created some of our most-loved varieties of fruits and veggies. It's also an old-fashioned way to preserve regional diversity and protect rare varieties of plants that have been pushed aside in favor of strains that are better suited for mass production. Here's a quick step-by-step:

1. Always start with open-pollinated or heirloom plants. Many conventional veggie varieties are hybrids, which means they were created by intentional cross-pollination. Since they won't reproduce true to type, this makes seed saving futile.

2. Pick easy plants. Peppers, peas, beans, lettuce, and melons are ideal for beginning savers since the plants don't require isolation or more fussy techniques.

3. Let the plant mature. In many cases, seeds don't form until later in the growing process, so we must allow at least some of the plants to mature completely. For example, I wait until my bean and pea pods are tough and fibrous before I collect the seeds.

4. Allow the seeds to dry (if necessary). Since I let my bean seeds dry on the plant, I can put them directly into storage. However, I like to rinse the debris off my pepper and melon seeds first. To do this, place the seeds in a jar with enough water to cover them. Shake well, drain the water, and let the seeds dry completely on a paper towel.

5. Store until next year. Seeds like to be cool and dark. I store mine in tightly sealed glass jars (to keep out moisture and pests) in the unfinished portion of our basement where it stays cool year-round.

Over time, seed saving will also allow you to select for certain traits that are most important to you. For example, if I save seeds from a tomato plant that ripened a little earlier than the rest, and I repeat this for several years in a row, I can slowly cultivate a strain of tomato that's better suited for our short growing seasons. This same process can be used for a myriad of traits—from color, to size, to flavor. A fantastic resource if you want to dive deeper into seed saving is *The Complete Guide to Saving Seeds* by Robert E. Gough and Cheryl Moore-Gough.

Benefits Beyond Tomatoes

By now you've probably sensed a bit of rebel in me. I admit, I not only love gardening for the many benefits it gives my family (and community), but I also savor how scandalous it feels to take an empty basket to the garden and return with all that loot. It's as if I'm secretly beating the system. It's victorious.

But healthier ingredients (and an adrenaline rush) are only the beginning of the reward, for there is much to be harvested from the garden besides just food. While some people find solace in the wilderness, I find mine in the garden.

I've never been able to cultivate much of an interest in a perfectly tamed flower garden. Resilient vegetables are more my style. My favorite time of year is August when my plants have almost gone rogue. At that point, I've forsaken all efforts to keep things tidy, so nature takes over. The sunflowers dwarf me by several feet, the squash vines burst through the fences, and the tomato plants tangle in the walkways, snagging my feet as I pass. For that brief moment, my utilitarian prairie garden takes a page from the feral spaces of *The Secret Garden*, and I couldn't love it more.

Last summer I found myself running on fumes. With our numerous family activities and multiple business projects, burnout was creeping in. I contemplated hiring more help (or taking a vacation), but ultimately, there was one thing that kept whispering to me. I was struck with an inexplicable craving to "go to the garden."

So that's exactly what I did.

Each night, as the horizon morphed with the sinking sun, I'd tuck the kids into bed and then steal away to my garden. But unlike daytime visits, I didn't use that time to water or weed or check another task off my never-ending to-do list. Instead, I just sat. And I listened.

As I tuned in to the sounds of my garden, I tuned out the

chaos in my mind. That's when I really began to hear the music: the chickens cooing in their run, thunder rumbling in the distance, bullfrogs singing their chorus. Around me, bean plants swayed in the breeze, white cabbage moths danced across the beds, and ants acted out their grand insect drama in the wood chips under my feet. These moments between my garden and me proved to be deeply healing, in a humble, organic way. By the time the sun sank each night, blanketing the farm in darkness, I'd walk back to the house feeling refreshed and full.

The garden used to be my last resort for handling stress. I'd always try zoning out on my phone or bingeing Netflix first. But now, it's my first line of defense when I'm feeling out of sorts. Excavating potatoes brings me back into my body on the days when my brain won't slow down. The labor of digging calms me, plus each time I unearth a fat, red globe from the soil, I'm rewarded with a little rush of dopamine. I often grumble about weeding, but once I start, it's hard to stop. Pulling a towering pigweed out by its roots is strangely soothing. When I lost one of my most beloved horses unexpectedly, the garden was the only place where I felt I could process my shock and grief. I can't fully explain it, but being close to the soil comforted me while reminding me of the circle of life. No, the garden won't fix everything, but I can't imagine a life without it. And I'm not the only one.

I was recently talking with the marketing director at a well-known greenhouse manufacturing company. He told me whenever the stock market dips or there's uncertainty related to the economy, their sales spike. At first glance, this doesn't make sense. When faced with financial or societal uncertainty, people are spending their hard-earned dollars on…greenhouses? But much like our innate desire to bake bread in the midst of a global pandemic, there's something deep inside us that inherently feels the pull to return to the garden when things feel shaky.

But maybe there's more to it than that. The true benefits of gardening go beyond simply being prepared for zombies (or whatever the latest threat may be). When humans return to the garden, it brings us to a place of internal balance—mentally, physically, and spiritually.

When we choose a life connected to the soil, even if that connection begins with a small windowsill pot of basil, we are changed. You'll plant that baby basil plant, and as it grows, it'll smell so delicious you'll want to find a recipe worthy of its flavor. And then, you might enjoy that dish so much that you'll plant a few more things and spend a little more time in the kitchen, which might lead you to the farmers market. There you'll meet like-minded people who will encourage creative experimentation. Your local food economy will blossom. And you'll walk with a little more pep in your step, thanks to your newfound passions (and improved diet).

And it all begins with seeds, soil, sunshine, and soaks. (I found my missing *s* word!)

The "Not from the Store" Challenge

Thinking about ingredients outside of the conventional supermarket routine can feel intimidating. Try breaking the process into baby steps to make it easier.

Baby Step #1: Make one component of a meal instead of buying it. Maybe you make your own bread crumbs instead of buying them, you mix up a roux for gravy instead of using premade packets, or you shred potatoes to make hash browns instead of using frozen ones. It doesn't matter how small it is. The goal is to start thinking outside of the usual supermarket shelves.

Baby Step #2: Source one ingredient without using the grocery store. You might forage it, grow it, trade for it, or buy it at the farmers market. Maybe you buy a carton of eggs from the neighbor down the street, you ask your mushroom-hunting friend to teach you the fine art of foraging, or you try a package of grass-finished ground beef from a local rancher.

Baby Step #3: Source an entire meal outside of the grocery store. This won't happen overnight, but you might be surprised how quickly it comes together as you repeat steps #1 and #2. For us, that first meal was a home-raised steak with mashed potatoes and green beans from our garden. It was a rustic meal, but let me tell you—*nothing* has ever tasted so good.

Becoming Old MacDonald

Becoming our own grocery store often starts with produce, but it can extend into the meat and dairy coolers, too. While I love my garden vegetables, thanks to our volatile Wyoming climate we have a much easier time harvesting eggs, milk, and meat here on our homestead. While most modern farms are highly specialized operations that focus on one cash crop, visits to historic farmsteads tell a very different story.

When I visit the ruins of old homesteads, I love to hunt out each piece of their homegrown grocery store. There's usually a milking stanchion in the barn, with a springhouse (a precursor to modern refrigeration) situated over a creek to keep the milk and cream cool. There are corrals for beef cattle and hogs, small sheds to house chickens, and smokehouses for preserving hams and bacon. Sometimes I can spot the remnants of orchards or feral asparagus or rhubarb patches. Occasionally I'll find musty root cellars littered with shards of stoneware crocks and sagging shelves that once housed rows of home-canned food. These old-fashioned farms feel quaint when compared to the high-tech agricultural operations of today, but they're beautiful examples of agrarian synergy that kept their families very well-fed. This interdependence of humans, plants, and animals is exactly what we seek to model on our own homestead. And our livestock plays a major part.

Beef cattle graze our pastures and turn the prairie grass into a sustainable protein source that graces our table year-round. Their fat becomes soap and candles, and their bones provide the base for nutrient-rich broth.

Our flock of laying hens transforms garden trimmings and kitchen scraps into orange-yolked eggs.

Our Brown Swiss cows provide us with milk, cream, butter, yogurt, and cheese for the house, as well as leftover whey and curdled milk for the pigs and chickens.

In turn, the pigs transform that leftover milk (and other food waste) into hams and bacon and sausage, as well as lard for baking.

And together, all of them give us one of the most precious resources of all: manure.

I am forever fascinated with this cycle of abundance that occurs on our little patch of prairie soil. While we're still dependent on some inputs from outside sources, by applying some of these long-forgotten farming practices, we're able to produce a staggering amount of food. I love how when food production becomes smaller and more local, everyone is happier, healthier, and more in line with nature. And that goes for the humans, the livestock, and the land. As you adopt an old-fashioned on purpose lifestyle, you can partake in this same cycle, even if you live in the middle of a city with no pastures or chicken coops in sight.

First, I invite you to consider the bigger picture of your personal food system. When we look at the food production systems of old-fashioned farms, we can see they were deeply interconnected and wasted very little. How can you bring some of those ideas into your own life?

Maybe it starts with learning how to use *all* the parts of the food you buy. (The chicken bones, the beet tops, the apple cores, etc.)

Repurposing Scraps

Use up every bit of those amazing ingredients with these old-fashioned tricks:

- Apple skins and cores can be used as a base for homemade vinegar.

- Stale bread turns into croutons or bread crumbs.

- Onion, carrot, and celery ends are the perfect starter for vegetable stock. Pop them in a baggie in the freezer until you've collected enough for a batch.

- Leftover beef, chicken, fish, or pork bones become flavorful broth. (See my recipe on page 122.)

- Random bits of meat (ground beef, leftover chicken or turkey, pork roast) can be mixed with a handful of veggies and topped with biscuit dough before baking for a quick yet filling potpie.

- Beet and carrot tops can be transformed into pesto, as can kale or spinach stems.

- Fruit that's slightly past its prime is ideal for homemade jam or fruit leather.

- Tomato skins can be dehydrated and blended to make tomato powder.

- Orange or lemon peels can be added to homemade cleaner. (See my recipe on page 163.)

- Used coffee grounds are fantastic additions to homemade exfoliating soaps and scrubs.

- Or, share your kitchen scraps with a chicken flock. (See my tips for creating a "chicken bucket" on page 106.)

Or perhaps you could start mimicking old-time farmers and use local compost or manures to feed your soil instead of commercial fertilizers (more on that in Chapter 9).

If you can't keep animals in your location, develop relationships with local farmers. See if local farms offer tours or volunteer opportunities, or better yet, like we talked about previously, buy your food directly from them.

Maybe you can bring more native plants back into your garden and landscaping or learn how to use the plants in your area that everyone considers to be weeds.

Beekeeping is a fantastic option for small spaces. The honey is great, but even more importantly, as pollinators decrease across the globe, beekeeping is one way to support their populations.

And of course, we can't have a conversation about homestead livestock without talking about the animals I affectionately refer to as the gateway drug for the homesteading lifestyle...*chickens*.

Our first flock of chickens was an impulse buy on a Friday night. I didn't have grand aspirations of building a sustainable food system. I just wanted better eggs. We'd lived on our property for a year or two at that point, and I decided our old yellow sheep shed would make an ideal chicken coop.

Christian had given me the green light for poultry acquisition (he's my enabler), but since it was summer, there wasn't a chick to be found at any of the feed stores (our chick season runs from March to April here). I couldn't fathom waiting another nine months, so I headed to Craigslist.

Within two hours, I was driving home with a flock of Rhode Island Reds in dog crates in the back of my Ford Taurus. In hindsight, I paid far more than I should have for mature hens. These were around three years old, which is exactly when egg production begins to decrease. Their previous owner was probably selling them to ensure he wasn't stuck with a flock of less-than-productive birds. But ignorance is bliss, and I was just thrilled to wake up to eggs in the nesting boxes that first morning. All these years later, there's still something special about an early morning stroll to the henhouse to collect eggs for breakfast.

Chickens are the perfect start to home food production for several reasons:

- They don't take up much space and can adapt to an urban environment.

- Since they are small, you don't need any previous live-stock handling skills to safely handle them.

- There's a big difference in the color and flavor of home-grown eggs as compared to store-bought. This makes them especially gratifying to produce at home.

- Aged chicken manure is rich in nitrogen and is perfect for adding to your soil.

There are plenty of fancy chicken breeds, but stick with a tried-and-true laying type for your first go-round. Rhode Island Reds, Australorps, Buff Orpingtons, or Plymouth Rocks are all solid options. These breeds have calmer dispositions and are consistent egg layers. And disposition matters... I once had a flock of Icelandic chickens—a rare, ancient variety. They were beautiful, but they despised confinement and insisted on flying out of their coop and roosting in the rafters of our equipment shed. It wasn't the end of the world (although Christian wasn't thrilled about them pooping on his tractors), but it would have been a nightmare if I had been trying to keep them contained in an urban setting.

Chicken feed is readily available at feed stores, but amending it with kitchen scraps cuts costs and makes the eggs even better.

Visitors usually eye the container by my kitchen sink with various levels of suspicion. I'm sure they're wondering why a bowl brimming with eggshells, carrot tops, watermelon rinds, and potato skins has earned such a prominent place on my countertop. Although it may be a curiosity in a modern home, the "slop bucket" was a mainstay of households for centuries—and for good reason. Not only did kitchen scraps sustain the family farm animals, they also reduced the need for reliance on outside grains, which drastically cut the family feed store bill. Our great-grandparents wouldn't have dreamed of sending nutrient-rich food scraps to a landfill. And you can follow in their footsteps:

First, find a sturdy bucket or bowl that's easy to wash and won't break if you tote it outside and accidentally forget about it. (Been there, done that.) Set it in a spot in your kitchen where it's easy to access. Some people keep their buckets inside a cupboard, but I know my weaknesses. If it's hard to reach, I won't use it.

Now toss all your unwanted food into the bucket. I'm talking apple cores, leftover bits of oatmeal, dried-out bread heels, floppy celery stalks, the bag of salad greens you swore you'd eat and then you didn't—yep, all of it. (And yes—you can include meat scraps, too. Chickens are omnivores and will happily devour any meat bits they can find, including grasshoppers, grubs, beetles, and any mice unlucky enough to venture inside the coop.) Offer your flock the contents of the scrap bucket daily. Then watch the spectacle that unfolds. You'll quickly learn their favorites—strawberry tops and tomato bits always go first, followed by any sort of bread. If one hen gets the prize, the others will chase her down and attempt to steal it. It's more drama than *The Real Housewives*. (And possibly more entertaining.)

Chicken Tractors

A chicken tractor (a mobile, bottomless coop or enclosure) is another option for housing your flock while also spreading the wealth (aka manure) around your property. While we have both stationary and mobile coops on our homestead, I find myself preferring the mobile options. Our current tractor is a simple contraption that Christian built out of two-by-fours and chicken wire. (It's much heavier than recommended for the typical tractor. But most typical tractors don't have to contend with hurricane-force winds.) We drag it to a new place in the yard each day to allow the birds to nibble at the grass and eat whatever bugs are unlucky enough to venture inside. The following year, you can see the previous path of the tractor is evident by grass that is taller and brighter than any other place in the yard, proof that the soil appreciates this natural cycle.

Chicken shelters don't have to be fancy (chandeliers and curtains aren't required, no matter what Pinterest says). In addition to an outdoor pen of some sort, your flock will appreciate a four-sided place where they can escape the elements and feel safe from predators. Add in a nesting box or two (old wooden crates are perfect for this), a place to roost, food, and water, and you're all set.

The old-fashioned act of growing our own ingredients gives us the gift of relationship with food and land. The homestead is a place where we stop fighting nature and, instead, immerse ourselves in it. And that applies whether your homestead consists of forty acres or a small backyard, balcony, or basement. One of the most satisfying pleasures of eating is in knowing where our food comes from. The more fully we understand that our food is tied to the soil rather than the store, the broader our perspective becomes. I love it when my ingredients remind me of the earth. I want to smell soil as I wash my potatoes. I want to see the tiniest bits of feathers on the chicken drumsticks. I welcome the bits of straw on my eggs. And I don't even mind the occasional bug bite in my freshly picked spinach. It's a welcome reassurance that my food is real and reminds me of my place in the bigger picture of things.

But growing our own ingredients does create one problem: once we bring these fresh, beautiful foods into the house, we must figure out how to use them. And they don't come with instructions...

Old-Fashioned Action Steps

- Grow something. In your windowsill. On your balcony. In your backyard. Or with grow lights in your bedroom or basement. If it feels like too big of an undertaking right now, start with sprouts on your kitchen counter. Whatever it takes, plant some seeds and watch them grow.

- Soil health is crucial, especially if you are growing food in containers. If you're using old, spent potting soil, your vegetable harvest will be scant. Amend the soil generously to keep production high.

- Instead of synthetic options, use organic compost or aged manure to fertilize your garden plot. Try 4-H clubs for leads on steer, rabbit, horse, or goat manure. (But be cautious of manure that may contain pesticides or herbicides. Horse manure is the most suspect since horse hay is commonly sprayed with aminopyralids—a category of herbicides that takes years to dissipate. This is the trouble I ran into a number of years ago, and I wouldn't wish that mess on anyone. More on this in Chapter 9.) Bagged manure from the garden store is better than nothing, but it's expensive if you need any quantity, so it's more cost-effective to go direct.

- If you can't raise your own animals, get to know local producers. Source honey from local beekeepers, eggs from your friend with the chickens, and meat from local ranchers and farmers.

- Think about the bigger picture of your ingredients, just like an old-time homesteader would. How can you put all the bits and scraps of the food you buy to good use? How could your garden and animals work together in a more holistic way?

- Strive to be a good advocate of the old-fashioned on purpose lifestyle, especially if you live in a populated area. When converting a front lawn to a garden, be mindful of the neighbors and HOA covenants, and keep it tidy and organized. If you raise city chickens, skip the roosters (many people don't share my affection for early morning crowing), and reduce unwanted aroma by using the deep bedding and composting methods. If you still have skeptical neighbors, never underestimate how far peace offerings of fresh vegetables and eggs can go.

CHAPTER 5

Cook Like Great-Grandma

My grandmother died when I was nine years old. Most of the memories I have of her are a little fuzzy and fragmented, but there's one part that remains vivid: her food.

Norma Christine Rising was a legendary cook, and I'm certain my penchant for overfeeding people came from her. She couldn't abide anyone leaving her table without first eating themselves into oblivion. As you crossed over the threshold of her red-gingham-draped kitchen, the aroma of beef and baked goods beckoned you to sit and stay awhile. Most of all, I remember her signature Saturday night roast suppers. There were buttery mashed potatoes smothered in thick from-scratch gravy, brown-sugar-glazed carrots, and angel food cake for dessert. But the star of the table was the beef. She had elevated the humble roast into an edible art form that fell apart on your fork before melting in your mouth.

When my interest in cooking and whole foods was kindled as an adult, Grandma's roast beef suppers were one of the first meals I attempted to replicate. And I failed miserably for years. My gravy was reminiscent of wallpaper paste, and I had to serve the roast with serrated knives so the unlucky eater could hack their serving into bite-size chunks. No matter what I did, I couldn't crack Grandma's code.

When my mom mentioned she had found Grandma's old

recipe boxes during a summer visit, I jumped at the chance to look through them. I was hopeful this collection would deliver a treasure trove of her trademark recipes and maybe even the much-anticipated secret of her masterpiece roasts.

As I thumbed through the yellowed three-by-five cards and obscure magazine clippings, I was devastated. Not only were her homemade bread and roast recipes absent, but there was a suspicious shortage of whole-food recipes in general. Nearly every recipe card called for the latest celebrated processed ingredients of her era: oleo, Jell-O, Cool Whip, Betty Crocker cake mixes, and Campbell's soup. Industrialization had struck again, offering a jarring reminder of the far-reaching effects of convenience food across the generations. Even a home cook of my Grandma's caliber hadn't been immune to the changing times. And so the kitchen is where we'll go to reclaim our next old-fashioned on purpose trait: *We cook from scratch.*

Our modern relationship with our kitchens couldn't be more different than that of our distant ancestors. Although premade food has been available in various forms since the early twentieth century, it didn't take center stage until World War II, when factories ramped up production of processed foods to feed the military. As a result, convenience foods like Kraft macaroni and cheese became a popular patriotic choice—it was cheap and meatless, and two boxes could be purchased for one rationing coupon. Eighty million boxes were sold in 1943 alone.

When the war ended, corporations had to get creative. So, they put their products into the hands of housewives instead of soldiers. The kitchen became the new frontline of marketing efforts focused on educating the American consumer about the wonders of factory foods. Commercials from the 1950s showcased picture-perfect families with wide smiles relishing the newly available convenience items. One Wonder Bread commercial touts the nutritional benefits of a daily sandwich: "As much iron as three lamb chops and as much niacin for mental health as six sardines!" In one Jell-O instant pudding commercial, the word "busy" is used thirteen times in seventy seconds to convey the time-saving wonders of the revolutionary dessert. A Betty Crocker muffin mix commercial waxes poetic over homemade muffins of old while passionately encouraging viewers to make their own baked goods "this modern way." Watch just a handful of vintage commercials, the message of the day is crystal clear—to be happy, healthy, relaxed, and modern, you must BUY. Only outdated, unhappy, frumpy housewives would make muffins from scratch. As the decades crept by, we forgot that our food ever came from the earth or the work of our hands. And our kitchens have never been the same.

We've become a culture that *celebrates* food instead of *cooks* it. Food blogs and cooking shows are more popular than ever, yet we're spending less time than any previous era in our kitchens. A 2016 study showed that we spend just thirty-seven minutes per day in food preparation and cleanup, as compared to nearly two hours a day in 1965. When divided over three meals per day, that equates to a mere twelve minutes per meal for modern families—less time than any other developed nation.

Industrialization has finally erased the monotony of food preparation. With access to fast food, takeout, microwaves, and convenience items in every size, shape, and flavor, it's no wonder we've learned to rely on these efficient options. Especially since corporate marketers yell at us from billboards, commercials, and banner ads: "Just add water! Frozen lasagna tastes like homemade! Grab our 3 for $5 special!"

> **In an era that tries to separate us from understanding how our food gets to our table, choosing an intimate knowledge of what we eat is revolutionary.**

Yet though we've been told that cooking is drudgery and we shouldn't be bothered with it, the exact opposite is true. *Cooking is power.* Of course, convenience isn't always a bad thing. But if we step back for just a second, we can see that we miss out on countless benefits when we relegate all our food preparation to manufacturers. In an era that tries to separate us from understanding how our food gets to our table, choosing an intimate knowledge of what we eat is revolutionary. Maybe even audacious. But most of all, it is transformative, not only in the way it empowers us to convert the raw offerings of the earth into sustenance, but in how it allows us to grasp a deeper understanding of ourselves and the world around us.

But before we can experience that transformation, we must first fall in love with our kitchens.

It's time for an old-fashioned kitchen revival, which is why I'll help you reclaim your family's kitchen in this chapter. Even if you've proclaimed a hatred of cooking or doubt your ability to boil water—take heart. We have more in common than you might think.

Rediscovering Grandma's Roasts

I've since figured out how to replicate my grandma's legendary roasts, and a roast beef dinner on a Saturday night remains one of my favorite meals. Here are my secrets for the best-ever beef or pork roasts:

- **Defrost it completely.** I used to try to cheat the system by putting frozen roasts right into my Crock-Pot. Technically it works, but the results are usually tough. It's worth it to take the extra step of defrosting ahead of time.

- **Season and SEAR.** Generously salt and pepper the roast, then sear it in bacon grease, lard, or butter until it's golden brown on all sides. This is the step I was missing in my early years.

- **Add extra flavor.** I cook my roasts in several cups of broth, with splashes of Worcestershire and generous additions of salt, pepper, garlic, onion, and sage.

- **Cook long and sloooow.** You can't rush it—trust me, I've tried. If you're using a slow cooker, cook on low for eight to ten hours. If using a Dutch oven, roast it at 300°F (with the lid on the pot) for three to four hours, or until it falls apart when you poke it with a fork.

The Unlikeliest Home Cook

Before moving to our homestead, I never gave my relationship with food a second thought. I was the quintessential consumer. Most of the food I purchased was encased in multiple layers of plastic packaging, traveling sometimes thousands of miles before being popped into my microwave. I bought blueberries in December and oranges in July. "Whipped topping" masqueraded as whipped cream in my freezer, slices of "pasteurized cheese product" impersonated cheddar in my fridge, and MSG-filled bouillons stood in for nutrient-rich broth in my cupboards.

The signature dishes of our newlywed years included such culinary delights as broiled Spam and cheese bread, frozen taquitos, and Tater Tot casserole. Nearly every food in our home was plastered with logos, filled with unpronounceable additives, and impervious to decomposition (in the traditional sense). But it all felt normal to me.

Then came the homestead.

Our budget was tighter than ever, and after a few months of living thirty-five miles from prepared food of any kind, I quickly discovered that if we wanted something *good* for supper,

I'd have to make it myself. Although my cooking was a choice made from necessity, not passion, hunger was a motivating impetus. And so I began to play in the kitchen.

I perfected from-scratch pizza crust and seasoned my own sauce for impromptu movie nights.

I mastered DIY hamburger buns since I never seemed to have enough when we wanted to have a cookout with friends.

I attempted to make french fries from raw potatoes, first in the oven, and then fried in golden beef tallow on the stove top.

I experimented with homemade bagels, soft pretzels, doughnuts, and French bread so I could whip them up whenever the urge arose.

I learned how to create my own cream of mushroom soup, enchilada sauce, and marinara, since they were never in my pantry when I needed them.

The Quick Pickle Formula

Quick pickling (also known as refrigerator pickling) is an easy way to preserve almost every type of vegetable. Simply cover fresh veggies in a brine solution and pop them in the fridge. This basic formula will make two pint jars of quick pickles.

Ingredients
- Vegetables of choice (approximately 1 pound); cucumbers, beets, carrots, tomatoes, green beans, or bell peppers are all good options

- Fresh or dried herbs, spices, or flavors of choice (think dill, mustard seeds, peppercorns, garlic, oregano, bay leaf, onion, etc.)

- 1 cup vinegar (either white or apple cider vinegar work well)

- 1 cup water

- 1 tablespoon fine sea salt (non-iodized is best)

- 1 tablespoon sugar (this reduces excess sourness, but isn't a requirement)

Instructions

Clean the jars and set them aside.

Wash and dry the vegetables, and peel if needed. You can pickle them whole or sliced—it's up to you.

Place your preferred flavors, spices, and herbs in the bottom of the jars. If using garlic, aim for 1 clove per jar. If using fresh herbs, add several sprigs to each jar. If using dried herbs, use ¼ to ½ teaspoon per jar. There is a lot of room for creativity here, so don't be afraid to experiment with amounts and flavor combinations.

Tightly pack the vegetables into the jars.

Make the brine: Combine the vinegar, water, salt, and sugar in a pot and bring to a boil. Stir occasionally to dissolve the salt and sugar.

Pour the brine over the produce in the jars, leaving one-half inch of headspace at the top.

Place the lids on the jars.

Let the jars cool to room temperature on your kitchen counter, then refrigerate.

Wait at least forty-eight hours before eating the pickled veggies to let the flavors meld together. The longer they sit, the more flavorful they'll be. Quick pickled veggies can be stored in your fridge for up to three months.

Some of my experiments resulted in mouthwatering meals I was proud to serve. Others became miserable failures. (I once exploded a pumpkin pie. True story.) But during that time, I made a shocking discovery: *the food marketers had lied*.

Making food from scratch wasn't *that* difficult. I mean, sure, biscuits and piecrusts required a little bit of finesse, but most of the recipes proved easier than I had thought. Even more shocking was my realization that *the more I created in the kitchen, the more I loved it.* By abdicating my cooking to corporations for so many years, I had been missing out on a supremely satisfying form of accomplishment.

The day I learned it was possible to make tortillas from scratch was transformative. Is that too dramatic a response for homemade tortillas? I don't think so. As silly as it may sound, until that moment, it had never occurred to me that certain foods could be made outside of a factory. Each time I'd stumble across a new recipe for making an item I previously believed to be accessible only from the store, it felt like I'd just discovered buried treasure. You can make yogurt at home? And crackers? And cream cheese? Why had no one ever told me this?

I found I could easily turn a pound of ground beef into a skillet meal with a little pasta and some veggies. I didn't need a cardboard box with mixes and prepackaged pasta to make it happen.

I discovered I could bring forth fluffy mounds of whipped cream from a splash of liquid cream in just a few minutes (and it didn't leave that chemical coating on the roof of my mouth, either).

I realized the cartons of brown liquid posing as broth were no comparison to nutrient-rich chicken stock that was simmered all day to extract all the goodness from the bones.

And from that point on, with every tortilla I rolled and every jar of yogurt I cultured, my confidence grew. My newfound obsession with the kitchen also fed my growing contrarian side. It felt deliciously rebellious to leave processed food in the dust and blaze my own trail.

Once I started to realize the miracles I could create in the kitchen with my own two hands, all while saving money and offering better nutrition to my family, there was no going back. A whole-food renaissance was underway. And if I can do it, so can you.

Beginning Your Kitchen Revival

The kitchen is the most magical room of a home. It's a stage where we shape raw ingredients into satisfying nourishment. It's a laboratory where we harness the chemistries of bacteria, yeast, salt, and fire. And it's a studio where we hone the arts of creating crusty loaves, bubbly ferments, and hearty stews.

> **The kitchen is the most magical room of a home.**

Your kitchen may be a sweeping space with top-tier appliances or a small nook in an urban apartment. It might feature granite countertops or faded Formica, boasting the most modern gadgets or basic workhorse tools. The color palette may be sleek and modern or a hodgepodge of decades-old trends. (Avocado green, anyone?) Regardless of size and aesthetics, your kitchen is the ideal place to claim your freedom from a world drowning in consumerism. A direct conduit between the garden and the table, your kitchen offers a ticket to self-sufficiency.

Like many kitchens, mine has undergone several face-lifts over the years, but it's not fancy. It's functional. While you may be picturing a sprawling farmhouse kitchen staged for social media selfies, YouTube videos, and photo shoots, my kitchen is actually a small space where my cultured foods fight for real estate and cookware adorns the wall. There's a sourdough starter by the spice rack, a crock of kombucha (fermented tea) on the island, and either vegetables fermenting or wheels of cheese drying in the corner, depending on the season. Scarred wooden cutting boards lean against the backsplash, mismatched knives cling to the magnetic strip above the sink, and my collection of well-loved cast-iron pans dangles over the stove. Eggs from the chicken coop wait in antique stoneware, feathers and bits of straw still attached. Filling the workspace, you'll find random garden produce—a solitary zucchini, a handful of unwashed potatoes, or a smattering of radishes. There are always dishes in the sink, always crumbs on the counters, always spills on my stove top, and always an excessive number of empty glass jars waiting to be put away.

I've come a long way from instant ramen noodles and microwave popcorn.

Now when people walk through the door of our home, the happy chaos of the kitchen draws them in. The very best conversations happen in the midst of stirring, chopping, and tasting. When we have a get-together, everyone gathers here, in the kitchen. It borders on ridiculous, but we can't help it. Sometimes halfway through the evening, someone will pause, look around the room, and declare, "Why are we all smashed in here when the couches are empty?" We laugh, but here we stay, perched on stools, leaning against the cupboards, and crowding around the island, as the chatter stretches long into the night.

But creating a life-giving kitchen doesn't require you to live on a farm. It can be established wherever you call home: an apartment, an RV, a single-wide trailer, a townhome, a split-level in the suburbs, or an old farmhouse on the edge of town. You don't have to move to a new house, wait for the perfect time of year, or start a new savings account to focus on food.

Food is far less complex than many people believe. Of course, there are plenty of ways to make it complicated or to procrastinate in the name of "research," but the truth is that preparing your own nourishing food can be a beautifully simple and rewarding practice. And you can start that practice right now, wherever you are today. But first, let's knock down some of the modern roadblocks that keep us paralyzed in the kitchen.

While our ancestors' lives revolved around food, weaving cooking into our modern routines can feel formidable. Overflowing schedules, tight budgets, and lack of culinary knowledge are just a few of the reasons we shy away from cooking at home. But these roadblocks aren't as impenetrable as you may believe. Let's address them one by one.

Roadblock #1: I don't have time
I mentioned earlier that in 1965, the average woman spent two hours per day cooking. But here's a secret: as old-fashioned as I may be, I rarely have two hours to devote to the kitchen each day. Homeschooling three kids, running multiple businesses, and keeping a homestead humming along is the ultimate juggling act. Every minute is precious. Yet, through the business meetings, book writing, product launches, and pre-algebra lessons, I still manage to put from-scratch meals on the table most days.

I lean heavily on a few strategies to accomplish this. First, I stick with the basics. This means the intricate homemade raviolis are reserved for special occasions (or let's be real—not at all). Thankfully, whole-food meals don't have to be fussy.

A few months ago, the kids and I came home from a full morning running errands in town. I was distracted wrapping up loose ends around the house and wasn't in the mood to deal with supper, but I remembered I had a whole chicken in the fridge. (Pro tip: always have *something* defrosting in the fridge—even if you're not sure when you'll use it.) I pulled it out and rubbed it down with salt and pepper before putting it in my five-quart Dutch oven. I shoved the pot into the oven at 350°F and went to the office to answer emails. About an hour before we ate, I scrubbed some of the potatoes I had previously dug from the garden and poked a few holes in the skins (because exploding potatoes are the worst). I placed the potatoes directly on the oven rack to bake, next to the chicken pot, while I went out to our garage gym and ran on the treadmill for a little while. About fifteen minutes before we were ready to eat, I pulled a bag of green beans out of the freezer and placed several handfuls in a saucepan with a splash of water, a dash of salt, and a squirt of lemon juice. The beans steamed while I carved the chicken and plopped the potatoes on a tray.

The result? A simple, home-cooked, nutritious meal. In less than fifteen minutes of hands-on time. All of the components were grown on our property, but you can easily find them at any supermarket in the nation. While there are certainly exceptions, most of the weeknight meals I make take less time to complete than a trip around the grocery store or a wait in a crowded drive-through line (even if you *don't* live thirty-five miles from town like I do).

Perhaps you don't work from home, so you can't pop in and out of the kitchen. No problem. This is where we can lean on the tools we have access to as modern folks. Instead of using a Dutch oven, put your chicken in the slow cooker before you leave the house that morning. When you get home, wash and cut a few potatoes (peeled or not) and place them in an Instant Pot with butter and salt. Or if you have a bit more time, cube them, toss with olive oil and salt, and roast them in the oven until tender. Add a salad, or steam some frozen veggies. Rustic meals like these are the essence of how I cook from scratch. They don't require fanfare or fuss, but they nourish the body just as much as a five-course spread.

Roadblock #2: Cooking is expensive
One of the common home-cooking objections is that junk food is so much cheaper that no one can afford to eat wholesome meals. I beg to differ. The substitute for processed food doesn't

have to be high-end produce or organic versions of potato chips or candy bars. (Those are indeed more expensive than their conventional counterparts.)

When I think of from-scratch food, I picture broths made with leftover bones and onion ends, bargain cuts of beef simmered long and slow, hearty stews made with bits of this and that, seasonal snack plates featuring vegetables from the garden or fruit from the grocery store, and bread crumbs from leftover bread ends. Homestead food is peasant food—a term I use with the utmost reverence. Peasant food is the best of humble ingredients, prepared with time-honored techniques to become something soul-warming and special.

Nourishing Homemade Broth Recipe

Ingredients
- 2 to 3 pounds beef bones, or leftover roasted chicken carcass

- 2 carrots, coarsely chopped

- 2 stalks celery, coarsely chopped

- 1 large onion, coarsely chopped

- 6 cloves garlic

- 3 tablespoons apple cider vinegar (optional)

- 2 tablespoons dried rosemary

- 2 tablespoons dried oregano

- 2 tablespoons dried thyme

- 1 tablespoon fine sea salt

- 10 black peppercorns

- 3 bay leaves

Instructions

Preheat the oven to 350°F. If you are using beef bones, roast them in the oven in a shallow roasting pan, flipping them once so they brown on all sides. If you're in a hurry, you can skip this step, but roasting adds an amazing depth of flavor, so I recommend it if you have time. The bones don't need to be cooked completely. You're just looking for that pretty brown crust on all sides. (If you're starting with beef bones that were previously cooked, you can skip this step.)

In a slow cooker or stockpot, combine the bones, veggies, vinegar (if using), and seasonings, and cover with 4 to 6 quarts cool water. Let sit for thirty minutes.

Set your slow cooker or burner on low, cover, and simmer, checking after 1 hour and skimming any scum or impurities from the surface. Simmer for twelve to thirty-six hours more. Strain the finished stock into jars, and store tightly covered in the fridge for up to two weeks. For long-term storage, freeze for up to twelve months.

On average, when compared to preparing a meal from simple ingredients at home, it costs five times as much to order a meal at a restaurant and three times as much to use a meal kit.

From the previous chapter, you know I'm a fan of organic, locally raised ingredients sourced from farmers markets and small farms. But I know that's not attainable for every budget—it certainly wasn't for us in the early years. So if your budget won't accommodate higher-end ingredients or strictly organic selections, start with the staples.

A single chicken can provide two meals for a family of four, plus a gallon of nutrient-rich broth. I'm a big fan of sustainably raised, pastured poultry. However, if that's not in the budget, start with a whole grocery store chicken. It's still better (and cheaper) than frozen dinners or chicken strips from the drive-through. Celebrate the baby steps.

> ### Stretching a Chicken
>
> While most modern recipes call for chicken breasts or thighs, I much prefer to buy whole chickens (or raise them myself), because they make meal planning much easier. For example, the first night, I'll roast the chicken whole and serve it with potatoes and vegetables. After we've eaten our fill, I pull all the meat from the bones and place the bones in my slow cooker or Instant Pot with water and herbs for broth. The next day, I can use the leftover bits of meat for soup, mixed with pasta and sauce, or in a casserole or skillet meal. A single whole chicken goes much further than buying the individual parts.

Seek out the less popular cuts of meat. There's more to a chicken than just breasts, and more to a steer than steaks. More economical cuts (such as beef shank or round steak) may be tougher, but with the proper cooking method (usually long and slow), they easily transform into melt-in-your-mouth meals.

At our local store, russet potatoes are three times cheaper than frozen french fries, and seven times cheaper than mashed potato flakes. Rolled oats cost half as much as the popular breakfast cereals, while fresh organic carrots cost three times less than frozen organic vegetables.

Dry beans (navy, pinto, black, red—you pick) are the original budget-friendly staple. The bigger the bag, the cheaper they are. (Although beans can become *too* dry after about a year, so don't stock up with fifty pounds unless you plan to eat a LOT of beans.) Soak beans overnight in tap water, and then cook in salted water the next day until they are smooth and buttery. My kids devour bowls of beans seasoned with garlic, onion, salt, and pepper for lunch. Then I smash the leftovers into refried beans or add them to stew or taco mix to stretch the meat.

Eggs come to my rescue on our busiest days. They shine as a quick protein source, especially when fried in a bit of butter or leftover bacon grease. They'll happily accompany any veggies you may have in the fridge, but my favorite is day-old bread, toasted and dipped in runny yolks. Of course, there's nothing like a farm-fresh egg, but if you don't have access to those, store-bought will do just fine. Eggs will last an impressively long time in the fridge, so stock up when they are on sale.

Cooking from scratch can indeed be expensive, but it doesn't have to be. There are so many ways to make affordable staples into delicious home-cooked meals.

Roadblock #3: I don't have anyone to teach me
I don't have a gourmet bone in my body. I haven't attended culinary school, and I didn't work in food service until we bought a restaurant (I'll tell you that story in the next chapter). I have a recurring nightmare about being on one of those TV cooking shows where they give you four slices of bacon, a kumquat, a can of anchovies, and a bowl of Cheerios and tell you to whip up a signature dish in thirty minutes or less to impress a Michelin-starred chef. The mere thought makes me break out in a cold sweat.

I entered adulthood with a deep-seated dislike for cooking. Mom tried...she really did. But I was more interested in horses than cooking back then. When I finally realized the kitchen was more interesting than I originally thought, I started at ground zero. I taught myself to make bread by reading books and got up the nerve to use my pressure canner after reading the owner's manual no less than eighteen times. (I even highlighted parts of it. Total nerd.)

DIY Sourdough Starter

Sourdough bread is the ultimate "must-have" in home industry. You're generating yeast from nothing. (Okay, not really nothing—the yeast resides on the flour and sometimes in the air. But it still feels magical.) Consider this your first step toward nutritious homemade breads.

There are a million and one ways to make a sourdough starter. Though I've tried many techniques through the years, I always come back to this solid, dependable starter. Once your starter is bubbly and ready to bake, visit theprairiehomestead.com and search "sourdough" to find my favorite recipes.

You Will Need:
- All-purpose flour

- Non-chlorinated water (see note below)

Instructions

1. Mix ½ cup flour with ½ cup water in a quart-sized glass jar. Stir vigorously, loosely cover, and then let sit for twenty-four hours.

2. Add an additional ½ cup flour and ¼ cup water to the jar, and stir vigorously. You want the starter to have the consistency of thick pancake batter. If it is too thick, add more water. Loosely cover and let sit for another twenty-four hours. You should begin to see bubbles in your starter at this point. If not, don't give up yet.

3. Discard half of the starter (regardless of whether or not you see bubbles), then feed again with ½ cup flour and ¼ cup water. Stir, loosely cover, and let sit for twenty-four hours.

Keep repeating step three until the starter doubles within four to six hours of you feeding it. If you still aren't seeing any bubbles after several days of this process, it's probably best to dump it out and start over.

Once the starter is bubbly, active, and doubling consistently after each daily feeding, it's ready to use in recipes.

Storage for Frequent Use

If you plan to use your starter every day (or every other day), it's probably best to keep it on the counter and feed it daily. To do this, discard half of the starter each day, then feed it a 1:1:1 ratio—1 part starter to 1 part water to 1 part flour (in weight).

You can get super technical and weigh this out with a scale, but I prefer to keep it simple. I usually discard all but ½ cup of the starter and then feed it with 4 ounces flour (a scant 1 cup) and 4 ounces water (½ cup).

Storage for Intermittent Use

If you'll only be using your sourdough once or twice a week (or less), you can keep it in the refrigerator. This will prevent you from having to feed it daily (and ultimately using a lot of flour!).

To transfer a starter to the fridge, first feed it as you normally would. Let it sit out for one hour, and then pop it in the fridge (covered). It's best to continue to feed it weekly in the fridge if you aren't using it much. However, I confess, I've sorely neglected my starter for many weeks (and even months) and I was still able to revive it.

Sourdough Notes

- Chlorinated water can kill your starter. If you have chlorinated tap water, run it through a filter first. Or, try boiling the water and letting it cool before proceeding with the recipe. (Boiling speeds up the evaporation of chlorine.) Bottled water is another option, although some varieties still contain chlorine, and there's no easy way to determine that.

- The key to successful sourdough is using the starter in the proper stage of activeness—this will prevent you from ending up with sourdough bread bricks. Most people run into issues because they try to use barely active starter to make full-rise breads.

- Having trouble? I have extensive troubleshooting tips over on theprairiehomestead.com. Just search "sourdough."

I'm living proof that even if you don't have Grandma around to teach you the ways of the kitchen, everything is learnable. You've got this. Start with simple recipes, whole ingredients, and basic techniques like boiling, searing, roasting, or sautéing. After that, venture a little further into meals that require you to caramelize vegetables, make a roux, or knead simple dough. If any of these feel intimidating, borrow a cornerstone cookbook like *Joy of Cooking* from the library or search for YouTube videos explaining the process.

When I'm browsing a cookbook and a recipe includes trademarked, brand-name ingredients, I either substitute those parts or skip the recipe entirely. Initially I did this to avoid the health issues associated with many processed foods, but I quickly learned I didn't need the industrial ingredients in the first place. A simple roux can replace canned cream soups, homemade cheese sauce can replace Velveeta, and whole milk or cream can (usually) replace evaporated milk.

Lean on recipes as long as you need to, and then don't be afraid to make adjustments. Change up the seasonings. Switch out the meat. Trust your gut and taste as you go—you'll make some mistakes, but you'll begin to gain "cook's intuition" along the way. And when all else fails? You can always scramble some eggs and call it good.

Creating Your Own Old-Fashioned Kitchen

While the heritage food practices of our ancestors weren't completely without issues, all combined, they created a web of nutrition, economy, community, and food security that was hard to match. So how can we re-create this in our modern era? It starts with making a few shifts in our pantries and cupboards. While most of us already have kitchens full of food and cookware, an old-fashioned kitchen requires a slightly different array of ingredients and tools.

Stock Foundational Ingredients

Before I started cooking, my pantry was loud. The shiny boxes and cans assaulted me with nutrition facts, slogans, instructions, and upsells as soon as I'd open the cupboard doors.

But now my pantry is peaceful. The glass jars of flour, beans, herbs, nuts, and rice quietly wait for me. They're in no rush. I love the humble beauty of food in jars.

Over the years I've homed in on my most-loved staples—the ones that allow me to make any of our favorite meals on a moment's notice. Your staples will be different than mine, but your best safeguard against processed food will be a well-stocked pantry.

The Missing Ingredient

Americans tragically underseason their food. I'm a firm believer in salting and seasoning food in the kitchen while it cooks (taste as you go to ensure it's right). This gives the salt a chance to mingle with the ingredients and create a depth of flavor that's impossible to achieve by sprinkling salt and pepper at the table. Choose a good-quality sea salt if you can (the kind with some color—pink, gray, or brown specks—is usually more

mineral-rich and flavorful), but if that's not in the budget, just use regular table salt for now and be generous.

Don't throw away what you have right now, but as it runs out,
replace processed convenience with wholesome basics.

These are the whole-food staples I keep in my pantry, along
with whatever meats/produce/dairy I have in the fridge and
freezer.

- Healthy fats (coconut oil, olive oil, lard)

- All-purpose flour

- Cornstarch or arrowroot powder

- Sea salt and black pepper

- Herbs and spices (oregano, rosemary, thyme, cumin, paprika, chili powder, and sage are my favorites)

- Dry beans (black, pinto, kidney, chickpeas)

- Vinegars (white, apple cider, balsamic, red wine, sherry)

- Healthy sweeteners (honey, maple syrup, unrefined cane
  sugar, molasses)

- Popcorn kernels (to grind into cornmeal)

- Rolled oats

- White or brown rice

- Nut butter

- Pasta (sometimes I make my own, sometimes I don't)

- Canned tomatoes (may be sauce, diced, crushed, etc.)

- Potatoes, onions, and garlic

Collect a Few Good Tools

Ever tried chopping onions with a knife that wobbles? Or flipping a six-ounce burger patty with a flimsy spatula? It's miserable. No wonder so many Americans hate to cook. The home cook is a craftsman, and as any artisan will tell you, proper tools are paramount. And not just for functionality, but also in how they *feel* when you use them. Wooden spoons should feel balanced in your hand, skillets should have just the right amount of heft, and knives should have the perfect balance of weight. The right tools make cooking downright pleasurable. Unfortunately, most of the cookware you'll find in a typical big-box store is anything but enjoyable to use.

My rule with kitchen equipment is similar to my philosophy of ingredients: the simpler the better. You'll never regret investing in timeless tools: cast-iron skillets, Dutch ovens, stockpots, quality wooden spoons and cutting boards, a few sharp knives, and stainless steel or ceramic mixing bowls. And it doesn't have to be expensive—I've snagged some of my most loved pieces at garage sales and thrift stores. Skip the latest "as seen on TV" gadgets, nonstick cookware, and plastic items. These more modern materials tend to leach into your food and usually don't last more than a handful of years anyway. It's fine if that's what you start with, but when you can, replace them with traditional, heirloom-quality pieces worthy of being passed to the next generation.

Cream of Anything Soup

Making a recipe that calls for canned cream soup? Whip up this quick substitute instead. The yield will be about one cup, which is roughly the same quantity as a can of condensed soup from the store.

Ingredients
- 2 tablespoons butter

- 3 tablespoons all-purpose flour

- ½ cup chicken broth

- ½ cup whole milk

- Salt and freshly ground black pepper, to taste

- Add-ins (see below for options)

Instructions

Melt the butter in a small saucepan. If making one of the variations below, mix in the add-ins now. Stir constantly until vegetables are softened, then whisk in the flour. Let the flour cook for around two minutes, whisking constantly. Pour in the broth and milk all at once, and continue to cook and stir over medium heat until thickened. Add salt and pepper to taste, then store in the refrigerator for up to one week. For long-term storage, this soup may be frozen for several months. However, it tends to separate a bit upon thawing, so you may need to blend it again.

Cream of mushroom: ½ cup finely chopped mushrooms and 2 tablespoons minced onions

Cream of celery: ¾ cup finely chopped celery and 2 tablespoons minced onions

Cream of chicken: ¾ cup finely chopped chicken and 2 tablespoons minced onions

Plan Ahead (Sort Of)

Most of the time when people (including myself) say they don't have time to cook, it boils down to a lack of planning ahead. When your fridge and freezers are filled with ingredients rather than ready-made meals, five minutes of prep can be the difference between a supper emergency and a hot meal on the table.

As much as I love cooking, and as full as our schedule is, many people assume I have a whiz-bang meal planning system.

But I don't.

I've tried the laminated planners, the printable meal plans, and the fancy apps. So far nothing has stuck. Yet I still manage to put three meals on the table most days. Truth is, my method is simple: I think ahead for a few days at a time, make sure I have what I need in the pantry and fridge, and pull out anything that needs to thaw. That's it. Sometimes I write it down, sometimes I don't. But my family gets fed most of the time, so it works for me.

Although I'm a happier cook when I'm not locked into a strict meal plan, I've collected a few practices over the years that help me put food on the table in a (mostly) consistent fashion:

- Build around the protein. Whether it's ground beef, pork chops, fish, chicken, or steak, combine it with some veggies (fresh or frozen) and maybe a starch (potatoes, pasta, etc.) and call it good.

- Keep a smattering of emergency convenience foods on hand. Sometimes I'm in the mood to make homemade pasta or tortillas, but other times I just need to feed my people. Premade tortillas and dried pasta are two of my favorite solutions when I need a semi-homemade meal on the table stat. Other quick staples are eggs (scramble or fry 'em), tomato sauce (homemade or otherwise for fast pasta meals), broth for simple soups, and frozen veggies for when I don't have time to cut up fresh ones or make a salad.

- Go for bulk. Buying in bulk not only saves time (fewer trips to the store) and money (items are often cheaper in quantity) but also creates a solid foundation for my meals. I keep large quantities of most of our staple foods. Knowing I have this base of ingredients helps me to create meals quickly.

- Create a list of fallback meals for the times your brain is tired. On the days when I have little energy and even less inspiration, we'll have tacos, spaghetti, breakfast for dinner, or "snack plates," aka random things from your fridge/pantry arranged tastefully on a plate. The kids will love it.

- Do a little extra. If you're cutting up onions, you might as well chop three or four at a time so you can have extra for the rest of the week. If you're browning ground beef, cook up several pounds at once and portion it for future suppers. The same idea can apply to everything from meal components to full dishes to desserts. But it's a simple trick that saves time and dishes.

Ultimately you get to decide what works best for you. If you are someone who rocks the pretty menu planners, that's fabulous. (And yes, I'm a little bit jealous.)

Do It for You

Home cooking takes effort. But it's worthy effort. There is a deeply intoxicating sense of accomplishment that comes from commanding a meal of the most nourishing order from rough ingredients. It stretches beyond the realm of "edible" and becomes something that is life-giving and soul-satisfying...even when no one sees what you're making.

If you live alone, if not a soul is coming for supper, if no holiday marks the calendar, and if you don't plan on posting a picture on social media, put forth the effort anyway. Do it for you. Make a pretty piecrust (or the best you can, anyway). Use the nice serving platter. Light a few beeswax candles. Ditch the paper plates. You'll be surprised at the ensuing sense of pride that will fill you, even when the only person to see it is you (or your family). There's a special sort of confidence that comes when you can say, "I created that piecrust... I mastered that beef roast... I brought forth this artisan loaf from nothing but salt, yeast, water, and flour." This is invigorating. It's empowering. And it's very worthwhile, even in an era when we don't have to.

Make It a Family Affair

Last, perhaps one of the most rewarding aspects of going to the trouble of cooking from scratch is that it more easily turns eating into a social event. Sharing food we've lovingly crafted with our own hands is, like Michael Pollan so elegantly states, the "difference between a Hallmark card and a handwritten letter." It's no secret that Americans are spending less time savoring our meals and more time eating while multitasking, driving, or working. Yet one of the most powerful acts we can do to take back our homes (and our lives) is to sit around the table to enjoy a meal together.

Regular family dinners have been shown to result in better diets, less substance abuse, lower rates of anxiety, and even better vocabularies for children and adolescents. Clear the table, turn off the TV, and sit down together. Candlelight, cloth napkins, and fancy dishes aren't a requirement. It's all about connection, and good food helps us connect.

The Beauty of Baby Steps

My kitchen transformation didn't happen overnight, and I recommend that yours doesn't either. Whatever you do, don't attempt to shift from the standard American diet to cooking fully from scratch in one fell swoop. I've tried that, and it didn't end well.

One fateful instance is forever seared into my memory. In

the early stages of our old-fashioned lifestyle, Christian and I had planned a weekend outing and needed to take sack lunches. Normally, that's not a big deal, except I was determined every single component of that lunch would be homemade, 100 percent from scratch, NO exceptions.

I baked several loaves of whole-wheat sandwich bread, cooked a beef roast to be sliced into lunch meat, and made a batch of homemade mozzarella to top the sandwiches. Determined not to use refined flour or sugar, I baked a pan of black bean brownies using cooked beans instead of flour (no sugar of course, only honey).

After two solid days in the kitchen, my results were...disastrous. The bread was so crumbly I could hardly slice it, the roast was reminiscent of shoe leather, the mozzarella was weepy and rubbery, and Christian made me promise to never, *ever* make black bean brownies again. They were *that* bad. I collapsed in a fit of despair, envisioning a bleak future of bologna, Wonder Bread, and Twinkies.

cooking doesn't have to be all or nothing.

Despite the dramatic end to my sack lunch escapade, I learned an important lesson that day—cooking doesn't have to be all or nothing.

If you make the sandwich bread but end up buying lunch meat and cheese to go on it, congrats! You made bread! If you craft homemade tomato sauce and serve it over store-bought pasta, that's fantastic. You made red sauce! Give yourself grace, focus on one thing at a time, and soak in the beauty of the process. If you fail in the kitchen (and you will), dust yourself off and try again. That is, unless you're attempting to make black bean brownies. In that case, it might be best to just admit defeat.

Top Ten Things to Start Making from Scratch

1. Bread crumbs—save dried-out bread ends and grind them in a food processor or blender.

2. Homemade condensed cream soups—I've included my quick recipe on page 131.

3. Broth—if you save vegetable scraps and leftover bones, it's basically free. Get my recipe on page 122.

4. Beans—buy pinto, black, or navy beans in bulk. If you have a pressure cooker (electric or otherwise), they cook up fast and easy. If not, a regular stockpot works just fine.

5. Biscuits—they use basic ingredients, take less than ten minutes of hands-on time, and taste so much better than store-bought.

6. Mac & cheese—if you whip it up on the stove top, it takes the same amount of time as the boxed versions and tastes so much better. Simply boil and drain the pasta, then add butter, milk or cream, and shredded cheese right to the pot.

7. Mayonnaise—an egg yolk, a cup of oil, and a pinch of salt. That's all it takes to whip up the best mayo you've ever had.

8. Salad dressings—homemade ranch is as easy as mixing mayo, buttermilk, and a handful of herbs in a jar. Vinaigrettes are even easier. A quick Google search will yield dozens of proven recipes.

9. Applesauce—wait until apples are in season or when you have a chance to buy a box or two at the farmers market. Peel, core, and slice them, then add them to a large cooking pot with a little water. They'll soften over medium heat, and then you can turn them into sauce with a blender or food processor.

10. Whipped cream—instead of buying the tubs of ar-

tificial whipped topping, use your mixer to turn heavy cream into the perfect dessert topping instead. Add a little sweetener (maple syrup is my favorite) and a splash of vanilla extract and you'll never go back to the fake stuff again.

In Praise of Balance

As you've probably gathered by now, I have strong opinions about the kitchen. But lest you think I'm a purist, allow me to assure you—I'm not. In fact, I have a confession to make. I have a microwave (gasp!). It's not my favorite appliance, but I haven't yet been motivated to ditch it entirely. No guilt allowed, remember?

I cut corners in other ways too, sometimes. For example, as much as I adore seasonal eating, I admit I occasionally purchase a gallon of milk to tide us through the bleakest of the milk famine months. I have no shame in eating fast food occasionally. I can make any type of bread imaginable, but sometimes I'll grab a loaf or two at the store during our busiest seasons. And if we're eating supper with friends and someone hands me a piece of store-bought pie buried under a mound of Cool Whip, I'll eat it with nary a complaint.

This may seem incongruent to some, but I see it as balance. We strive to eat well 80 percent of the time, but I don't sweat that other 20 percent. Stress is just as detrimental as processed foods, and I'm not interested in perfection. The key? Don't allow the industrialized food model to own you. Know its tricks; be wary of the siren call of convenience; opt out as much as you can. And then, if you need to take advantage of periodic shortcuts to keep your sanity intact, do it. With no shame.

My hope is that as you dust off the mixing bowls and break out the bread pans, you'll experience a new type of meditation—a chance to slow down and take inventory of who you are and what makes you tick. Processed foods aren't evil, but when they're all we eat, we miss out on the sacredness of making things for ourselves. There's a humble beauty in those small moments when we brush egg wash over the rolls before sliding them into the oven or when we take the extra care to sprinkle paprika over the deviled eggs. When we apply intention to the mundane, it has a way of becoming magical. These little things matter, and they slow down time, even if just for a moment.

The kitchen is a life-giving place. I love when our spaces are filled with things brewing, fermenting, rising, bubbling, stewing, simmering, aging, curing, growing, sprouting, and germinating. Those are action verbs—they brim with life. They sparkle when you say them. A microwaved TV dinner mummified in plastic doesn't have that same effect. Its energy is flat and empty. While I'll never claim to have all the answers, I do know this: you won't go wrong by cooking. Even just once per week to start. Even simple meals. Even with grocery store ingredients. It's a worthy way to spend your time, and you won't regret it.

Old-Fashioned Action Steps

- If you're brand-new to cooking, set simple goals, such as making one meal from scratch each week, or skipping breakfast cereal on Mondays and making scrambled eggs instead.

- If you're already savvy in the kitchen, but want to give your foods an old-fashioned twist, focus on making components of meals. Tutorials abound for homemade butter, yogurt, tortillas, soft cheeses, all manner of breads, condiments, gravies, sauces, and more. You'll level up your skill set with each new food you master while keeping the kitchen interesting at the same time.

- Keep an eye on thrift stores, garage sales, and online marketplace groups for solid used kitchen equipment. I've bought canning pots, mason jars, dehydrators, stoneware pans, slow cookers, cake pans, cast-iron skillets, and knives all secondhand. People are prone to discard "old-fashioned" gear in favor of the latest gadgets. Their trash is your kitchen treasure.

- Learn how to cut up a whole chicken. It will save you money, get you in touch with your farm roots, and give you (almost) free broth.

- Speaking of broth, learn how to make it. I know... I've referenced it many times in this chapter, but I'm obsessed. I can't think of a homemade food that is more drastically different than its store-bought counterpart.

- One word: eggs. They are my number one fallback when I'm out of supper ideas. Make egg salad, fried eggs, baked eggs, poached eggs, or just scrambled eggs. Yes, it absolutely counts as a from-scratch meal.

- When you do cook from scratch, double the recipe and freeze half of it. There's no shame in making your own shortcut foods.

- Mimic our early days on the homestead and make a rule that you can eat whatever you like, *if* you make it yourself. Homemade versions of favorite treat foods (french fries, ice cream, pizza, breads) might not be ultra-nutrient-rich, but odds are good they'll be better than the store-bought versions, plus you'll be expanding your skill set in the process.

- When I'm not in the mood to cook, this helps: Clear the countertops of junk mail, Hot Wheels cars, stray pencils, and the thirty-eight drinking cups scattered around.

Take a deep breath, close your eyes, and count to ten. Pull out your favorite cutting board and the knife that feels just right. Turn on that podcast or playlist you've wanted to listen to. Tune out the chaos of the day and sink into the task at hand. I'm not saying chopping vegetables is as relaxing as a day at the spa, but it does bring me back to center. Quite often, in fact.

- I've included several of my favorite recipes in this chapter, but you can find my full kitchen playbook in *The Prairie Homestead Cookbook: Simple Recipes for Heritage Cooking in Any Kitchen*.

CHAPTER 6

Work with Your Hands

Once upon a time, we bought a restaurant. A 107-year-old soda fountain, to be exact. Am I a restaurateur? Not at all. In fact, I'd never even worked a job in food service. (My high school employment was changing oil at a Jiffy Lube.) But the passion I carry for restoring old things is unyielding, so after daydreaming about that vintage soda fountain every time I'd drive by (and many months of preparing), we finally bought it.

I feel like this should be the part of the story where I say, "And we made milkshakes and lived happily ever after." But that's not how it went. At least not yet.

The week we signed the papers to take ownership was one of the hardest weeks I've ever had. Not only were we thrust into the wilds of restaurant ownership ("The internet is down! We're out of fries! There aren't enough quarters in the drawer!"), but our homestead was hit with a series of unexpected losses. We lost our two-week-old dairy calf for unknown reasons, a set of goat triplets was stillborn, another baby goat mysteriously disappeared, and I discovered the compost I was using in my garden was poisoning the soil.

Mixing these sudden tragedies with the stress of a new business venture was overwhelming, to say the least. I couldn't get my head above water. As soon as I'd resolve one pressing issue, the next one would punch me in the face. I struggled to sleep and wondered if we'd made a huge mistake. I felt beat-up and depleted.

So I decided to make a wheel of gouda.

Most people would argue that cheese was the *last* thing I should have been worrying about that week. And they would have a point. But this homestead life has taught me that one of the best ways to reduce stress is through the act of creation. That's what I was seeking that day as I set out my pots and cheesecloth. Cheese was simply the by-product. And handicrafts and projects like these play a more important role in our mental health than you might think.

As I watched the curds knit together in the pot, my mind became still. My tension melted away as I carefully set the cheesecloth in the mold and spooned the warm curds inside. And my soul, which had felt so defeated those past few days, swelled with joy as I lifted the finished wheel out of the press and admired its shape.

Even as our life has become busier over the years, I've learned (often the hard way) that leaving margin for creative, hands-on pursuits is nonoptional. Creativity breathes life back into me, so I can then go manage the rest.

But this isn't just my own personal quirk. We're all wired to create, even though it's become increasingly easy to lose touch with this most basic of human instincts. We now live in a world where we can go an entire lifetime without having to create much of anything for ourselves. This modern routine of consumption, not production, feels so normal, it's hard to imagine anything different. It never occurs to us to question it. However, when we do, we open a new world of possibilities and happiness. And therein lies the next trait we can adopt as old-fashioned on purpose individuals: *We seek out opportunities to work with our hands.* As we saw in the last chapter, the kitchen is one of the most intuitive places to start, but it's only the beginning.

The Hidden Rewards of Using Your Hands

It wasn't my imagination that my cheese project reduced my stress during the worst week ever. There's a fascinating process driving it all at a biological level. Neuroscientist Kelly Lambert calls this cycle the effort-driven rewards circuit, and it could partially explain why we sometimes feel so out of sorts as modern people who lack hands-on activity.

In her book *Lifting Depression*, Lambert explains that every symptom of depression (a disease that is affecting our society at staggering rates) correlates to a part of this circuit. The official name for it is the accumbens-striatal-cortical network. (Yeah, I know—it's a mouthful.) It's easier to remember if you think of it as the system in your brain that connects motion, emotions, and thought processes.

Our hand movements are crucially connected to the motor cortex in our brains. When we use our hands for complex, real-world tasks (aka not just typing or pressing buttons), it starts a neurological chain reaction, which causes the reward center of our brain to release dopamine and serotonin (often called the "happy chemicals"). Even more compelling is the fact that this type of manual activity may even stimulate the production of brand-new brain cells. It's not hyperbole when I say we are wired to create.

Working with our hands has also been proven to reduce stress. In one study, researchers tested the cortisol levels (our body's main stress hormone) of a group of adults before and after they worked on an art project. Not only did the participants report feeling more relaxed after the craft was complete, their cortisol levels were significantly lowered. In another study, 1,300 men were observed over the course of eighteen years to see if certain personality traits contributed to lifespan. They discovered that while the traits of openness (a willingness to try new things) and intelligence did not predict mortality, *creativity did*, even more than smoking, age, or health status.

These findings are fascinating, but we don't need scientific studies to prove the value of creativity—we can feel it. There's a marked difference in how we feel after bingeing a Netflix series versus working with our hands. While watching TV may be the path of least resistance, I think we could all agree that we feel more deeply satisfied after spending time doing something meaningful.

It's similar to how we might feel when we grab a candy bar to quell our hunger. While the sugar boost is hard to resist, there's no denying we feel better long-term when we choose a more nourishing option. Just as our bodies crave healthy nutrients for lasting satisfaction, our brains crave challenging cognitive stimulation, and they reward us handsomely when we heed the call.

In *Shop Class as Soulcraft*, author Matthew Crawford uses the words "quiet and easy" to describe the way manual tasks make us feel. That phrase has stuck with me ever since I first read it. It's the perfect way to explain how I feel after weeding my onion rows. I'm tired and dirty on the outside, but content and calm on the inside.

It encapsulates the pride I feel after a canning session in the kitchen. By the end of the day, my kitchen is sticky and I have peach juice in my hair, but seeing my jars of food lined up on the counter is deeply rewarding. It describes how Christian feels after he makes hay. He says there's nothing like turning around on the tractor and seeing all the bales lined up in neat rows across the field.

It even applies to animals. Our dog, Jed, has a reputation for being a troublemaker. But after he completes a job, like helping us herd the goats back into their pen, his entire demeanor changes. His expression shifts from one of mischievousness to a look that could only be described as "quiet and easy." The rapid rise of industrialization has changed the world around us, but our brains remain the same. They are ancient organs wired to light up when we immerse ourselves in meaningful, tangible work. Manual tasks build our confidence and competence. We walk a little taller because we know we're capable. We don't have to tell the world who we are—the results are self-evident.

In Benjamin Franklin's autobiography, he observed the effects of lack of physical creation among a crew of men tasked to build a stockade. When rain continued to interrupt the project, he noted:

> ...*when men are employ'd, they are best content'd; for on the days they worked they were good-natur'd and cheerful, and with the consciousness of having done a good day's work, they spent the evening jollily; but on our idle days they were mutinous and quarrelsome, finding fault with their pork, the bread, etc, and in continual ill-humor...*

I can't help but think that "quarrelsome" and "ill-humored" serve to describe many aspects of our contemporary society as well. Our tech-heavy life is robbing us of opportunities to use our hands outside of tapping a screen or pressing the remote. We're losing our feel of the real world—the one that exists in living color, not pixels. We've accidentally outsourced our very ability to experience the world around us.

> ## being a producer is a birthright that belongs to us all.

Yet, being a producer is a birthright that belongs to us all. And perhaps, while not the ultimate cure-all, building and creating things may remedy the sour mood of our contemporary culture, just like it did for Franklin's men. The "consciousness of having done a good day's work" is powerful medicine. Friends, it's time to weave creation and production back into our everyday lives. Here's how.

Reclaiming Your Birthright

Obviously, refusing to ever consume anything again is impossible. Therefore, it's wise to adopt a nuanced approach. The conversation isn't "production *versus* consumption," but rather, how we can incorporate *both* ideas into our everyday lives. "The responsible consumer," according to Wendell Berry, "must also be in some way a producer."

Personally, mixing these two concepts has resulted in the most fulfillment for me. I make, create, and produce things. Yet I also buy items. And to take it one step further, I even market and sell products. It's possible to dwell in all these spaces without losing our integrity—the key is *awareness*.

Buying items isn't inherently bad. Only when we purchase without conscience does it become a problem. Becoming specialized in a trade or skill is admirable, as long as we don't abdicate every other part of our life to someone else in the process. Fair exchange of value isn't evil. It's when we drift into over-consumption that the trouble begins.

So what does becoming a responsible consumer-producer look like? We can start by reviving a few time-honored ideas:

Become Unspecialized

Historically, humans have been generalists. That means we knew how to do stuff. And lots of it. Basic survival demanded that a person be able to hunt, grow, and prepare food, understand simple medicinal knowledge, make tools and weapons, find safe water, and handle animals. However, as the idea of specialization became popular (about the same time that factories entered the scene), the need to possess a vast collection of skills no longer felt necessary.

Adam Smith first introduced the notion of specialists in *The Wealth of Nations*. The idea is that if you can teach people how to do single, small tasks very well, they can come together to produce things in a lightning-fast, cost-effective way. Smith famously underscored this point by using the example of a straight pin factory. While a single pin-maker might only be able to make a handful of pins on his own each day, if the process is broken down into distinct operations, the process becomes much more efficient. Smith estimated that if pin making was divided into eighteen different steps, a group of ten men could produce roughly 48,000 pins each day.

It's a pretty cool concept, isn't it? In fact, it was so compelling that it revolutionized our entire culture. And it certainly makes sense if you're going to start a production line. The problem is, like so many aspects of industrialization, it's gotten a little off balance. Over time, we've hyperspecialized every part of our lives, and our skill sets have atrophied as a result.

As Wendell Berry highlights in *The Unsettling of America*, the average citizen now abdicates the problem of food production to agriculturalists, the problem of health to doctors, the problem of education to teachers, and the problem of conservation to conservationists. We even have "entertainment specialists" to keep us amused when we're not at work in our specialized careers.

Please understand that I'm not picking on specialization. There's nothing wrong with possessing a lot of specific knowledge in a certain field. I deeply admire anyone who has devoted a lifetime to understanding everything they can about a particular topic. But I love how an old-fashioned on purpose life invites us to broaden our skill sets. And in doing so, we become more competent, balanced individuals.

The next time you're faced with a menial task—changing your oil, fixing the handle on the toilet, planting a tree, replacing a missing button—use it as a chance to shift your perspective. Instead of viewing these tasks as annoying chores, reframe them as a chance to expand your repertoire of skills. Your brain will reward you for participating in these humble tasks just as much as more traditionally creative ones. Recently, after a long day in the office, I entered the house and came face-to-face with a five-gallon bucket brimming with freshly picked green beans. I groaned. In my rush of deadlines and paperwork, I had completely forgotten about them. Snapping beans was the *last* thing I wanted to do after my hectic day. But since they had to go into the freezer that night, I resigned myself to my fate. I recruited my children, set up bowls, and begrudgingly grabbed a handful of legumes. *Snap, snap, plop! Snap, snap, plop!* The beans began to fill our bowls. A few minutes into our project, we decided to have a contest to see who could fill their bowl the fastest. We laughed as the puppy pounced on a wayward bean, only to spit it out a second later. We talked about yellow beans, purple beans, dragon tongue beans (the kids' favorite), and which ones we should grow next year. In less than twenty minutes, the bucket was empty. I portioned the beans into bags, vacuum-sealed them, and labeled them with the date. As I tucked them into our freezer and shut the door, I couldn't help but notice how *good* I felt. I had been productive in the office that day, but the satisfaction I felt when I closed my computer was different than the accomplishment I felt looking at the shiny packages of beans in my freezer. I was thankful to have both.

The Old-Fashioned Skills Bucket List

When it comes to becoming a generalist, it can be difficult to know where to start. I encourage you to make a list of all the skills you'd like to learn.

To help you brainstorm, I've included an example here of an "Old-Fashioned Skills Bucket List," but try to tailor a list that fits your specific interests. (Tip: Don't worry if the skills seem too out of reach. Learning something new is half the adventure.)

☐ Take a first-aid or CPR course

☐ Know how to clean and dress a wound in case of emergency

☐ Put together a seventy-two-hour kit for emergencies

☐ Collect a stash of shelf-stable food that could last for several weeks in case of emergency

☐ Learn to use non-electric lighting

☐ Know how to purify water

☐ Add alternative energy sources, for example, solar and wind, to your home or homestead

☐ Change your own oil and/or tires

☐ Safely handle, shoot, and clean a gun

☐ Sharpen a knife or axe

☐ Harvest, split, and stack firewood

☐ Build and fix a fence

☐ Tie a variety of knots

☐ Build a fire

☐ Cut, bale, and stack hay

☐ Make your own soap and/or candles

☐ Make your own laundry detergent

☐ Darn a sock

☐ Learn to knit, quilt, or crochet

☐ Spin wool

☐ Weave cloth

☐ Sew clothing

☐ Drive a vehicle with a manual transmission

☐ Drive a tractor

☐ Drive and back up a trailer

☐ Understand basic mechanic and carpentry skills

☐ Understand basic plumbing skills and how to unclog a drain or toilet

- [ ] Dry laundry on a drying rack or clothesline
- [ ] Learn how to tan a hide
- [ ] Make your own skin care and beauty supplies
- [ ] Make your own cleaning supplies
- [ ] Weave your own baskets
- [ ] Tap trees to harvest maple syrup
- [ ] Store food in a root cellar or basement
- [ ] Compost kitchen scraps and animal manure to feed your garden
- [ ] Know how to properly prune and graft a fruit tree
- [ ] Know how to safely cut down a tree
- [ ] Start your own seeds
- [ ] Grow heirloom varieties of your favorite vegetables
- [ ] Identify and forage for wild edibles in your area
- [ ] Save seeds from vegetables you grow for next year's season
- [ ] Make herbal extracts, tinctures, and infusions
- [ ] Know the difference between poisonous and edible mushrooms
- [ ] Propagate plants through root cuttings
- [ ] Milk a goat, cow, or sheep
- [ ] Give an animal an injection (in the muscle, vein, or under the skin)
- [ ] Assist with kidding, lambing, or calving
- [ ] Understand how to help an animal in a difficult birth situation
- [ ] Trim the hooves of a goat or sheep
- [ ] Butcher and pluck a chicken
- [ ] Incubate fertilized eggs and hatch your own chicks
- [ ] Learn the basic cuts of meat for beef or a hog

☐ Take a hunter's safety course

☐ Learn how to fish

☐ Keep bees and harvest the honey

☐ Use composting worms to make rich compost for your garden

Make Your Home a Hub of Creation

I love walking into the house of a producer. Their homes have a special sort of energy. There are projects tucked into every corner. Their handiwork is on display in various ways throughout each room. The countertops are crowded with living foods, jars, and experiments. There are braided rag rugs peeking from under the couch, hand-poured candles flickering on the table, and an eclectic mix of thrifted, refurbished furniture dotting the rooms. These spaces radiate a feeling of movement, excitement, and *life*. It's a throwback to a time when homes were vibrant ecosystems that set the stage for production and growth.

Prior to the industrial revolution, the home, not the factory, was the place of industry. And it was a family affair. While women performed certain tasks like cooking and laundry, men also played an integral role in household functions, such as caring for livestock, chopping wood for cooking fires, and making tools. Men grew the wheat that the women turned into bread. Men gathered and chopped the wood used to fuel the hearth where the women made stew. And of course, the children pitched in and helped with chores all day long.

We've drifted away from this dynamic, and the stereotypical gender roles that go with it. If you're picturing me as the perfect doting 1950s-era housewife...that's not me at all. I'm more Ma Ingalls meets Calamity Jane. But our homes are still one of the easiest places we can cultivate an old-fashioned mindset. They can be havens of inspiration, corners of creativity, and retreats that recharge us after a stressful day. It simply starts by reframing how we think about them.

One helpful shift is to think of all the new, exciting things happening in your home as sources of "nonmonetary income"—a term I gleaned from a podcast interview with Shannon Hayes, author of *Redefining Rich*. She defines nonmonetary income as "any need that can be met without having to shell out dollars for it." It's easy to assume all the effort we're putting into our old-fashioned skill sets isn't worthwhile, but if you start adding it up, it might just surprise you.

Homemade Slow Cooker Candles

Nothing comes close to the soothing, old-fashioned ambience of candles, especially when they're homemade. A slow cooker streamlines this simple project, but if you'd rather use your stove top, that works as well. You can find the wax and wicks at your local craft store or online.

Supplies
- Beeswax chunks or pellets (about 6 to 7 ounces per half-pint jar)

- Wicks

- Essential oils (optional)

- Small mason jars (half-pint or smaller) or nonporous repurposed containers (check your thrift store for old teacups or unique jars)

- A slow cooker

Instructions
Fill the slow cooker with three inches of hot water. Fill

the containers or jars completely full with beeswax, then place them in the slow cooker with the lid on.

Turn the heat on high and let the wax melt, stirring occasionally. The wax will shrink down as it melts, so continue to add more wax until the jars are filled (leave one inch of space at the top).

It takes about two hours for my slow cooker to completely melt all the wax, but yours might be slightly faster or slower, depending on the model. You don't have to babysit the cooker, just check it when you think about it.

Once the wax is completely melted, remove the jars from the slow cooker and let them cool for five to ten minutes.

If you are using essential oils, add *at least* sixty to eighty drops to each half-pint jar. (Keep in mind that essential oil–scented candles will not be as aromatic as those made with synthetic scents.)

Position the wick in the center of each container and keep it in place by winding it around a small dowel or pencil, or propping it up with small dowels, pencils, or strips of tape. The goal is to keep the wick straight and centered in the jar.

Allow the candles to cool and set up completely before trimming the wick to one-fourth inch.

For us, our nonmonetary income includes the money we save in doing our own vehicle maintenance, making DIY cleaners and skin care, cutting the kids' hair, growing our own meat, baking our own bread, and even the money we save by working at home rather than driving to town for employment. Once you start to crunch the numbers, focusing on home-based skill sets feels much more tantalizing. It only takes a few minutes to realize how much you are (or could be) contributing to your family's bottom line through small, simple actions. Try it!

Another way I cultivate a space for creativity is to make our home uniquely "us." It's easy to get swept away in what we're told a stylish home *should* be, but if we only ever let trends guide us, our home will struggle to find its personality. You possess a sense of style that's unique to you. It will shine through as you allow your creativity to guide you. And as a bonus, this provides an endless supply of projects where we can use our hands in tangible, rewarding ways.

I find my best inspiration far from the home decor aisles of big-box stores. Garage sales and thrift stores are my hunting grounds, followed by the junk piles that accumulate on rural properties (including my own), and nature itself. Over the years, I've decorated with cast-off barn doors, crusty windowpanes, dried flowers, birds' nests, tractor parts, dilapidated furniture, glass jars excavated from the soil, wagon elements, interesting rocks and sticks, and of course, windmills. Some treasures require tinkering and paint before they're display-worthy, while others go right on the shelf after a quick cleaning. Another favorite strategy is to decorate with things you use on a regular basis. Allow the functional to become the celebrated. Instead of mass-produced knickknacks, my kitchen decor consists of glass jars filled with dry goods, cast-iron skillets on the wall, and crocks filled with rolling pins, wooden spoons, and sourdough starter. Our firewood box is one of the focal points of our living room. The mustard-yellow box with its chipped paint came from a 1936 carriage house and was salvaged from a dumpster. It's an eye-catching addition but also serves an important purpose. Of course, I still have some traditional decor pieces in my home, but hands down, my favorites are the quirky treasures with a story. A cozy home is created in layers over time, but it's worth the wait. Plus, I've noticed the more I craft, build, and produce in my home, the easier it is to be creative in the other areas of my life.

And finally, you can foster a creative atmosphere in your home by taking a hint from history and making projects a family affair. Our affinity for personal screens drives us to be isolated from each other, even when we're all in the same building. Thankfully, it doesn't take massive effort to change this. Some of our most fulfilling family times have come when we're working with our hands *together*. Christian and I often joke that our love language is projects, and that hasn't changed as the kids have grown. As we renovated the soda fountain, the kids were along for the ride. They helped us haul junk out of the basement, demolish walls, take measurements, paint the exterior, and tidy the courtyard. As chaotic as that project was, I think back to those days with fondness. There was something precious about the weekends we spent together, cleaning, painting, building, and dreaming. We were coming together to create something bigger than us. And that's a dynamic even the tiniest children can appreciate.

But you don't have to buy an old restaurant to find meaningful ways to spend time as a family. Your own special memories can come in the form of raking leaves, hunting for thrift store treasures, painting the garden shed, making pizza together, or stacking firewood. It doesn't have to be complicated to be transformative.

Honey Mint Lip Balm

If you have lips (which I'm assuming you do), this one is worth trying. I've made all sorts of variations of homemade lip balm recipes over the years, but I particularly like this formula. It's velvety smooth and glides on like a dream. Plus, it'll help you avoid all the petroleum-based balms out there. These ingredients are readily available online or at most health food stores and can be used for a variety of DIY projects, so they're worth having. This recipe will make around ten tubes.

Supplies
- 3 tablespoons coconut oil

- 1 tablespoon beeswax pellets

- 1 teaspoon shea butter

- 1 teaspoon honey

- 6 to 8 drops peppermint oil (optional)

- Repurposed and cleaned lip balm tubes or tins

Instructions
Place the coconut oil, beeswax, and shea butter in an oven-safe dish or cup (I like to use a small Pyrex measuring cup—it makes for easier pouring) and place this container into a small saucepan filled with water over medium-low heat.

Gently heat, stirring occasionally, until the mixture is completely melted. Then stir in the honey.

Remove from the heat and stir in the peppermint oil. Carefully pour the liquid into tubes or tins, stirring frequently as you go. (The honey likes to sink to the bottom.) Let the balm set up for one hour.

Create to Relax

The first time I read Cal Newport's description of "high-quality leisure" in his book *Digital Minimalism*, I felt strangely validated. For years, I'd noticed that I felt more recharged after a day spent working around the homestead as compared to a day spent vegging on the couch. Yet based on the conversations I had with people around me, I had secretly begun to wonder if I was the only one who felt this way.

"Don't you EVER relax, Jill?" The question was usually accompanied by an incredulous look.

"Of course," I'd reply, before launching into a short description of the prior weekend when I had stained some trim for the soda fountain remodel and repotted pepper seedlings. While those experiences had felt genuinely *relaxing* to me, my answers never seemed to satisfy my inquisitors. I'd usually get a withering glance as they quickly changed the subject.

It's a commonly held belief that passive activities are the only valid form of relaxation, but I'm determined to redefine that. The act of creation can be far more regenerative than a day spent on the couch. The more effort you devote to a pursuit, the more value you gain from it. Low-effort activities, like scrolling a phone or watching TV, require very little energy from us. Therefore, they provide very little value. In contrast, when I fill my free time with meaningful pastimes, I'm mentally energized at the end of the day, even after strenuous activity. Rethinking how we relax also frees more time for creative pursuits since relaxing and creativity don't have to be mutually exclusive; they can be one and the same.

> **when I fill my free time with meaningful pastimes, I'm mentally energized at the end of the day, even after strenuous activity.**

Even though the path of least resistance can seem more appealing at first, if we're honest with ourselves, we can admit that doing nothing can be overrated. Often when I've finally achieved the blank calendar I was craving, it wasn't as gratifying as I thought it'd be. I usually fall into mindlessly wasting time on my phone instead of relishing the emptiness like I thought I would.

For an activity to fit into the category of active relaxation for me, it has to meet the following criteria:

1. It can't be too strenuous mentally. I feel the most relaxed when I give my brain a chance to rest. This is also when I come up with some of my best ideas, so I want to make sure I'm not trying to solve complicated problems or struggle through complex instructions during these times.

2. It needs to involve some sort of motion. Nothing too taxing, but a little movement helps bring both my mind and body back to center.

3. There must be a result I can see at the end of the day. Because nothing feels more gratifying than looking back at a completed project.

Some of my favorite tasks that fit this bill are weeding, simple food preservation (with recipes I know well), cleaning the barn or chicken coop, organizing my cupboards or fridge, repainting an old piece of furniture, moving around furniture or decor, or chopping vegetables for the week.

So while sometimes I absolutely take a nap, or sit on the porch swing and stare at the clouds, I find active relaxation to be my secret weapon for *really* recharging at the end of the day. It's multitasking at its finest—I give my brain a break from its usual tasks and flex my creativity muscles at the same time.

Escaping Excess

A major piece in fighting back against overconsumption is becoming a producer. However, we can also play a role in consuming *less*. Here are a few strategies I use:

1. Wait 24 hours. The allure of the perfect impulse buy

is powerful. However, if I make myself wait a day or two before buying, I usually find I really don't need the item like I thought I did.

2. Avoid duplicates. Do I *really* need another Dutch oven? (Even if it *is* that shade of spring green I've been wanting?) Probably not. But it can be hard to resist. One way I combat the temptation to buy more than I need is to give myself storage space boundaries. For example: I have one cabinet to hold my cooking pots. Once that space is full, then I don't buy more (unless something breaks). Turns out, I didn't really need five Dutch ovens after all. (We all have different points of buying weakness. Yours may be tech gadgets, shoes, or handbags. Mine happens to be pretty cookware. Yet the strategies are the same.)

3. Buy better quality. I know, cheap items are tempting, but they usually break or wear out prematurely. Therefore, I've learned to save until I can invest in the longer-lasting version of things, even if they're a little more expensive on the front end. For example: Cheap nonstick skillets are a dime a dozen, but they only last for a year or two (plus they emit fumes when you use them). Cast iron is a timeless alternative that costs a little more but never needs to be replaced (except under extreme circumstances). Simple choices like this combat our throwaway mindset and help limit the amount of junk in our landfills. The website buymeonce.com features durable goods that are made to last a lifetime—it's a good place to start.

4. Resist planned obsolescence. It started with a group of light bulb manufacturers in the 1920s (the "Phoebus cartel") that banded together and agreed to collectively shorten the life span of their bulbs to encourage more purchases. And it's still going strong today. But planned obsolescence isn't just for cell phones that no longer hold their charge or appliances that break after a handful of years; it also happens with clothes ("This isn't in style!") or the latest gadgets ("That phone has a better camera!"). Be aware of the marketing messages that surround you and ask yourself if getting the latest and greatest version will *really* improve your life or merely scratch the itch to buy something.

5. Buy used. Buying secondhand saves money and gives old items new life (which saves them from the landfill). This is one area where the internet can help us, whether it's community buy-and-sell groups on Facebook, eBay, craigslist.org, or websites that sell gently used books and clothing. Or look for websites like renttherunway.com that allow you to rent clothing instead of buying it.

Creating YOUR Way

"But I'm not a creative person!" Some of you may be thinking this as you've read these pages. I want to assure you that you are indeed creative. We all are, in our own way.

When most people think of working with their hands, they usually envision master craftsmen or professional artists. The "creativity" shelf at many bookstores is packed with books written by woodworkers and mechanics, which might lead you to believe you must immerse yourself in an advanced craft to reap the rewards of a creative life. However, while installing cabinetry and rebuilding motorcycles are worthy pursuits, they don't hold a monopoly on creativity.

The act of creating and producing is highly personal. I find joy in making pies and renovating old buildings, while others find it in repairing vehicles, painting with watercolors, knitting socks, decorating their homes, throwing pottery, taking a dance class, playing guitar, baling hay, welding metal, working with wood, or making jewelry, just to name a few. The path toward becoming a producer rather than just a consumer will be unique to you—the key is finding your "flow activities."

This is something I happened to stumble across as a young mom. During my early years of motherhood, I was caught off guard by how isolated I would feel with only an infant to keep me company in a house thirty-five miles from town. And I struggled. Activities like baby yoga classes and infant swim lessons were one possible remedy, but since our gas budget was tight and the winter roads didn't always offer a safe route to town, these typical new mom boredom-busters weren't realistic for me.

In a moment of serendipity, I went to the library and borrowed the book *The Complete Tightwad Gazette* by Amy Dacyczyn. Its promise of "promoting thrift as a viable alternative lifestyle" felt well-suited to our situation. Although I decided to skip the advice of separating two-ply toilet paper to make single-ply rolls, some of the other ideas caught my eye, namely the ones that involved making homemade alternatives to store-bought products. As I tried my hand at making cleaning products and pantry staples, I experienced a weird charge of excitement. It delivered the same thrill I felt when I bought something, except I wasn't buying—I was *making*. Before long, I found myself craving the rush. Each afternoon during nap time, I couldn't wait to try something new.

I experimented with as many new kitchen techniques as I could find, from milling my own wheat, to making yogurt from scratch, to making crackers. I became captivated by the secret world of bacteria that fermented the vegetables on my counter and made my homemade loaves rise (and sometimes didn't). I decorated our home with salvaged and refurbished furniture. I attempted herbal salves, tinctures, and lotions. I learned what household chemicals you could mix together (vinegar + castile soap = a slimy mess; always add lye to water, not the other way around) and concocted toilet bowl scrub, laundry detergent, and carpet cleaner. My kitchen resembled the laboratory of a mad scientist (especially when I'd don safety glasses and rubber gloves to make soap), but I loved it.

In essence, I was giving myself a crash course in preindustrial-era skills, but I had no concept of that at the time. It just felt like play.

Citrus-Infused All-Purpose Cleaner

This simple DIY cleaner captures the spirit of kitchen creativity by mixing trash (citrus peels) with a common household item (white vinegar) to make a frugal all-purpose cleaner that smells amazing. It was one of the first homemade cleaners I ever attempted, and it made me feel like a rock star.

Supplies
- Peels from 2 oranges (grapefruit, lemon, or lime peels also work)

- 4 cups white vinegar

- 1 quart-sized glass jar

- Spray bottle (a repurposed one is fine)

Instructions
Place the orange peels in the glass jar and fill to the top with vinegar. Seal tightly, shake well, and set the jar aside for four to six weeks (or longer) to allow the citrus to infuse into the liquid.

After time has elapsed, remove the peels from the mixture (you can compost them) and strain to remove any bits of citrus that might be floating in your vinegar. Dilute the mixture 1:1 with water (one part citrus vinegar to one part water) and place in a spray bottle. Use on countertops, floors, bathrooms, and other hard surfaces.

In my own weird way, I was experiencing what psychologist Mihaly Csikszentmihalyi calls *flow*, which he defines as "the state in which people are so involved in an activity that nothing else seems to matter." I'm guessing Dr. Csikszentmihalyi wasn't thinking of the euphoria that comes from repainting an old chair or mixing up bathtub cleaner when he was writing about flow, but I absolutely felt it during those early creation sessions. As time has passed, I've felt flow doing plenty of other (slightly more sophisticated) things, too. And it's these moments of stretching our abilities and working toward mastery that bring us "as close to what is usually meant by happiness as anything else we can conceivably imagine," writes Csikszentmihalyi.

I couldn't agree more. The only catch is that flow states won't happen during passive consumption—you must be *doing something* to invite them in.

Your ventures don't have to fit into a category at the craft store, nor should you create out of obligation to someone else. Think about what lights *you* up and chase that interest. The more curious you are, the more doors will open.

If you're still stuck, ask yourself, "What's something I buy that I could make instead?" or "How can I simplify an area of my life?" My personal desire to shift away from extreme consumerism has informed much of what I make and do. (Making homemade floor cleaner feels more exciting to me than knitting. Don't ask me why...) This is when looking back to history becomes especially useful. What did people clean their homes with before there were cleaning aisles at the store filled with hundreds of products? Vinegar, lemon juice, and baking soda were the stars of the show. How did our ancestors care for their skin? With olive oil, beeswax, and rose water. When you start to dig, you just might be surprised at how little we really need to be happy.

For those who spend most of their day at a desk (I absolutely fall into that category during certain seasons), making time for manual activities is even more important. As I've thrown myself into the writing of this book, I've found myself craving hands-on projects more than ever. The best way to spark my creative juices is to get out of the office and work with my hands, even just for a handful of hours. Stepping away from the screen feels counter-intuitive when you're under a deadline, but it works for me, almost every time.

Old-Fashioned Skin Care

The beauty industry tells us we need a lot of fancy products to keep our skin healthy. And I've tried a lot of them. There are scrubs, masks, cleansers, lotions, under-eye creams, anti-wrinkle potions, and toners and serums of all kinds. My bathroom cabinets were full. The products worked well enough, but after a while I couldn't help but wonder, do I *really* need all of these? When I started thinking about what was available before the advent of ad campaigns and fancy marketing, everything became much simpler.

Fast forward to today. My skin care regime centers around one main ingredient: beef fat. Yep, you read that correctly. Beef tallow (rendered beef fat) is an amazing moisturizer since it closely matches the composition of our skin. It's readily available as a by-product of the beef industry and doesn't require an elaborate industrial process to manufacture it. It's incredibly sustainable (if we're going to eat beef, it's important to use all the parts) and makes my skin glow. When I have fat left over from butchering a steer, I make my own balm. Otherwise, I purchase a tallow balm that's mixed with olive oil (another natural oil). I can use the same balm on my face and body—no special face formulations required. For a simple face wash, I use a bar of homemade soap, or a bit of mild castile soap mixed with a few drops of face-friendly essential oils (Roman chamomile, tea tree, and lavender are my favorites). My skin care product shelf has shrunk from fourteen products to two, my budget has plummeted, and my skin has never been happier. All skin is different, so I can't guarantee my exact routine will work for you, but I encourage you to rethink your personal care products. Life becomes so much simpler when we cut out the influences of consumerism.

Man vs. Machine

I won't buy an air fryer, but I love my slow cooker.

I refuse to heat my greenhouse with fossil fuels, but sometimes use a machine to milk the cow.

I insist on making popcorn on the stove top, but use my microwave for reheating leftovers.

I'm cautious of the consequences of progress, but I'm not a Luddite.

When should we resist the influences of modern machines, and when should we welcome their benefits? I don't have a black-and-white answer for that. Appliances or machines aren't inherently evil; however, sometimes they can steal joy from us and we don't realize it.

Start by asking yourself: *What is this appliance or machine taking away from me?*

Bread machines can save precious minutes, or they can rob us of an opportunity to use our hands for a worthwhile manual task.

Dishwashers can lessen our load at the end of a stressful day, or they can steal a moment when the family can come together to wash and dry plates and put them away.

Microwaves can be lifesavers when we need to quickly reheat leftovers, or they can lull us into believing that turning on the oven is too much effort.

If you're hoping I'll conclude this section with a tidy list of appliances that are recommended for an old-fashioned on purpose life, you won't find it. The practices that make you feel more alive may not have the same impact on me, and vice versa. Why do I reject bread machines but not Instant Pots? I don't have a good reason—only personal preference. We're not developing doctrine here. Rather, we're giving ourselves permission to tailor a life that best fits each of us, no matter how different our choices may look from anyone else's.

When I'm deciding which machines to use and which ones to skip, there are two questions I ask myself:

1. Does the old-fashioned version of this activity help me to slow down and be more mindful, or does it make me feel more agitated and stressed?

2. Does doing this by hand create superior results or a higher level of personal satisfaction?

Dandelion Salve Recipe

I always fancy myself an ancient medicine woman when I'm out in my yard foraging for dandelion blossoms. Dandelions are thought to help relieve arthritis and joint pain, so this salve is a soothing option applied to your hands and body. It's also a very versatile salve (I've even used it as an udder balm for our milk cows).

Step One: Make Dandelion Oil

Ingredients
- 1 cup dandelion blossoms (Only pick dandelions from areas you know have not been sprayed with herbicides.)

- 1½ cups olive oil (or other liquid oil such as almond oil or apricot oil)

Instructions
Spread the blossoms on a tray and allow them to dry for one to three days to remove some of the moisture. Place the wilted flowers into a pint-sized glass jar. Add

the oil and gently stir. Cover the jar with a paper towel or coffee filter affixed with a rubber band.

Place the jar in a cool, dark place for three to four weeks. Strain out the blossoms (you can compost them) and store the finished dandelion oil for up to one year.

Step Two: Make Dandelion Salve

Ingredients
- ½ cup dandelion oil

- 2 tablespoons beeswax pellets

Instructions
Place the dandelion oil and beeswax in an oven-safe dish or cup (I like to use a small Pyrex measuring cup) and place this container into a small saucepan filled with water over low heat. Stir until the beeswax is fully melted.

Remove from the heat and cool for several minutes. Pour into small glass jars or tins. Allow the dandelion salve to set up for several hours.

Store in a cool, dry place for up to nine months. Use the salve to soothe achy joints or chapped skin.

Notes:

- After the beeswax has melted and the mixture has cooled, I like to add essential oils. I prefer marjoram and fir oils if I'm targeting joints, or lavender for a calming, soothing salve.

- For a firmer salve, add a little more beeswax.

Let's compare two examples. First, firewood.

Our house is equipped with a propane furnace, but we rarely use it. We prefer to use our woodstove, especially throughout the depths of winter. This is partially because there's nothing like sidling up to a woodstove on a frigid day, but also because we enjoy the entire process of heating with wood. Dealing with firewood requires effort, but it's worthy effort.

Since trees are sparse here on the prairie, semitrucks bring us loads of logs from the mountains, and it's up to us to do the rest. The logs must be cut into rounds with the chain saw, then split into kindling. Christian built a tractor-powered hydraulic log splitter to make this process a little easier (yes, a machine!), but there's still a considerable amount of wood-handling required. Our firewood days are family projects. We take turns carrying the heavy rounds to the splitter, running the hydraulic levers, and stacking the pieces into our firewood bunk. When the kids were smaller, they carried the small pieces, but now they are adept at stacking and even running the splitter. It's hard, dirty work, but there's something about cutting firewood that makes us feel deeply contented. And the work doesn't end there. During the coldest months, the fire must be tended throughout the day. Sometimes it burns out during the night, so someone must walk across the freezing living room first thing in the morning to start a new blaze. Yet no one complains. Nothing beats the sight of a full woodbox when the snow is flying outside or the pride on the kids' faces when they build a fire with the wood they stacked themselves. The entire process of heating with wood—from splitting to stacking to tending the flames—is just as enjoyable as the fire itself. Flipping the switch on the furnace can never provide that feeling. For all these reasons, heating with wood is an old-fashioned on purpose task we happily continue, even as our family's schedule becomes busier.

Now, let's contrast that with laundry. Washing clothes by hand is certainly a homesteader task.

I could procure an old-fashioned wringer washer or adopt the "plunger in a bucket" method that's featured on many off-grid and survival blogs. Either of those options would get the job done in a retro way.

However, when I consider hand-washing my family's clothes each week, my blood pressure rises, and I start to feel a little clammy. Hours spent with a bucket and plunger isn't my personal idea of time well spent.

Hanging laundry outside might be romantic in the summer, but it becomes almost impossible in the winter—especially with our extreme winds and violent storms. (Our sheets and socks would be halfway to Nebraska within ten minutes of being on the line.)

Perhaps the process of manually washing would bring some meditative joy, but all I can think about when the thought crosses my mind is STRESS. (Plus, I'm not convinced I could do a better job than the washing machine.)

Therefore, even though I'm partaking in the task of stacking wood and building fires along with a whole other host of old-fashioned practices, I have no qualms about my very modern choice of owning a washer and dryer.

But just because this is *my* choice doesn't mean it will be right for you. Your path will look different than mine. Perhaps scrubbing dishes by hand is your jam. Or maybe hand-washing clothes DOES bring you peace. Or the idea of turning the soil over in your flower beds with a shovel instead of a rototiller fires you up. Only you will know the hard things that will feed your soul.

No matter how digitally advanced we become, we'll always need pursuits that keep us grounded in the real world—things we can touch, mold, craft, shape, and feel. That will never change. When you assume the role of a producer, you'll find that it pairs beautifully with the other ideas in this book. Take knitting, for example. By making your own socks or hats, you're not only resisting strict consumer culture, you're supplying your closet with new items, and activating your brain's effort-driven rewards cycle at the same time. It's a triple whammy. And it's just one example of how an old-fashioned on purpose life brings us back into balance.

When we awaken out of the mindset of overconsumption and own our role as a creator, whatever that may look like, we'll find our lives are filled with deeper levels of satisfaction, confidence, competence, and accomplishment. But creating is just one way we can step out of the unnatural spaces of our modern lives.

Old-Fashioned Action Steps

- Be mindful of the pull of advertising and how it affects your buying choices.

- Seek out activities with a physical, hands-on component to stimulate your effort-driven rewards circuit.

- How can you despecialize your life? Make a list of all the skills you'd like to learn.

- Try your hand at making your own cleaning products, skin care, lip balm, dandelion salve, and sourdough bread using the recipes I've included in this book.

- Practice active relaxation. There's certainly a time and place for a nap or a Netflix show, but when you do have spare time, don't let passive consumption always be the default. Find activities that fill your cup in other ways.

- Use your newly cultivated skill sets to create meaningful homespun gifts to share with others.

- Start thinking of your home as a place of production, not just consumption. How can you bring more life and creative pursuits into your home?

- Think outside of the box when it comes to home decor. If you love it, display it—no matter what Pinterest says.

- Try a few recipes that go beyond your usual kitchen comfort zone, particularly ones that are cultured or fermented.

CHAPTER 7

Escape the Human Zoo

I picked at the pile of pale scrambled eggs on my Styrofoam plate, adding salt as I sat at the particleboard table in a hotel dining room. Fluorescent lights cast an industrial ambience over the vinyl ferns that adorned the edges of the crowded space. Instead of the usual ruckus of kids and dogs, my soundtrack was composed of commercials blasting from the oversize TVs in both corners.

As I dipped my plastic spoon into a cup of grainy yogurt, I turned the container around to read the ingredient list: nonfat milk, cane sugar, cornstarch, artificial sweeteners, and a bunch of other things I couldn't pronounce. No wonder it tasted so strange. I guess something had to make up for the missing fat and flavor. I pushed the yogurt aside and took stock of my surroundings. From the food, to the furniture, to the floors, to the fixtures, I was surrounded by...synthetic.

Whenever I travel, the thing I miss most about our homestead is the rustic imperfection. After back-to-back days of sitting in antiseptic conference rooms, I ache for something, *anything* natural. I find myself longing for food not wrapped in plastic, spaces not infiltrated by bright lights, grass without green dye and a perfect haircut, and any space where nature isn't forced to bend under our boot and stay within prescribed borders. On the homestead, I'm constantly reminded that we're part of a bigger picture and that we humans don't have the final say. It's oddly reassuring. For me, unpolished reality always trumps flawless synthetic.

But plastic ferns and pseudoyogurt are only the beginning of our new artificial age. As I write these words, headlines are buzzing with excitement over laboratory-grown meats, the coming virtual universe where we can "live a second digital life," and even a "molecular beverage printer," dubbed the "Netflix of drinks." We've revolutionized transportation. We've streamlined manufacturing. We've visited the moon. We've digitally connected humanity. And now, we're determined to create a manufactured world.

Yet as we leap toward the synthetic, many of us sense a mismatch. Something doesn't feel right. Many of the most important parts of what makes us human are being pushed aside as we race toward the cutting edge, and our bodies know it.

One researcher who was studying depression described modern populations as "overfed, malnourished, sedentary, sunlight-deficient, sleep-deprived, and socially-isolated." How's that for a cheery thought? Some have even dubbed our modern world a "human zoo"—a place where we exist in artificial environments distant from our original habitat.

Yet as disheartening as this feels, there is hope. When we peel back these synthetic layers, we can thrive. This is how I've learned to bring myself back to center, time and time again. And that brings us to the next principle of an old-fashioned on purpose life: *We partner with nature to stay healthy and grounded.*

It sounds easy enough, but how exactly can we accomplish this?

Well, one option is to buy an off-grid cabin one hundred miles from civilization, forage for all your food, only drink spring water, light your house with candles and kerosene lamps, and refuse to wear shoes.

Yeah, I know. That's not gonna work for me, either.

Thankfully, there's another way. We don't have to shun our modern world completely. Rather, we need to understand our limits and seek out regular opportunities to return to our natural environments. We're biological creatures, after all. If you're still not sure what that might look like, the past holds valuable clues.

I don't know much about the family who homesteaded our property before us, but I've patched together pieces of their story from scattered memories shared by locals. I know their last name was Hansen and that they built their tiny stucco house in 1918. They had four daughters and a baby son who is buried in the pioneer cemetery up on the flats. One visitor told me they paid their daughters twenty-five cents for every rattlesnake they killed. (Legend has it that our property was crawling with rattlers back in the day, though we only see them occasionally now.) I have no doubt they had more than the ordinary measure of grit and vision to put down roots in this ocean of grass.

Sometimes I imagine time to be like a tracing paper overlay. I picture the Hansens and me, like overlapping ghosts, walking the same paths on this homestead a century apart. But while we both milk our cows and gather eggs on this piece of prairie, the similarities of our lives end there. The Hansen family lived in a different world. They rose with the sun and went to bed when it sank below the horizon. Soil and sweat were their constant companions as they built fences, erected buildings, cultivated the garden, and cared for their animals. There was no temptation to sneak glances at their cell phones as they walked to the barn, because the present was their only reality. Work was never-ending, so expending precious energy running on a treadmill would have seemed ludicrous. Social interactions were sparse, but sacred. It took a lot of effort to get to town or the grange hall, so they would have made every visit count.

Since every bit of their existence required massive effort, one could easily make the argument that my version of homesteading is superior to theirs. After all, I have post-hole diggers, refrigeration, running water, and light at the flick of a switch. However, even though I may have the Hansens beat in terms of convenience, I must work much harder for things that came easily to them, such as solitude, peace, physical movement, and connection to nature. Even on a homestead many miles from civilization, I must diligently guard against the influence of the human zoo.

Yet once again, it's not about pitting one against the other (a modern life against subsistence farming). But rather, it's asking the question, "How can we capture the best parts of both?" There are several ways we can accomplish this. None of them are complicated. They simply require a sense of curiosity and a few mindset shifts. Even if your day-to-day involves office buildings, asphalt, and conference rooms, it's very possible to reclaim your natural birthright.

Move Your Body

I know, you've heard this one before. It's hard to find a health article, blog post, or guru that doesn't recommend exercise. Yet as we embark on this old-fashioned shift, I'm going to invite you to rethink how you move. Let me explain.

Recently, I cleaned out the chicken coop. It wasn't on my schedule, but after spending several hours in the office and rewriting the same sentence eleven times, I gave up. I slipped on my muck boots, grabbed my work gloves, and headed outside. As I cleared out the accumulation of old bedding, I squatted, stretched, and lifted until I was covered in dust, chicken manure, wood chips, and sweat.

I didn't look like I'd come from the gym, but I felt like it. My muscles were warm and trembling, and my heart rate had increased. My face felt sun-kissed, and my mind was clearer. And the solution for that stagnant sentence popped into my mind on the second load to the manure pile. Sweeping the cobwebs out of the coop had seemingly swept them out of my mind as well.

This sort of natural, built-in movement is what our bodies are adapted to do. Yet we've accidentally outsourced most of our opportunities for motion. While our world is now designed for us to be sedentary, our bodies are not. As convenience has increased, so has the incidence of heart disease. Prior to the twentieth century, cardiovascular disease was extremely rare as most people were active as a part of their day-to-day lives. However, as industrialization made life easier, rates began to skyrocket. One cardiologist at Johns Hopkins reported seeing a 98 percent increase in heart disease in just a ten-year period at the beginning of the twentieth century. Fast forward to today, and heart disease tops the charts as the number one cause of death. But with the way our world is now structured, sitting can feel like an inescapable aspect of the human zoo. So how do we counteract this side effect of modern life?

The gym is one option. I'm thankful for the small home gym in our shop when it's too cold to do much outside (walks in −30°F windchill aren't my idea of a good time). But as soon as the seasons change, I almost always opt for homestead chores over gym routines. There's something about accomplishing a task while moving my body that is more satisfying than even the best days on the treadmill or rowing machine. And science even backs this up.

In a study of communities with the longest-lived people, researchers discovered each group had lives full of natural movement. Rather than compartmentalizing movement as "exercise," it was built into their daily routines. They maintained their homes, kneaded bread, worked in their gardens, and walked *a lot*. Science shows that this sort of steady, consistent movement that combines cardio, strength, and flexibility is preferable over exercises that only focus on specific muscle groups.

In fact, there's a growing movement of fitness professionals who are recommending exactly this. Instead of focusing on isolated moves at the gym, they recommend movements that more closely mimic how humans would have moved before industrialization took over. I try to work some of these movements into my regular routines (although some are easier than others!).

- **Lifting.** This one is the easiest, since there are plenty of things to lift on a homestead. Buckets of grain, firewood, rocks, hay bales, saddles, etc.—it's all fair game. Combination strength movements required in real-life situations are more effective than only working one muscle group at a time. Yard work is a fantastic place to practice lifting if you don't have a homestead.

- **Carrying.** Instead of always grabbing the wheelbarrow to carry a bag of grain, or using the hose to move water, I often carry things myself. (In gym-speak, carrying a heavy object in each hand and walking for a distance is called the "farmer's carry," which I think is very fitting.) If you don't have a reason to carry buckets, try walking around your yard with a milk jug of water in each hand. You can also try wearing a weighted backpack when you walk (see sidebar on page 178).

- **Squatting.** Squats are a gym favorite for their ability to strengthen the tendons and ligaments in our legs, as well as reducing knee injuries. Working in the garden and yard provides plenty of opportunities to squat with a purpose.

- **Crawling.** It's not just for babies. Natural movement proponents recommend crawling for adults to increase core strength and bolster neural connections. I end up crawling a lot when I'm weeding in the garden or yard.

- **Balancing.** Balance exercises encourage the structures in our body to work together as one unit, prevent injuries, and may even improve cognitive function. Granted, this one is a little harder to facilitate during your regular chore routine. Try walking across boards like a balance beam, standing on one foot, or crossing fallen trees when you're on a walk.

As we shift our perspective on movement, chores take on a whole new meaning. Raking leaves elevates our heart rate while collecting fodder for our compost piles and making the backyard look tidier. Watering the gardens builds strong arms and legs if you're carrying the water in buckets. (I'm telling myself this right now as I'm lugging five-gallon buckets to water tiny fruit trees every day.)

Weeding encourages healthy squatting and bending. Sweeping the house provides an opportunity to increase our heart rate and flexibility (especially if we go all in and move furniture). Even washing dishes can be meditative when we allow ourselves to sink into the soapy moments and just be. A definite plus for our mental health.

Of course, these are just some of my examples—you can come up with your own "old-fashioned workout" routine, depending on what tasks you have around your house.

As you pursue many of the old-fashioned activities in this book, you'll notice that healthy movement is a side effect. While there's nothing wrong with scheduling gym time, as we become more engaged with the world around us, many of our exercise goals could start taking care of themselves.

The Magic of Walking

There's nothing better for giving yourself a mental reset than going for a walk.

If you live in a place with minimal yard or garden work, walking is a simple way to weave movement into your everyday routine. Sometimes I'll use earbuds while

I walk, but other times I leave my phone at home so I can log some quiet solitude at the same time. To increase the difficulty level, look into rucking (wearing a weighted backpack while you walk). Start with a weight that's about 10 percent of your body weight (this can be adjusted depending on your fitness level). Because rucking combines weight with cardio, it's a low-impact exercise with big benefit. And you can do it anywhere you'd normally take a walk.

Stay in the Dark

It's easy to underestimate how unnatural our environments truly are. One aspect of my life I never considered until we started homesteading was the *light*.

While the Hansen family would have lit their little house with candles and kerosene lamps, I now illuminate it with the flip of a switch. The incandescent bulb changed our world for the better in many ways, but never have humans had so much exposure to nonstop light. Our ancestors went to bed not long after the sun set with only the glow of a campfire, candle, or lamp to illuminate their way. Now, streetlights shine in our windows while LED lights stare at us from electronics and appliances all night long. Even though we're thirty-five miles from the closest town, I can see the haze of its light on the horizon when I look to the south at night. Nighttime has never been brighter. And that's not a good thing.

I first noticed this by accident. I realized whenever I'd look at my phone too late at night, I'd sleep horribly. I was sure it was coincidence at first, so I kept testing the theory. (Yes, I'm stubborn.) Sure enough—the more I used my phone before bed, the more I tossed and turned.

Our TVs, phones, and e-readers give off blue light—a type of light that's especially problematic when we're exposed to large doses at night. This is why we sleep poorly after we've been scrolling Facebook in bed (even if we're watching kitten videos and avoiding Aunt Martha's political articles).

While we're exposed to blue light through natural sunlight, blue light has the shortest wavelength and the highest energy. In nature, we need blue light to cue our brains when it's time to be awake, alert, and focused. But when we surround ourselves with fluorescent lighting, TV screens, computer screens, and smartphones at all hours, the overexposure to blue light disrupts our circadian rhythm, causes eye damage, decreases melatonin production, and tricks our bodies into thinking it's daytime, which doesn't bode well for a good night's sleep. Perhaps this is part of the reason modern society is chronically sleep-deprived. (The CDC reports that one in three Americans don't get enough sleep.)

This extra artificial light adds up. In a study by Harvard University researchers, blue light was found to suppress melatonin for about twice as long as green light and to shift circadian rhythms by twice as much, in addition to increasing our cortisol levels. High cortisol levels make it difficult to experience deep sleep, which in turn lowers our immune system's ability to fight illness and disease. (Ever notice how you get sick almost immediately when you're sleep-deprived?)

But light exposure doesn't have to be a point of stress. It's an easy place to recapture a more old-fashioned balance. When in doubt, think about your great-great-grandparents' relationship with light and follow their lead: use blue light (especially sunlight) in the morning and warm light (or minimal lights) at night, and keep your bedroom as dark as possible when you're sleeping, perhaps adding light-blocking curtains to your windows. This is just another way the simplicity of an old-fashioned on purpose lifestyle helps bring us back into balance. Little steps like these add up in a big way.

Here on the homestead, the biggest step we've taken to regulate our exposure to unnatural light is dimming the lights inside our house in the evening. Once supper dishes are washed and the kitchen is put to bed (usually around 7:00 p.m.), we congregate in the living room. We turn the bright overhead lights off and use a small chandelier in the corner of the room instead. It's bright enough to see what we're doing without feeling like we're sitting in the middle of a hospital operating room. It makes the room feel cozier anyway (especially when the woodstove is burning), so it's not a sacrifice. We also disconnected our outside yard light, which had an obnoxious way of shining into our bedroom windows, and we removed all light-emitting devices from our bedrooms. If you do use screens at night (which I still do sometimes—I'm not perfect), FL-41 tinted glasses have been shown effective to filter both blue and green wavelengths.

Of course, we don't want to keep ourselves in the dark all the time. A healthy dose of sunlight first thing in the morning is good for us. If I'm feeling drowsy in the morning, nothing wakes me up better than heading outside (especially when it's −3°F—a far more effective approach than coffee). Taking an old-fashioned approach to light is a simple shift that can make a huge difference in how you feel throughout the day.

Light Pollution and Animals

Humans aren't the only ones affected by artificial lights. Bright beaches disorient sea turtles that are trying to lay eggs, city lights disrupt migratory bird patterns, and lit-up night skies confuse bats and pollinating insects.

The quickest fix is to turn off any outdoor light that's not absolutely necessary (bonus: it'll save your electricity costs). For outside lights that must stay on, here are a few tips:

- Use wildlife-friendly bulbs that give off amber-colored light.

- Point outdoor lights down, not up into the sky.

- Use lights with shields or coverings to reduce glare and contain the light.

Soak in Natural Spaces

When my daughter Sage was four, we rushed her to the emergency room one afternoon after what we thought was a simple head cold resulted in her tiny body having to fight for each breath. When the doctors in the ER saw her labored breathing, they immediately admitted her.

She suffered an excruciating few days of breathing treatments, tests, and oxygen, and thankfully, the problem ended up being a regular respiratory virus—nothing abnormal. Although Christian was the one who opted to stay with her at the hospital, my adrenaline-fueled stress levels at home were still high as I attempted to care for our other two children and manage the homestead animals while impatiently checking for updates.

When Sage finally walked through the door, relief flooded over me. She was her usual confident self, proud of her hospital stay and eager to show off her new collection of stickers and coloring books. After lots of hugs, catching up, and throwing a load of laundry in the washing machine, I was struck with a very specific craving. I knew what I needed. As the kids settled in to watch a movie, I slipped on my jacket and headed outside.

The November air was sharp and the soil frigid, so I made a beeline for the greenhouse, where the warmth enveloped me like a giant blanket. When I knelt to pluck weeds from the rows of spinach and plunge my fingers into the soil, my body released its last threads of tension. My breathing slowed. My muscles, tight and sore after days of stress, began to loosen. I could finally form a full thought.

At the time, I didn't know that *Mycobacterium vaccae* bacteria in the soil might have been reducing my stress as I weeded the spinach, or that multiple studies have found that surgery patients who viewed plants and trees had quicker recoveries and reported less pain than those without exposure to nature. I'd never heard of the healthy fatty acid hidden in soil that can help lower anxiety levels, boost immune function, and reduce inflammation. All I knew was that as I raked, weeded, and pruned, the soil brought me back into balance. Once again, as it had so many times in the past, the earth nurtured me as I cared for it.

The yearning I felt for soil the day Sage came home from the hospital wasn't an isolated incident. It manifests itself whenever my life becomes extra stressful or when I'm immersed in artificial environments for too long. Biologist E. O. Wilson called this craving "biophilia," which he defined as the connection that humans subconsciously seek with the rest of life. I believe we're all starving for this connection. While Americans now spend over 90 percent of their days inside buildings or vehicles, the practice of existing within man-made structures for the bulk of our lives is very new. Prior to that, nature was our home.

Even if you haven't connected with the natural world since childhood, the desire to connect with the living world around you is still there. Your body will tell you what you need when you give it a chance.

Ask yourself: Do you feel more alive when you're shopping in a sterile grocery store, or when you're walking through a garden? Are you more refreshed after a walk outside or after binge-watching YouTube videos? While grocery stores and screens may be our default, when we consciously choose connection with the world around us, we feel *different*.

There's fascinating research surrounding "earthing" or "grounding," which is simply the practice of allowing our bodies to be directly connected to the earth. It's thought that by putting our foot or skin directly in contact with the ground, we experience a myriad of benefits, from pain relief to better sleep. Some companies sell special "grounding" mats designed to mimic the electrical current of the earth, but you don't need a gadget to ground yourself. Just take off your shoes, walk barefoot in the grass, or spend your lunch hour sitting under a tree. You'll feel the difference immediately.

We all have an innate need to be a part of our natural habitat, though it's easy to miss these whispers in our fast-paced modern lives. And these healing moments in nature don't have to happen in a grand place. I'm far from being a "mountain woman." While I'd love to do more camping and hiking in the future, I find my doses of nature in smaller, simpler ways. Some of my most satisfying moments have taken place in my garden or during walks on the roads near our home. They can be cultivated in your backyard or the local park. You can find them by going on walks and noticing the native plants and birds (or bugs!).

> ## *While modern life dulls our senses, nature awakens them.*

While modern life dulls our senses, nature awakens them. The more time you spend outside, the quicker you'll be to notice slight weather changes, tell a warm wind from a sharp one, and understand how much life really lives in the soil beneath your feet. "As human beings we need direct, natural experiences," writes Richard Louv in *Last Child in the Woods*. "We require fully activated senses in order to feel fully alive."

It's no coincidence that nature is a part of the equation with each of the previous practices in this chapter. The natural world offers us engaging ways to move our bodies. It provides us with the exact type of light we need throughout the day. And when we immerse ourselves in the world around us, we become more synced to the cycles that keep our world turning. It's no coincidence that we feel better in our natural habitat. We're supposed to be there.

Making Peace with the Zoo

I don't like how junk light disrupts my sleep, but I still look forward to occasional movie nights with the kids. I work outside as much as possible, but am still thankful for my treadmill on the coldest days. I try to avoid plastics in my home, but I wouldn't have a greenhouse if not for the miracle of polycarbonate panels. I love spending the afternoon with my fingers in the soil, but there are plenty of days my hands are pounding on my laptop instead. As appealing as nothing but a rotary phone and candlelight seems at times, I still have one foot planted firmly in the industrial world. I don't see that changing anytime soon. Yet when we explore creative ways to fulfill our modern obligations while honoring our biology, everything aligns.

But don't take my word for it—let your body do the talking. That's ultimately what convinced me. The first time I really felt it was during a thunderstorm.

Although I was a newcomer to the prairie, when you live in a drought-prone place, you quickly learn rain is always to be celebrated. That evening I watched with anticipation as the clouds darkened. They didn't disappoint.

As lightning flashed and water poured from the sky, something came over me. I flung open the kitchen window, sat on the floor, and rested my chin on the windowsill, watching the storm put on the most spectacular display. The cool air rushed in through the window as goose pimples covered my arms. Rain spritzed through the screen and splattered my face as puddles formed in the thirsty grass. The smell of wet earth was intoxicating.

> **as I connected to the natural world around me, I became more connected to myself.**

From the top of my head to the tips of my toes, I felt alive in a way I hadn't before. My senses were awakening. And it was in that moment something shifted for me. I hadn't yet read any of the research about biophilia or soil microbes or blue light or screen time. All I knew was that as I connected to the natural world around me, I became more connected to myself. And when we let that simple principle guide us, it's hard to go wrong.

So may we step away from the synthetic, feel the air on our skin, move our bodies for the joy of it, wiggle our fingers into the soil, shed the overly civilized parts of our lives, and *listen* to our bodies. These are some of the best experiences life has to offer, and when we sink into them, everything aligns.

Old-Fashioned Action Steps

- Expose your body to natural light, especially in the morning.

- Dim the house lights at night and avoid blue light–emitting devices before bed.

- Add blackout curtains to your bedroom to give your body the gift of darkness.

- Turn off outdoor lights to protect the dark sky for wildlife.

- Find natural ways to exercise by doing chores.

- On the days you're sitting more than normal (traveling, long office days, etc.), be extra intentional about finding even thirty minutes to move your body.

- Go on long walks regularly. Look up, listen, think, and observe.

- Try to touch the earth or soil every single day.

- Walk barefoot outside.

- If you work in an office building, take your breaks outside as much as possible (yes, even if it's cold!).

The chicken coop needed TLC when we bought our property

Every roof on the property had to be redone

Our little farmhouse after many years of renovations

A windmill given new life

My real-life homestea

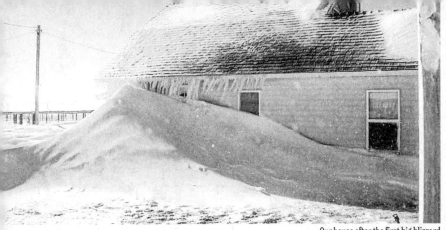

Our house after the first big blizzard

A below-zero day on the prairie

Is handle the cold well, as long as they have plenty of hay

A tornado a few miles from our homestead

Growing sprouts on the counter

Store-bought butter (top) and homemade butter from o

Tomatoes ready for planting

Our raised garden beds

Weeding the cabbage midsummer

A bountiful garlic harvest

Becoming our own grocery store

Freshly dug potatoes

Our chicken tractor

Bagging our home-raised meat birds

Homegrown ingredients

The working kitchen

Homemade pizza

Old-fashioned apple pie

Home-canned cherries

My homestead pantry

Homemade mayonnaise

From-scratch biscuits are easier than you think

Drowning in milk and making cheese

The Chugwater Soda Fountain before we bought it

The soda fountain after our renovations

The interior of the soda fountain after many months of updates

Honey mint lip balm

Homemade candles made in the slow cooker

Dandelion salve

Cutting firewood as a family

Seeking solitude in the greenhouse

My preferred form of exercise

es provide endless opportunities to move our bodies

The peace of the late-summer garden

Sinking into the quietness of winter

Playing in the buffalo wallow

The humble chicken bucket

A tomato plant that has been damaged by herbicides

Gathering our cattle

Using the deep-mulch method

Warming a calf in the mudroom

Our kids start building fires around age seven

Running on the hay stack

Working cattle with our local friends

Mesa and her steer at

A family baseball game in Chugwater

CHAPTER 8

Unplug to Connect

It'd been a hectic week. An overload of projects had converged to produce a frenzy of emails, documents, deadlines, and Zoom calls. I was fried. But all day long I'd kept my momentum, knowing I'd eventually get to spend time in the garden for a much-needed reset.

After the day's scorching temperatures, the evening air had become mellow and soft on my face. Savoring my alone time, I admired the lush vegetables and vibrant flowers with a deep sense of satisfaction. I bent to pluck a few lamb's-quarters from the cabbage bed, allowing myself to sink into the silence. Until...

BUZZ! The phone in my pocket vibrated. Without thinking, I reached for it. Someone needed a link for a call tomorrow. I dashed off a quick email and then refocused on my tomatoes. I plucked a few suckers from between the stalks, until...

BUZZ! A friend texted about getting together over the weekend. I didn't want to forget, so I shot back a quick reply. I moved to the next tomato plant, as I noticed the way the dusky light danced across my strawberry blond calendulas. "That's Instagram-worthy," I thought. Out came the phone again. I fiddled with the camera settings until the composition was just right. As I uploaded the picture to the app, I scrolled by a photo of the most impeccable English flower garden I'd ever seen. I squinted at the screen, comparing their pristine heirloom roses to my scrawny prairie calendulas. I guess my blooms didn't look as good as I thought. Come to think of it, my tomato trellising left a lot to be desired. And why were the holes in my cabbage leaves so big?

My mood flattened. I hacked at a weed with my hoe. Thirty minutes into my garden session, and I'd spent more time with my screen than the soil. My solitude had been broken by comparison and distraction. I was feeling just as fragmented and distracted as I had been in the office earlier that day. Technology had struck again.

Ironically, as counterproductive as my phone can be, my garden wouldn't exist without it. As a stay-at-home mom in the middle of nowhere, the internet has long been my connection to the world. From it, I've learned how to amend my soil, diagnose pest problems, manage stubborn weeds, and cultivate new crops.

But technology takes as much as it gives. While I may be immune from most of the trappings of modern life here on the prairie (smog, sirens, and crowds aren't an issue, and my only traffic issues are when the neighbor's cows lie down in the middle of the road), I still constantly battle the lure of technology. My phone shatters the stillness, whisking my concentration away from the magnificence of this prairie life and off to faraway places. I understand the dangers. I've read the research. *I know better.* Yet it's still a temptation. And that brings us to our next old-fashioned on purpose tenet: *We use technology as a tool, but it doesn't own us.*

And this may be our toughest task yet.

If you had to guess, how many times would you say you look at your phone each day? Twenty times? Forty times? Sixty times? Maybe you're squeamish to admit it because those numbers seem high. But odds are, those are extreme underestimates. A 2022 survey of one thousand Americans found that participants checked their phones an average of *344 times per day.* That means we're checking our screens approximately every four minutes.

Another survey estimated average daily smartphone use to be from 3.6 to 5.7 hours per day (varying by state). Mississippians reported the most hours spent on their phones, with a total of eighty-six days per year consumed by smartphone technology.

In other words, if those residents stepped away from their phones, they could gain back eighty-six days each year for other activities. What could you do with an extra three months of time?

Yet ignoring our phones is easier said than done, because these devices are designed to exploit the weaknesses of our biology. Tristan Harris, a former Google design ethicist, likens phones to having "a slot machine in your pocket." The irresistible urge to check, swipe, tap, and like isn't accidental; this technology was engineered that way. The designers knew exactly what they were doing. As a result, it's almost impossible to resist the temptation of tech. Dopamine floods our brains every time we drag our thumbs to refresh the screen. We can't get enough. It's an addictive cycle that some experts compare to using cocaine.

And it's not just cell phones that keep us addicted. The average American household now has twenty-five connected devices. We turn to tech to track everything from calories and exercise to heart rate, blood pressure, and sleep. Smart homes allow us to adjust the lights and thermostat without getting off the couch, smart refrigerators tell us when we're low on milk, and smart washing machines send a message when we need to switch that load of laundry. We stream video content at all hours, and we even meet with our health-care providers online, not to mention turning to screens to access education, church services, dating apps, and social networking.

But our newfound love affair with screens isn't harmless. In one survey focusing on screen time, nearly all participants reported problems stemming from phone use, including everything from eyestrain and reduced productivity to narrower worldview and back pain. Even more concerning, more than 68 percent said screen time had a negative effect on their mental health, with nearly a quarter of users linking smartphone usage to increased anxiety and depression.

But perhaps the aspect that frightens me the most is the evidence that the internet is rewiring our brains. Our brains have the amazing capability to reorganize and make new connections based on experiences. This works in our favor when we're trying to learn new skills (yes, at any age!), but this can also work against us.

Thanks to the never-ending supply of data streaming through our devices 24/7, our attention spans are shrinking. Our ability to focus on meatier concepts is waning as we're faced with fewer opportunities for deep thought. I noticed this in myself when I began researching this book.

As I dug into mountains of peer-reviewed articles and stacks of books, *I couldn't get in the groove.*

I had to read sentences over and over to grasp their meaning. I struggled to stay focused for more than a few pages at a time. I began to wonder if my attention span was decreasing with age. However, I couldn't quit, so I persisted, haltingly.

Then something happened.

The more I dug into scientific journals, nerdy research papers, psychology texts, and hefty nonfiction books, the easier it became to focus. Light bulbs came on. I felt like I was riding a high of new ideas and connections. My brain was tired, but *happy.* But it left me wondering—why did I struggle so much at first?

I suspect my phone had a lot to do with it, and the research backs that up. Digital technology is "rapidly and profoundly altering our brains," writes Dr. Gary Small, professor of psychiatry and director of the UCLA Memory and Aging Center. When we only consume information in the form of sound bites, posts, tweets, and skimmed articles, our ability to focus atrophies. This affects our cognition and our capacity to think deeply.

This bothers me. I cringe to think that my scrolling, skimming, liking, and tapping might be changing my brain in ways I don't even realize. I've considered ditching my phone many times. I've thought about going back to a flip phone or one of those new hybrids that has smartphone features without the allure of apps. But I haven't canceled my contract just yet. As a business owner, the benefits of my phone still outweigh the costs, but it's a balancing act. Is it possible to be a mindful, old-fashioned on purpose person *with* a phone? I think it is, as long as we're intentional. Here are some of the strategies I use to keep tech in check in my life.

Seek Out Solitude

One of the biggest problems with phones is that they rob us of the opportunity to think our own thoughts. Prior to the advent of smartphones, solitude was much less elusive. Sitting at a long stoplight, walking down the street, waiting in line at the grocery store, or driving long stretches of highway gave us valuable space to ruminate on various concepts. Now, when faced with the tiniest hint of boredom, we fill the seconds with a constant feed of *someone else's* ideas.

Have you ever noticed that the best ideas come when you're showering? There's nothing magical about the shower—it's simply one of the few distraction-free spaces we have left. Being alone with our thoughts is crucial for allowing our brains to reboot, increasing our ability to concentrate, coming up with our own ideas, expanding creative thought, and solving problems.

When solitude is absent from our lives, we are more prone to be overwhelmed, both physically and emotionally. Daily quiet time alone has been shown to help lower blood pressure, decrease heart rate, improve breathing, reduce muscle tension, and increase focus and cognition.

And the busier you are, the more you need it. The more time I take off, the more I get done. The more blank space I have, the more creative I become. It sounds backward, but it works. Some of the greatest artists and inventors in history credit stretches of alone time with their genius. "The mind is sharper and keener in seclusion and uninterrupted solitude," wrote Nikola Tesla. "Be alone, that is the secret of invention." Our brains are capable of amazing things when we simply give them room to breathe. In fact, at this very moment, you already have the answers to some of the problems you're struggling with right now. *You just can't hear them* because they're being drowned out by podcasts, iTunes, Facebook, and Netflix.

Thankfully, even though finding solitude in our full lives isn't always easy, it's very possible.

The first trick is to schedule it in. If we wait for the perfect time to appear, it's never going to happen. So I schedule it in— just like a hair appointment or dental checkup. If I don't, the open stretches in my schedule quickly become cluttered with other obligations. And make no mistake—time alone with your thoughts is just as important as getting your teeth cleaned.

The second trick is to think outside of the box. Scheduled quiet time is great, but that's not the only way to find it. Your session of solitude doesn't have to be a thirty-minute meditation session. It can be five minutes of quiet in the car before you pick your kids up at school. It can be shutting off the music or podcasts for part of your drive so your brain has a moment to just *be*. It can be leaving your phone at home when you go on a walk. It can be lying in your backyard staring at the clouds. I can't believe I'm admitting this, but sometimes I sit on a bucket in the garden and watch bugs after I'm done watering or weeding. (This past summer I saw a ladybug larva cram an entire aphid into its mouth. It was spectacular.) We all have more opportunities for quiet than we think—we just fill them with our phones without realizing it. See how your brain exhales when you give it the slightest bit of margin. I think you'll be pleasantly surprised.

Good Ideas Can Be Shy

When you're attempting to coax an idea out of hiding, you must be sneaky. Ideas like to appear when you're thinking about other things, especially when you're working with your hands.

When I'm stuck on a problem, I "seed" the idea in my brain, and then I leave my office and try not to think about it. Creativity is best cultivated in a wandering mind. For example, if I'm trying to come up with the perfect story for a section of this book, I'll remind myself of the core principle I want to communicate as I walk to the barn. Then I'll get to work with my wheelbarrow and manure fork while letting my subconscious do the rest. It'll turn that seed of an idea upside down, flip it around, and play with it a little. And usually, once I become engrossed in whatever mindless physical activity I'm doing, the solution appears. It feels like magic, but it's really just the power of the subconscious. See what brilliant ideas brew while you're,

- Taking a shower

- Driving long stretches of highway

- Weeding the garden

- Mucking out the barn or coop (manure is the best fertilizer for blossoming ideas)

- Enjoying a long walk

- Folding laundry or washing dishes

- Mowing the lawn

- Painting or sanding wood

- Partaking in hands-on hobbies like watercolors, knitting, or pottery

- Reading a book

Conquer the Compulsion

Replace the urge to check your phone with something better. For me, that's usually reading. I keep books sprinkled all over the house, which makes it easy to grab one while I'm waiting for the pasta to boil or the kids to clean their rooms. While I do consume ebooks and audiobooks, there's something luxurious about flipping actual pages. I remember more information when I read it on a sheet of paper (especially when I can highlight it and make notes in the margins). Therefore, I can't think of anything more delightfully old-fashioned than leaving your phone in another room and losing yourself in a book. Read nonfiction. Read books that make you think. Read books that answer some questions and create others. Read stories that inspire you to step out of your comfort zone. Read books printed on actual paper. Read books with which you don't agree. Read outside in the grass. Read in waiting rooms and the airport. Read books written in old-fashioned language (yes, it takes more work to decipher them, but it stretches your deep-thinking muscles). Reading is the ultimate old-fashioned default activity instead of the phone.

Other default activities I've tried when I feel the urge to zone out on my phone are quick cleaning tasks (washing a window or two, decluttering the dining room table), three minutes of deep breathing, watering plants, or even exercises. One winter I tried doing ten air squats whenever I felt like surfing my phone. I blew past my goal of fifty squats per day without even doing an official workout.

While default activities are handy, you might not need them if you keep your phone out of sight. I often reach for my phone just because it's in view. I'll scroll and "wake up" fifteen minutes later feeling disoriented and distracted. Keeping my phone out of sight breaks this mindless habit. As I write this chapter, I've banished my phone to another room entirely. If I keep it on the desk, I know I'll reach for it as soon as I get stuck on a sentence.

Nix the Notifications

Our phones are needy little creatures. They flash, ding, buzz, and do everything they can to steal our focus with their incessant red notification bubbles. It's time to break this codependent relationship. To start taking back control, I regularly go through each app on my phone and ask myself, "Is this doing more harm than good?" For example, one way I stay motivated during certain monotonous tasks is by listening to audiobooks or podcasts. Over the years, this habit has introduced me to some of my favorite authors, sparked new passions, and challenged old ways of thinking. It's been refreshing and healthy. I keep my listening in check by sometimes leaving my phone in the house and working in silence. This gives me the best of both worlds and is easy to manage.

In contrast, there's Facebook. I can be quick to justify my account considering I have business groups and profiles there. If I'm honest, however, most of my time on Facebook is spent scrolling, watching random videos that contribute very little to my life, or feeling agitated over negative comments. The little bit of good I get from Facebook isn't worth the constant distraction. So I deleted the app. I can still access my pages and groups through my laptop when I want to stay connected with my online community, but mindless scrolling is less of a temptation. My Facebook usage has since plummeted, and I don't feel like I've missed out on anything at all.

I'll be honest—all of this is a moving target for me. I won't claim to have mastered it. Some days I'm so engrossed in real life I forget my phone exists, while other days I catch myself falling into old habits and mindlessly scrolling. You get to decide what your relationship with social media looks like—it may serve you to leave it entirely. But regardless of the path you choose, we don't have to be victims of technology. We can take charge and make it work for us. And when we do, the rewards are many.

Stop Gambling with Your Time

Here are a few more ways I keep the addictive draw of my phone in check:

- **No noise.** I've turned off all noise on my phone, except for the alarm. The dings and buzzes give me a sort of Pavlovian response I can't ignore, no matter how hard I try. If you need to be able to hear calls from certain numbers, most phones have selective settings to allow specified numbers to ring while silencing the rest.

- **Do not disturb.** I keep my phone on "do not disturb" or airplane mode when I'm working or sleeping.

- **Leave it.** When I see my phone, I pick it up without thinking. To avoid this, I often leave it in another room, especially when I need to focus on a project or when I'm spending time in nature.

- **Delete apps.** I've deleted as many apps off my phone as possible, including Facebook and email, and I use an app that reminds me when I'm over my daily allocation of social media time.

- **Batch it.** As much as I'd like to get rid of email entirely, that's not a possibility right now. So I try to check once or twice per day (on my laptop, not phone). And shockingly, the world has kept spinning.

- **Audit yourself.** For a jarring wake-up call, use a time-tracking app on your phone to audit the amount of time you're spending with your screen. Your findings might be painful, but once you're armed with information, it's easier to implement changes.

Prioritize People over Phones

It's trendy to complain about social media these days. And let's face it—it makes an easy target. Declines in empathy, nonexistent conversations, skyrocketing anxiety and depression...with a list like that, it seems obvious that social media is inherently dangerous. Yet as tempting as it is to draw hard lines (Phones are bad! Social media is bad!), it's not quite that simple.

In a book about old-fashioned living, you might expect me to shun social media entirely, but the reality is, the retro homesteading movement is growing *because* of social media. Families are rethinking their priorities, eating better food, learning new skills, and connecting to the land thanks to the inspiration they're seeing on their feeds. I think that's incredible.

The debate over social media comes down to *how you use it*. Think about that long-lost friend from college you never would have found without Facebook. Or the resources and inspiration you've discovered via Instagram. Or the way you were able to send a heartfelt direct message to a long-distance friend who needed some encouragement. Those types of interactions count for something. One study concluded that social media can be beneficial *when we are using it to communicate in a personalized, intentional way*. And therein lies the key. Social media can play a role in helping us build community, as long as we're not allowing it to replace real interactions.

One way we can foster this is to make sure we're balancing our screen time with real-life relationships. In his book *Bowling Alone*, Robert Putnam digs into the data to determine why we've pulled away from each other as a culture. In eras past, civic involvement was much more popular. Clubs and activities were all the rage for our grandparents' generation. From Rotary and Lions Clubs to church groups and bowling leagues, they spent many hours each week involved in their communities. Yet participation in these sorts of activities has been on the decline for decades. While Putnam discovered a variety of culprits, there was one element he called the "single most consistent predictor" of civic disengagement: *dependence on television*. The trend of increased TV watching "coincided exactly with the national decline in social connectedness." As television sets became the new centerpieces of family life, community engagement plummeted. Of course, smartphones increased this disconnectedness a hundredfold. We may think our craving for community is being satisfied digitally, but screens are a cheap substitute. We still desperately need real people, real conversations, and real life.

It's crucial that we refuse to let phones take center stage when we're with other humans. Resist pulling out your device when you feel those initial hints of boredom in a group of people. Our unwillingness to be uncomfortable, even for just a second, prevents us from having the types of impromptu conversations that allow us to explore new ideas in a vulnerable and unscripted way. Think back to a time you made an unexpected connection with another person—maybe you caught their eye at just the right time and you both burst out laughing, or you discovered the two of you share a surprising similarity. These sorts of interactions are nonexistent when our phones are our focus.

One study showed that people who used their phones while out to supper with friends enjoyed their experiences *less*. Participants said their phones made them feel distracted, which dampened the mood of the gathering and made the evening feel boring. Make it a personal rule to keep your phone off the table and in your pocket, purse, or car when you're enjoying a meal with friends or family. Seek out opportunities to connect with people in real life. Invite friends over for supper, have a conversation at a coffee shop, or just look people in the eye and smile when you're running errands. These simple, old-fashioned steps can do so much to create connection and conversation in our screen-based society.

Navigating Our High-Tech World

I remember the first time I drove through a city using GPS.
Christian and I had borrowed a friend's first-generation Gar-
min for a multistate road trip, and I was enthralled. That gadget gave me a navigational confidence I'd never had before. To
this day, I punch every new address into my phone with little
thought of exact routes or directions. I've learned to trust the
wisdom of the disembodied voice.

I'd never given my GPS dependence a second thought until
recently when I arrived in an unfamiliar city and realized my
phone battery had dropped to 3 percent. I panicked. Without
my phone, I had no idea how to get home. I had completely
ignored all the highway names and landmarks on my drive in,
thinking I didn't need to know them since I had my trusty GPS.

Once upon a time, I drove alone across Wyoming with nothing but printed directions. But now, my navigational instincts
had disappeared. I eventually borrowed a phone charger, but
for the rest of the drive home, I was unnerved at how helpless
I'd become. And it made me wonder, what other instincts had
I left behind as technology became the driving influence in my
life? I don't want to live so much through a screen that I neglect
to live an actual life.

But like every other concept in this book, we have a choice.
We don't have to be victims of technology; we can take control and make it work for us. It's okay to use tech and its trappings as tools, *as long as they don't become our masters*. I still plan
to use my GPS, but not all the time. On some trips I might use
a paper map or ask someone for directions, just to test my wits.
And when I do use the app, I now take note of the landmarks
along the way. I still use my phone to learn new gardening techniques, but I am careful to leave it in the house when I'd benefit
from a stretch of solitude. I listen to podcasts and audiobooks
but reach for printed books as much as I can. And I enjoy the

connections I make on social media but make time for plenty of face-to-face conversations, too. These are small steps, but they preserve important pieces of what makes us human. And that's worth keeping.

Old-Fashioned Action Steps

- Choose face-to-face conversations over screen-to-screen ones.

- Occasionally use a paper map to navigate instead of always relying on GPS.

- Keep your smartphone out of sight whenever possible.

- Turn off notifications on your phone (except from emergency contacts).

- Set your phone to airplane mode when focusing on a project or trying to sleep.

- Remove any extra apps from your phone (especially social media).

- Reach for a book when you feel the urge to check your phone.

- Use a whiteboard, notepads, or sticky notes to break away from the computer.

- Instead of Google, seek answers from a book, library, or friend, or do your own experiments.

- Savor quiet solitude as an opportunity to unwind and discover original thoughts.

CHAPTER 9

Tread the Earth Lightly

Our homestead is smack in the middle of what used to be bison country. While the massive herds have long since vanished, hints of their existence remain. The weathered sandstone bluffs that rise out of this endless prairie were once used as "buffalo jumps" (cliffs that bison were herded off so they could be harvested at the bottom) by Indigenous tribes. And I suspect there's a "buffalo wallow" in our back pasture where, in the spring and early summer, the clay-bottomed depression collects several feet of water that remains long after the rainstorms pass. Impromptu watering holes like these were once popular bison hangouts, although now they just attract dogs, kids, and the toads that appear out of nowhere.

A prehistoric aura lingers in this valley. When I squint just right, I can block out the road signs, fence lines, and power poles to imagine the landscape the way it was before modernity left its mark. But despite the timeless feel of the land itself, most of the original inhabitants are missing. Over the past century, most of the elk, deer, and wolves have gone the way of the bison. Antelope, coyotes, and scattered mule deer are the lone remnants of what was once a diverse ecosystem filled with ruminants and predators.

When I show my kids the grainy black-and-white photos of bison skulls piled high by hunters, they become quiet. They whisper, "Mom, I wish the bison were still here." As their home-school teacher, it's hard for me to explain how this fixture of the prairie was eliminated in such a short period of time. While mass killings may not be the only reason bison nearly went extinct (there's some evidence that diseases may have been partially to blame), the role humans played in their disappearance is chilling. It's estimated that 30 million bison were exterminated during the latter part of the nineteenth century. All I can do is share this knowledge with my children and emphasize that sometimes we study history so it can show us how to live. Other times, we study it to learn from others' mistakes.

But the story of destruction and change goes well beyond the bison. Even before the rapid transformation of the last one hundred years, this land has never been static. At one time, these grasslands were a part of the "American Serengeti," and home to dinosaurs, mammoths, and camels. (Yes, camels!) Over the millennia, wind, water, extreme weather, and raging fires have shaped its topography time and again.

Of course, the human inhabitants have shifted, too. Early records show this portion of the plains was predominantly Crow territory. They were followed by the Kiowa, who were later pushed out by the Cheyenne and the Sioux. It seems that with or without modernity, change is inevitable. And while my wistful daydreams can't rewind time, they do bolster my resolve to tread lightly so I can leave this majestic land better than when I found it.

While some of our modern leaps into the realms of technology and machinery have been beneficial, many have created a swath of unexpected damage in their wake. Pollution clogs our air, islands of trash fill our oceans, species become extinct, and delicate ecosystems vanish a little more each day. The earth groans under the weight of what we deem to be progress.

I'm ashamed to admit that I never thought much about these issues before we started homesteading. But embracing the practices from the previous chapters finally gave me a reason to care. As I became more connected to the land, I began to embody the next trait shared by old-fashioned on purpose individuals: *We care for the earth and tread as lightly as possible.*

As we seek ways to be better stewards of our planet, ideas like biking to work, recycling plastic bottles, or planting trees usually top the list. These are a place to start, but I would argue that it's time to consider not just how we can "do less harm," but also how we can "do more good."

It was the homestead that first opened my eyes to this possibility. It happened by accident at first. As I started making more meals, there was less packaging to throw away. As I harvested vegetables from my backyard, I became more aware of the resources required to ship food to my table. As I made homemade candles and cleaning products, I started to pay attention to the chemicals I was inviting into our home. But most of all, as I made the shift from instant gratification to old-fashioned satisfaction, I discovered many ways I could give back to the earth that sustains us. And a few of them just might surprise you.

Eat More Sustainably

Let's start with food since we eat three times a day (at least). How we grow and purchase our food can be a powerful tool for good in this world. But first, it's vital that we understand why we eat so much differently than we did in centuries past.

In the last two hundred years, farming has morphed from a personal, family affair to a corporate one. Much of this shift was made possible by the darlings of our new industrial system: corn, soy, and wheat.

Until very recently, grains were an expensive, labor-intensive crop to grow. While humans have cultivated them for millennia, they were produced in much smaller quantities. However, thanks to advancements in technology, cheap oil, and government subsidies, we now have a seemingly endless supply of grain. And when you have an abundance of something, it makes sense to use it in everything. And so we do.

We've trained cattle to eat large amounts of grain. We've figured out how to cheaply produce chicken and pork (prior to the twentieth century, chicken was a luxury food and pigs were considered the garbage disposals of the farm). We've built cars that run on corn. We feed farmed fish grain-based pellets. And the labels of our processed foods read like a thesaurus entry for grain: high fructose corn syrup, cornstarch, sorbitol, dextrose, hydrolyzed wheat protein, brewer's yeast, malt, hydrolyzed soy protein, and the list goes on.

In many ways, this system is extremely efficient. The shift to the high production/high input industrial model has allowed us to grow more food on less land and with fewer farmers. We continue to develop more efficient irrigation technologies and more fuel-efficient tractors. We have used traditional crop breeding practices to develop crop varieties that are resistant to common diseases and pests, and require fewer pesticides. We know more about animal nutrition and health and can produce more meat and milk per animal. But there's more to the story. And this industrial system comes at a cost.

As food allergies and sensitivities become more and more common, it would seem that humans aren't thriving in this grain-based paradigm. And neither is the environment.

Conventional production of corn, wheat, and soy requires heavy use of fossil fuels and a staggering amount of synthetic fertilizers and pesticides (about 3 million tons per year). Monocultures don't exist in nature, so it takes a lot of effort to keep them running. But it's not just the inputs that are concerning—this system produces problematic outputs as well. It's estimated that industrial farms (also known as confined animal feed operations or CAFOs) in this country produce 788,000 tons of dry waste (manure) per day, which poses a major management challenge when it's concentrated in small spaces and not returned to the soil right away. There's also evidence that the greenhouse gases emitted from our industrial models of farming are contributing to climate change.

Many of our modern techniques are causing air and water pollution, soil loss and degradation, a loss of species biodiversity worldwide, and a rise in human health concerns. Scientists are sounding the alarm that if our topsoil deterioration continues at its current rate, we eventually won't have any left. When it goes, so does our food supply.

This is a delicate topic. While it's trendy to blame farmers for everything, I don't think that's fair. The world is an intricate place, and the people growing our food are human and imperfect. As with any industry, there are early adopters of new ideas, and there are those who are slow to change. Farmers and ranchers (big or small) face complex pressures and challenges. Some choose farming and ranching because of their love for the land and the lifestyle. Some choose this line of work because it is all they have ever known.

Those who want to move toward more regenerative (or even sustainable) practices face many barriers including pressure from lenders, neighbors, and family (to stay the same); lack of capital to invest in new tools or equipment; and difficulty in finding mentors or the time to pursue education.

But it's crucial that we ask better questions of the system, and one of the most important is, how can we produce food without damaging the planet that sustains us? And if we take it one step further, how can we produce food in a way that heals the planet and builds resilient communities?

I believe a part of that answer is to eat regionally and seasonally as much as possible, like we talked about in Chapter 4. But that's just the beginning. It is possible to work with nature instead of fighting against it, as long as we're willing to think outside of the industrial farming paradigm. These alternative approaches not only reduce agriculture's environmental impact, but also allow us to take a more proactive role in stewardship, especially when the conversation turns toward emissions and carbon. Let's take a quick trip to the prairie and this will make more sense.

Here on the Great Plains, trees are in short supply, but we have plenty of grass. The blue grama, needle, thread, buffalo, and western wheatgrasses that cover this land are packed with nutrition. And these undulating hills of waving forages play a crucial role in the preservation of our planet.

According to the National Park Service, "No other ecosystem in America removes as much carbon from the atmosphere as prairie grasslands." Most of the carbon in grasslands is stored in the soil, while most of the carbon in forests is stored in the trees themselves. The plants of our American Plains work as an air purifier of sorts, pulling carbon dioxide from the atmosphere through the process of photosynthesis and sending it down through their roots, where it feeds a complex web of fungi and microbes who support plant life. The healthier the soil, the more plant growth it can support, and the more carbon is removed from the atmosphere.

When we disturb the soil with tillage, use excessive amounts of nitrogen fertilizer, or overgraze and leave bare soil, some of this hard-earned soil carbon is lost back into the atmosphere as carbon dioxide.

When their roots run deep, the plants work together to form a "carbon sink" or "grassland carbon storage system." This captured carbon returns the favor by holding water, cycling nutrients, and supporting a lush ecosystem aboveground. As with all things in nature, this interconnected process works seamlessly when we don't disrupt its balance.

As I first began to learn how important grasslands truly are, my knee-jerk response was that we should put them in a glass case and not allow anyone to touch them ever again. Yet that's the *exact opposite* of what they need to thrive. In fact, grasses are like us—they flourish when they're exposed to healthy doses of challenge. And when you're grass, challenge comes in the form of hooves and teeth.

When Lewis and Clark explored the West, they were astounded by the massive herds of bison that covered the landscape. "And if it be not impossible to calculate the moving multitude, which darkened the whole plains, we are convinced that twenty thousand would be no exaggeration number," Lewis wrote in his journal. These migratory herds didn't stay in one place for long. Their impact was intense, but quick. After moving through an area and eating and trampling the grass, they'd often not return for years. It's within this cycle that the prairie thrives. When grass isn't eaten, it oxidizes and decomposes slowly, doing little to help the soil. But when ruminants graze that grass in an intensive way, followed by a long period of rest, good things happen.

And here's the cool part—while bare ground and poorly managed pastures can contribute to an increase in greenhouse gas emissions, soil erosion, and pollution, grasslands that are managed in a way that mimics nature have the opposite effect. "Mother earth never attempts to farm without livestock; she always raises mixed crops," wrote Sir Albert Howard, one of the fathers of the organic farming movement. The old-fashioned solution isn't banning ruminants or growing space-age meat in a test tube, but rather employing animals in the ways nature intended.

A new generation of sustainability-minded farmers is doing exactly this. Operations that focus on diversity rather than monoculture are growing in number, and this time-honored model pays off in big ways. An in-depth study conducted with White Oak Pastures, a regenerative farm in Georgia, showed that through mimicking the natural grazing patterns of animals like bison, they were able offset 100 percent of their farm's carbon emissions from their grass-fed beef. But the benefits don't end there. While carbon might be the word of the day, if we look beyond this singular view, there are other notable side effects to a more holistic approach to meat production: animals' quality of life and health improves, topsoil is recovered, biodiversity increases, water and air quality improve, fewer industrial inputs are required, food is more nutrient-dense, and our rural communities thrive. Livestock and crops can be managed in a damaging way, or they can be managed in a beautiful, restorative way. As the saying goes, "It's not the cow, it's the how." These regenerative systems are built on the idea that we as humans can be a force for good. It's a hopeful story, and one in which we can all participate.

So here's where you come in. Now that we're aware of the power of pasture, our role in restoration starts with what we're putting on our plates. One of the easiest steps we can take is to reduce our consumption of processed food. Spend your dollars on more food and less packaging. Since industrialized foods are usually comprised of grain derivatives, encased in many layers of plastic, and shipped long distances, they tend to leave a much larger environmental footprint. I'm not anti-grain by any means— I eat them on a regular basis and couldn't live without sourdough bread. But if I'm going to eat wheat, I prefer to do so in moderation, much like our ancestors would have. And I opt for locally grown options whenever possible. (Also, look into heritage wheat varieties or ancient grains like einkorn, spelt, or emmer if you're one of the many who have trouble digesting modern wheat.)

If you can find local regenerative farmers who are using practices that build soil, that's ideal (think rotational grazing, reduced tillage, multispecies farming, cover crops, use of compost and manure, etc.). Pastured, grass-finished beef and lamb can be regenerative since they are raised with zero grain input. These operations also improve pasturelands by stimulating new growth and naturally spreading manure in the process. Pastured poultry and pork operations will typically still feed some grain (pigs and chickens are omnivores so they can't survive solely on grass), but most provide a more natural diet to these animals while allowing them to live like nature intended. All that said, if you're struggling to find regenerative or pastured farmers in your area, don't rule out conventional beef. Almost all cattle live on grass for at least the first half of their life, and some feedlots use crop residues or by-products of the food industry (like cornstalks or beet pulp), which is more sustainable than grain-intensive pork or chicken.

It is always nice to know your farmer, buy regionally and in season, raise some of your own food, and support the businesses that share your values. Yet not all of these options are available in all areas. Remember—this isn't about perfection, but rather making the best buying choices you can in your current situation. Keep in mind that unlike USDA Certified Organic, terms like "sustainable," "grass-fed," and "regenerative" are not regulated. This means anyone can use these words for marketing their products regardless of practice. When available, look for third-party certification labels like Certified Naturally Grown, Food Alliance Certified, Rainforest Alliance Certified, or Salmon-Safe. I don't necessarily expect small, local growers to secure these labels, but knowing the differences can help you navigate grocery store shelves.

Regeneratively raised meats often cost more, but when we look at the overall cost of cheap meat to our health, the soil, and the environment, the extra expense can be justified. Buying in bulk (a quarter of a grass-finished cow or a half of a pastured hog) as well as becoming familiar with the more economical cuts (roasts, pork shoulder, beef shank, spareribs, oxtail, etc.) are two ways you can offset these costs.

It's hard to do justice to this topic in just a handful of pages. If you're interested in continuing this discussion (and I hope you are!), I highly recommend the book *Sacred Cow: The Case for (Better) Meat* by Diana Rodgers and Robb Wolf. Their factual, data-driven approach is a solid place to start, and they aren't afraid to tackle the hard questions.

> ## when we care for the soil, it cares for us.

So while I can't do much about global topsoil loss or excessive pesticide use, I do have a say in what my family eats. As consumers, every dollar we spend is a vote for our values and the world in which we want to live. You can choose to support the farmers and ranchers whose practices match those values. And that matters. These are little steps, but they add up in a big way. Because when we care for the soil, it cares for us. And another way we can care for the soil is to feed it. What does soil like to eat, you ask? The answer to that question is likely hiding in your garbage cans at this very moment.

Isn't Grass-Fed Beef Tough?

Can pastured beef be tough? Absolutely. If you fry up a steak from a ten-year-old milk cow the day after she's processed, expect your jaw to feel tired a few bites in. But other than that, pastured beef can be unbelievably tender if you handle it properly. Here are a few tips:

- Never microwave meat to defrost it. This holds true for any type of beef, but especially grass-finished cuts, which dry out more quickly since they have less external fat to trap steam.

- The very best steaks I've ever eaten have been grass-finished—the key is to avoid overcooking them. Sear steaks in a hot pan until they are browned on both sides, then finish cooking them in a 400°F oven. I pull mine out when a meat thermometer reads 135 to 140°F and let them rest for ten minutes before cutting.

- Grass-finished roasts shine when cooked long and slow. You can find my favorite technique for grass-fed roasts on page 113.

- Grass-finished ground beef is usually lean. This means you probably won't need to drain it after browning. If you're making burgers, you can treat them like you would any other patty—just avoid smashing them while they're cooking. We want to keep all those juices inside.

Putting Waste to Work

Currently there's a lot of concern over the methane produced from cow burps. (Keep in mind that the earth has always been home to tens of millions of burping ruminants. It's nothing new; it's simply a part of the carbon cycle.) However, there *is* a historically new contributor to methane emissions that is often missed—mountains of rotting food. In the United States, we throw away approximately 80 billion pounds of food each year, which equates to a staggering one-third of our total food supply. When I try to picture what that looks like, I feel queasy.

> *In the United States, we throw away approximately 80 billion pounds of food each year*

The Food and Agriculture Organization estimates that this waste "contributes to 8 percent of greenhouse gases emitted, more than all U.S. animal agriculture and nearly as much as total U.S. agriculture."

But once again, an old-fashioned life is a perfect match for this modern problem. These solutions turn trash into treasure (aka food for your soil), and they happen to be especially fun. (Although I may have a weird definition of *fun*.)

The first solution? The humble chicken bucket we talked about previously. Yes, it's a way to reduce your feed costs, but it's also an effective way to keep your kitchen waste out of the landfill.

A study conducted by Dr. Maureen Breen showed that, on average, a chicken consumes roughly 1.6 pounds of food waste each week. This adds up to over eighty-two pounds over the course of a year. And that's just one chicken! Considering the average American wastes around one pound of food per day, a small flock of backyard chickens could easily handle the waste produced by a typical family. This would not only keep methane-producing scraps out of the landfill but also fuel a healthy protein source in the form of eggs, create manure to feed flower beds and gardens, and accomplish all these important tasks in a sustainable way. Once again, old-fashioned solutions just make sense.

If you don't have chickens, make friends with someone who does. It's not uncommon for our friends and family to bring bags of broccoli stems or buckets of watermelon rinds when they visit. Most backyard flock-keepers will happily accept offerings of kitchen scraps and might even give you a carton of eggs in exchange.

Even if you can't find a flock to share your scraps with, there's still no reason to toss your garbage gold into the trash can.

Composting is another way to turn scraps back into soil. Whenever someone asks me how to improve his or her soil, my answer is almost always, "Compost." Have sandy soil? Compost. Have clay soil? Compost. Have low-nutrient soil? Compost. Properly made compost is naturally balanced, provides organic matter to the soil, and is slower to release nutrients than synthetic fertilizers. It's another instance when, when we resist the urge to be high-tech, things are simpler, are more affordable, and result in much happier gardens and soil.

You don't have to live on a homestead to become a composting convert. If you have a backyard, simple bins can be built out of upcycled pallets or scrap lumber (Pinterest has tons of prototypes). If you don't want to build your own bin, there are brilliantly designed, self-contained compost tumblers and bins on the market today that anyone can use—even if you live in an apartment. Vermicomposting (composting with worms) can help you create compost even faster, without taking up much space. (Just be sure to house your worms in a stationary bin—they don't like being tumbled.)

While plenty of complex composting formulas exist, keep in mind this is a natural process that has been happening without human intervention since the beginning of time. It can be as simple or as complicated as you'd like it to be. I take this very relaxed approach to composting:

$$(\text{Brown} + \text{Green}) \times \text{Time} = \text{Compost}$$

Things in the brown category would be high-carbon materials like dried grass clippings, leaves, shredded paper, sawdust, cardboard (the kind without a shiny coating), or straw.

Things in the green category would be high-nitrogen materials like animal manure, fruit or veggie scraps, coffee grounds, weeds (with no seed), or fresh grass clippings. (Avoid adding meat, fat, or dairy products to your mix, as well as any food that contains excessive salt.)

Mix the materials together, add a little water, and that's it. Compost gurus recommend using a 4:1 ratio of browns to greens. However, my ratios are never dialed in. And somehow, I still magically end up with compost.

As far as the time part of the equation, it depends on how much attention you want to give to your pile. You can speed up the decomposition process with more frequent watering and turning (ideally in a sunny spot), but even if you neglect your pile entirely, it will break down eventually. Finished compost will be crumbly and smell fresh (not like rotten food or manure). Once the process is complete, spread it on the top of your soil or mix it in.

Once you're ready for a more in-depth approach to this topic, my two favorite books are *The Gardener's Guide to Better Soil* by Gene Logsdon (this one is wonderfully accessible and doesn't make me feel like I need a chemistry degree to decipher it) and *The Rodale Book of Composting* edited by Grace Gershuny and Deborah L. Martin.

The Original Miracle Fertilizer

In a world obsessed with blasting all bacteria (both good and bad) into oblivion with antibacterial everything, we've lost our fondness for manure. I'm always caught off guard when I see city friends tiptoeing around our barnyard. "What's wrong?" I ask. They give me an uncomfortable look while pointing at the ground, and then I realize...oh. The poop. A little manure on my boots doesn't bother me, partially because it's just grass and water, but also because I've fallen in love with the stuff. Where manures were once the beacons of fertility for large-scale producers and home gardeners alike, we now attempt to sanitize our gardens like we do our homes, using miracle sprays and synthetic fertilizers designed to take the "ick" out of growing plants. And it seems to work...for a time, at least. But our soils are begging for the good stuff. It's time we reignite our passion for manure—because it's magical stuff, my friends. With current markets seeing a severe shortage of nitrogen-based fertilizer, I think it's a perfect time for manure to experience a renaissance. If you don't have animals, try sourcing manure from local farms. (You

can take your pick of the variety—rabbit, chicken, goat,
sheep, cattle, or horse manure are all great options.
Skip manure from pigs, dogs, and cats as it sometimes
contains pathogens.) Fresh manure is high in nitrogen,
which can damage your plants, so you'll want to compost it before applying it to your garden. (The one ex-
ception is rabbit manure—it can be used immediately
without issue.) Even if I didn't eat eggs, I'd still keep
chickens, just for their ability to eat kitchen waste and
make manure for my soil. It's that valuable.

If you're not feeling excited about building a designated compost pile in your backyard, trench composting is even simpler.
Dig a hole in your garden or flower beds, dump in the kitchen
scraps, and cover with soil. The end. You can hasten this process
by using a blender to grind up the scraps (add plenty of water
so you don't burn up your machine), but even if you don't, the
food will still break down over time. Some of the best, direct
amendments are,

- Eggshells (crush them up and sprinkle throughout your
  gardens)

- Coffee grounds (coffee is acidic, but the grounds are not)

- Fruit and veggie peels (chop them up for faster decomposition, or just bury them)

- Used tea leaves

Beyond composting, there's another eco-friendly way to put
nutrients back into the soil without commercial fertilizers. It's
a solution that came to me during a garden conundrum when
I was once again forced to consider the bigger picture instead
of running to the store to buy a quick fix. I haven't looked at
gardening the same since.

Cover Your Soil

When we built our raised beds, most of the boxes ended up with beautiful black topsoil—every gardener's dream. But the last four beds got the short end of the stick. They unintentionally got filled with the clay from the bottom of our dirt pile.

If you've never dealt with heavy clay soil, count yourself lucky. Contrary to popular belief, it's nutrient-rich and grows decent vegetables, *if* you can get the seeds into the soil. And that's a big *IF*.

Preparing those beds for planting each spring was like sticking my shovel into concrete. Each four-foot-by-eight-foot bed required at least an hour of hard digging before I could plant. It was agonizing, and each year seemed to get worse. After my third spring, I'd had enough. Either I had to come up with a new plan or I'd have to remove thousands of pounds of soil by hand. Was there a way I could make the soil happier and make my life easier in the process? My unlikely answer came in the form of cover crops.

> *Covered soil may seem unimportant, until we realize how much the earth dislikes being naked.*

Cover crops are exactly what their name implies—plants used for the sole purpose of keeping the soil covered. Covered soil may seem unimportant, until we realize how much the earth dislikes being naked. The only places left bare in nature are industrial farmland or deserts—neither of which is a stellar example of vibrant soil health.

Cover crops are often used in large-scale regenerative agriculture but can work miracles in a home garden, too. My favorite garden covers are winter rye and clover, but you can also use alfalfa, mustard, radish, field peas, winter wheat, buckwheat, and countless others. By keeping the ground covered during the dormant months, they prevent the soil from being depleted of nutrients when it's vulnerable to sun, weather, and wind. They also reduce soil compaction, reduce erosion and runoff, add organic matter, and discourage weeds. But here's my personal favorite. Some cover plants partner with bacteria to capture nitrogen (an important soil nutrient) from the air and pull it in the soil. If that's not magic, I don't know what is.

Instead of fighting with my beds, I decided to change my battle plan. After I'd cleared the vegetable plants that fall, I sprinkled winter rye seeds over my troublesome soil and watered the emerging shoots until the snow came and the hydrants froze. The fledgling blanket of rye protected the soil as the winter wind raged. And then, as spring crept closer and the soil temperature rose, the rye awoke and shot to eighteen inches tall. "That's a nice crop of grass you have," Christian would tease.

But as pretty as my rye was, it couldn't stay. I had forty-eight tomato starts waiting for that space, and the clock was ticking. The most common way to transition from cover crops to regular crops is by tilling the cover into the soil. But since I couldn't use a tiller in my raised beds (and had no desire to dig it by hand), I opted for a more unorthodox method. If I was going to fail, I might as well do it with flair. In late May, I trimmed the rye as short as possible with a Weedwacker. As the stubble turned yellow, I dug small holes and planted my tomato seedlings amid the rye carpet. I scooped up the rye cuttings left over from the trimming session and arranged them around my transplants to act as additional mulch on top of the stubble. It looked bizarre. I wondered if I'd sentenced my poor tomato seedlings to instant death.

But they didn't die. In fact, they flourished. The rye root mass repressed weeds and slowly decomposed throughout the summer. By that fall, evidence of my rye crop was mostly gone, and softer, more workable soil remained. No hard, miserable digging required. And I had a bumper crop of tomatoes as a bonus. My clay beds are still a work in progress, but the more I cover them, the better they get. And once again, I am reminded that working with nature, instead of against it, is a beautiful thing.

As we seek to lessen our environmental impact, small actions like saving our food scraps or planting cover crops add up for big results. The compound effect can work in our favor, although sometimes the opposite happens. I learned that lesson the hard way one year.

Plants for Pollinators

Avoiding pesticides is one way to help our pollinator friends; another is to cultivate their favorite plants. This list barely scratches the surface of all the options, but it's a good place to start. You'll want to do a little research to determine which plants are best suited for your area.

- Dandelions
- Sunflowers
- Coneflowers (aka *Echinacea*)
- Goldenrod
- Marigolds
- Calendula
- Borage
- Yarrow
- Lavender
- Lilac
- Milkweed

Cancel the Chemicals

I had been growing vegetables for several years the first time it happened. After stumbling across *The Ruth Stout No-Work Garden Book*, I'd become a zealous convert to the world of deep mulch. My newfound revelation prompted me to bury my entire plot in ten inches of old hay that spring. The results were astounding. My vegetables flourished, my weeding and watering chores were cut in half, and the soil was filled with earthworms. (Covered soil is happy soil!) It was the best garden I'd ever had. I couldn't wait to repeat my success the next year. When spring came, I added more mulch, planted my seeds, and waited for another victory. But something was terribly wrong. The leaves of my tomato plants twisted into gnarled clumps, the green beans refused to germinate, and the potato plants were stunted and squatty.

I panicked. Was it a bug? A fungus? Some exotic plant disease? Too much water? Not enough water? After dozens of articles and web searches, I came across a photo of a tomato plant that looked exactly like mine. "Herbicide poisoning," the caption read. But that couldn't be it. I didn't use herbicides, and neither did our neighbors. Where could it have come from?

I kept reading. These particular herbicides belong to a category called "aminopyralids." They are designed to kill broadleaf plants, but since they don't harm grass, they're commonly used for weed control in hayfields.

My heart sank when I made the connection. *It was the hay.* My precious mulch was poisoning my garden. Despite my most valiant organic growing attempts, industrial chemicals had still crept in. The good news? My garden and I eventually recovered. The bad news? It happened again several years later, but this time with contaminated manure. I later learned that these herbicides can pass through an animal, sit in a compost pile for an extended period, and *still* damage vegetables years later. (Soil microbes will eventually break down the chemical, but it takes several years. My plants never died from the contamination, but they stopped growing, their leaves became deformed, and they didn't produce fruit.) Even concentrations as little as one part per billion can damage a tomato plant. As devastating as the loss of my vegetables was that year, even worse was the knowledge that the manure and mulch I depended on to feed my soil was now poisonous.

These experiences left me with so many questions. What other consequences are well-intentioned actions (like keeping weed-free hayfields) having? Are there ways we can work *with* nature, instead of against it? It was a brutal lesson, but it started me down the path to being more mindful of the choices I was making in my garden and yard. I also earned a healthy respect for how quickly the balance of nature can be disrupted. Since then, it's been my goal to keep herbicides and pesticides away from our homestead. Though sometimes that's easier said than done.

The idea of working in tandem with nature has a way of capturing the imagination. It's all Bambi, and butterflies, and bucolic garden scenes, but then…the bugs arrive. And the romance fades ever so slightly. There are grasshoppers, squash borers, potato beetles, and, maybe worst of all, the indomitable cabbage worm. Before you know it, your strict organic ideals suddenly feel less compelling, and you can't stop fantasizing about bombing the whole garden with a bottle of Sevin Dust. Full scorched-earth? Sure, why not. Anything for a taste of revenge against the army of grasshoppers that stripped your precious kale crop down to stems in a matter of hours.

The struggle is real. The longer I garden, the more sympathy I have for commercial vegetable farmers attempting to salvage their crops.

But despite the sweet temptation of revenge, I resist the urge to head to the pesticide aisle. Did you know that more than 70 percent of fruits and vegetables on store shelves have been sprayed with pesticides? As a result, more than 90 percent of Americans have these toxic compounds in their bodies. It's the price we pay to keep our produce bug-bite free. But as I learned in my garden, agrochemicals like these tend to give us short-term benefits and long-term consequences, the full effects of which we may not realize for years. According to a 2019 report, there are 310 problematic pesticide chemicals currently in use today. Some of these are known to cause cancer, endocrine problems, and reproductive problems, as well as being hazardous to the environment.

Beyond the damage to our own health, rampant use of pesticides has serious consequences for the insect population. One particularly striking problem is the fact that pollinators are vanishing. Each year since 2006, US beekeepers have lost 30 percent of their colonies. When the pollinators disappear, so does our food supply. Like most gardeners and farmers, I don't want to contribute to the diminishing pollinator population, but I also need to be able to defend my crops from the hordes of hungry pests. After years of learning by trial and error, I've collected a few proven techniques to defend my garden without using harmful chemicals:

- **Restore the balance.** Often one species will explode when their natural predators are eliminated. Therefore, instead of only asking ourselves, "What can I *subtract* (or kill) to make my garden thrive?" we need to be asking, "What can I *add* to my growing space to bring it back into balance?" In our modern fervor to banish all bugs, we've thrown many insect populations off-kilter. Instead of focusing on eliminating as many insects as possible, consider what animals or bugs you may need to invite in to bring balance to your garden ecosystem.

Try planting more flowers and native plants, building bird- or bat houses, or creating watering holes for frogs, toads, and lizards. This isn't a quick fix, and it won't eliminate your pest problems overnight, but it pays off in the long run.

- **Rotate plants.** Growing the same plant in the same place year after year depletes soil nutrients, increases the chance of disease, and encourages pest infestation. To avoid this, rotate your annual crops to a different spot each season. This breaks the life cycle of problem insects that might be living in the soil (although flying pests can still find their way to their favorite treats). Also—remember that monocultures don't exist in nature. The more variety you can bring to your growing spaces, the better.

- **Cover up.** Many garden supply stores sell insect barrier cloth, which can be affixed to floating row covers or draped over plants. This is a surefire way to win against cabbage moths and grasshoppers. Anchoring it down in our Wyoming wind can be a problem, but you may find it useful in your (less hurricane-prone) garden.

- **Bribe the kids.** I'm not ashamed to admit that I've bribed my children to pick bugs off my vegetables. (And yes, the kids enjoy it. Seriously.) Cabbage worms, hornworms, and potato beetles are all the perfect size for little fingers. Handpicking won't eliminate all of them, but it can make a dent. (And chickens will love any of the insects you collect. It's a good protein source.)

- **Make a spray.** Sprays are my last resort, since even homemade ones can be harmful to bees and other pollinators. However, if you must use a repellent spray, a nontoxic DIY version is preferred over the chemical solutions found at the garden store. Neem oil (made from the seeds of the neem tree) and diatomaceous earth (a fine powder made from fossilized algae) are two organic pesticide alternatives. However, since they can be harmful to bees, I use them very sparingly, if at all.

- **Don't sweat it.** Produce doesn't have to be picture-perfect to be delicious. While I draw the line at grasshoppers stripping my kale plants down to bare stems or aphids sucking the life out of my lettuce, I don't mind the occasional spinach leaf with a few bug-bite marks here or there.

I used to view my garden in terms of what I could extract from it. It gave and I took. But a garden will teach you what it needs if you'll listen. I'm still an imperfect grower, but my perspective has changed. I now see it for the ecosystem that it is. As the gardener, it's my job to nurture the entirety of this space, from the insects buzzing in the air, to the soil beneath my feet. When we view our gardens, as well as our planet, as living systems, everyone benefits: the environment, the plants, and most certainly us.

> *When we view our gardens, as well as our planet, as living systems, everyone benefits*

Will the choices I make in my yard and garden reverse all the issues on the planet? No, they won't. But when people like you and me make better choices, they add up. And who knows what sort of ripple effect they can have.

Easy Organic Pest Spray

Makes 1 quart of spray

Ingredients

- About 1 quart water

- 1 to 2 teaspoons biodegradable liquid soap (castile soap or dish soap works)

- 1 tablespoon cayenne pepper

- 20 to 30 drops peppermint oil

Instructions

Fill a quart jar or sprayer with water. Add the soap, cayenne pepper, and peppermint oil. Other essential oils can also work, but peppermint is a solid choice since most bugs dislike the menthol it contains.

Shake gently, then spray on plants that are struggling with pests. It's best to spray in the evening, as applying during the heat of the day may damage more sensitive plants. Repeat as needed or after heavy rainfall.

Reduce the Rubbish

In the early years, our homestead's most defining characteristic was the garbage we inherited from the previous owners. From the outbuildings brimming with rusty mechanical parts, bags of worn clothes, and boxes of broken Christmas decorations to the sinkholes filled with old cars, it's taken years for us to purge the junk.

The trend has continued as we've renovated other properties. If life was a video game, we'd have reached triple-star expert status in "dumpster loading." Over the course of three renovations, we've filled at least twenty construction-sized dumpsters with other people's leftover stuff. The sheer volume overwhelms me every time. It's disheartening. If there can be an upside to any of it, the process has motivated me to be more mindful of the trash I personally contribute to landfills.

> ## On average, Americans produce 4.4 pounds of trash per day per person.

Unfortunately, our junk-filled renovation projects aren't an anomaly. On average, Americans produce 4.4 pounds of trash *per day per person*. And that's just here in the States. Part of the way we can combat this is by putting our food waste to good use. But what about the rest?

I like to look to generations past for inspiration. Before the advent of mass-produced goods, possessions were cherished. Dishes, clothing, and furniture were passed down through generations and lovingly preserved. If something broke, you repaired it. Big purchases, like washing machines, refrigerators, and televisions, were long-term investments. But thanks to mass production and cheap goods, we've become a throwaway culture. How can we reverse this trend?

One of the biggest causes of our global waste problem is, of course, plastic. Many of these products, such as plastic bags and food wrappers, are used for just a few minutes but will remain in our environment for hundreds of years after we're gone. (Did you know your old toothbrush has a life span of five hundred years?) And it's not just an issue for our soil and oceans. A particularly alarming study recently showed that "human exposure to plastic particles results in absorption of particles into the bloodstream." Yep, you read that correctly. Researchers found plastics *in the blood* of 77 percent of the study's participants.

I don't want plastic in my blood, nor do I want it languishing in the soil. Recycling is better than nothing, but it's not always as effective as we may believe. Roughly 90 percent of plastic destined for recycling still ends up in the landfill. So instead, I've set my sights on stopping trash at the source. If you implement any of the ideas in the previous chapters, you're well on your way. Homemade food doesn't have as much packaging, homegrown vegetables aren't wrapped in plastic baggies and wrap, and handmade goods tend to last longer than their mass-produced counterparts. Here are other steps we've been taking to use less plastic and generate less garbage on our homestead:

- Instead of individual tea bags, I buy loose-leaf tea in bulk and use stainless steel strainers or tea balls.

- When I host large groups, I use pint-sized mason jars instead of plastic cups, mismatched silverware from the thrift store instead of plastic cutlery, and enamelware camping plates (nonbreakable and cute!) instead of paper plates.

- We've stopped buying toothpaste in tubes and have opted for toothpaste tabs instead. The kids love them, and they're less messy. Our floss is compostable and comes in a refillable glass container. (See the resources in the back of this book for some of my favorite companies.)

- Homemade skin care products aren't difficult to make, contain fewer chemicals, and cut down on waste. I often make our own soaps, lotions, toners, and moisturizers.

- Instead of disposable razors, I invested in a stainless steel razor with recyclable blades.

- Hundreds of millions of laundry detergent bottles are thrown away each year. To avoid adding to the problem, I use plastic-free detergent tabs or refillable systems. The same can work for dishwasher soap.

- Wool dryer balls scented with essential oils work just as well as dryer sheets (and are less toxic, too).

- More and more companies are popping up that provide refillable cleaning products in compostable packaging. Sometimes I use these options, or I just make my own concoctions with simple household ingredients.

- I use a lot of herbs in my cooking but can't grow them all myself (at least not yet). To avoid throwing away a million small plastic containers, I buy herbs in bulk and use them to refill my collection of glass jars.

- Washable bamboo cosmetic pads work just as well as the disposable ones and are easy to pop in the washing machine.

- Instead of using paper towels for everything, I keep a generous collection of dish towels and rags.

- I'm a believer in keeping a home library with useful books, and I like to purchase them secondhand whenever possible. Thriftbooks.com and abebooks.com are two of my favorite online sources.

- Glass storage containers will last much longer than the plastic ones, plus they don't leach into your food. Mason jars are also a slick way to store leftovers.

- Whenever possible, I buy our groceries in bulk to reduce packaging waste. Azure Standard carries a wide selection of dry goods in paper bags. I buy flour, beans, popcorn, sugar, and more this way. When it arrives, I transfer the food into food-grade five-gallon buckets (to deter rodents and bugs) and then burn or compost the paper bags.

- Canning food saves money and cuts down on waste. However, new canning lids must be purchased for each batch, unless you opt for special reusable lids. I've been using the reusable lid sets from Harvest Guard for several years with great results.

- The Ziploc baggie habit is hard to break, but reusable silicone baggies have helped.

- I'm still working on a good plastic wrap alternative. I've tried the silicone covers and beeswax wraps, and I don't love either option, so the hunt continues.

I'm far from perfect. Someday I'd love our family to be completely zero-waste, but we're not there yet. We still must take out the trash each week. But it's a start.

Native Plants

A few years into living on our homestead, I drove to a Colorado nursery to purchase some fruit trees. The sales associate warned me that the four pear and apple trees I'd chosen needed more sheltered environments. I listened politely, while thinking, "Whatever. I'll make this happen. Watch me."

While sheer willpower yields fantastic results in many areas of life, I'm sad to report that it does not apply to trees. The first three gave up the ghost immediately, although one lone apple tree valiantly clung to life. It lingered for years, never really growing, but at least coming back each spring. I sweet-talked it. I bought special fruit-tree oil and fertilizer. One year I even hand-dug it out of a snowdrift so the weight of the melting snow wouldn't break the branches. But my efforts were futile. Finally, I laid it to rest, along with my dreams of ever having an orchard.

But once again, the old-time homesteads in our area held the solutions to my fruit-growing problems. What fruits did they plant in an era when sprinkler systems and synthetic fertilizers weren't available? My answer came in the form of buffalo berries, native plums, chokecherries, serviceberries, and currant bushes.

It's been a pleasure to watch these varieties grow on our homestead. The early frosts and late blizzards don't faze them—they come back each spring stronger than ever. It's been another reminder that when we work with nature, instead of against it, things often become easier. And after years of thinking apples were impossible, I added several cold-hardy, prairie-proven varieties to our homestead this year, as well as a variety of pear (fingers crossed). I'm already dreaming of the pies. As you're looking for ways to tread lightly (and make growing easier), don't underestimate the power of native plants. They're much lower maintenance and provide an important habitat for other species in your area. The National Audubon Society has an extensive database of native plants organized by region. Type in your zip code at https://www.audubon.org/native-plants.

It's All Connected

When I initially outlined this book, each topic had a tidy place. But as I've started writing, the subjects have resisted my organization and insisted upon leaking into neighboring chapters. We can't talk about healthy food without also understanding good soil. We can't restore soil without bringing animals into the picture. We can't raise healthier animals without talking about their feed. And we can't consider better feed without taking manure and the carbon cycle into account. But that's the beauty of these ideas—they're inextricably connected—just like our environment and us. And it's this holistic mindset that has the most potential to restore our world.

When we focus only on reductionist talking points, we miss out on this stunning complexity. If we can resist the urge to compartmentalize life, the more connected and whole we will become. Many old-fashioned ideas "accidentally" help the earth and our health in the process, which usually means we're on the right track. We can start this process of connection by asking ourselves—how can I be more aligned with the natural world around me? As we become more connected to our unique places, answers tend to present themselves in the most interesting ways. Just watch and see.

My own path of treading more lightly has been imperfect. I'll never be able to fully restore our prairie to what it once was. There are things I could do better and connections I have yet to make. I don't have all the answers, but I know as I take more halting steps backward, I feel better. As I focus more on the bigger picture, choices feel easier, my footprints are lighter, and the natural world around me thrives. Sometimes the most impactful changes are the humblest. It's a restorative process both for us and for this amazing place we call home.

Old-Fashioned Action Steps

- Use your food waste to fuel a flock of chickens.

- If chickens are out of the question, compost food waste instead. If you don't have a garden, use it in potted plants or donate to a friend or community garden.

- Whenever possible, choose pastured meats and be mindful of how much grain-based food you eat and buy.

- Avoid herbicides and pesticides in your yard and garden. If you really need a bug spray, consider nontoxic homemade sprays instead.

- Plant trees and flowers that feed pollinators.

- Buy in bulk to reduce the amount of household trash you produce.

- Seek out locally grown food that doesn't have to be shipped thousands of miles to reach you.

- When the weather is nice, line-dry your clothes to save on electricity. Or if you're really hard-core, you can buy indoor drying racks and skip the dryer year-round.

- Opt out of junk mail. There are several services you can find with a quick internet search that allow you to bulk unsubscribe from credit card offers and catalogs.

- The average American throws away eighty pounds of clothing each year. Donate your unwanted clothes and buy used whenever possible.

CHAPTER 10

Let Them Play

When they were ten and eight, two of my kids accidentally locked themselves in our stock trailer. They were deeply involved in one of their imaginary adventures and didn't realize the trailer door doesn't have an interior latch. And so, they found themselves prisoners in the back pasture for a solid twenty minutes before we walked by and heard them hollering. At first, they were rattled, but after a reassurance they weren't in trouble and a reminder to be aware of their surroundings, something clicked.

The next day, they packed a backpack with various tools (and snacks) and headed back to the trailer with the intent of locking themselves in again. This time, *on purpose*. In fact, they were so inspired by their trailer incident, they turned it into an "escape room" and couldn't wait to lead their friends through various sequences (involving ropes, buckets, and a lone horseshoe) that allowed them to reach through the holes to the exterior latches and free themselves.

As the kids tested their wits against the door latch, the stock trailer became an incubator for critical thinking and problem-solving, while providing a healthy dose of adventure in the process. Shenanigans like this abound on our homestead. At any given time, you'll find my children taking dunks in the algae-filled stock tanks, loading up their backpacks for walkabouts in the pastures, harnessing the dogs to wagons, building playhouses out of firewood, turning cardboard boxes into forts, maintaining their elaborate mud pie kitchens, and floating homemade boats in the buffalo wallow. As I'm writing this chapter, the incessant pounding of my nine-year-old son hammering together boards for his new tree house is serenading me. He showed me his sketched plans during breakfast this morning as he announced, "I'm gonna need to go to town to get some boards and maybe a few hinges." Not too long ago, they baked a batch of hardtack (a rock-hard survival bread made from water, flour, and salt) for an upcoming adventure game they were planning. (Their idea, not mine. Hardtack has never been high on my snack list.)

In the context of modern childhood, my crew's homespun adventures are a little unorthodox. And once again, I suspect the homestead is to blame.

My accidental path to unconventional parenting started the day we brought home our first child from the hospital. Before taking her inside the house, we made a quick detour to the barn to introduce her to the animals. (First-time parents do weird things, y'all.) It was silly, but symbolic. In our own way, I guess we were saying, "This is your home, and you are now a part of this bigger picture." We've stuck by that philosophy ever since.

The kids have had a front-row seat to all our escapades since day one. It was a choice made from necessity at first. Since there was a shortage of available babysitters, I quickly learned if I wanted to do anything but sit in the house, the babies had to come along. And so they did. I've nursed them in barns, in pastures, and in horse trailers. My diaper bags were full of sippy cups, diapers, and rattles, but also baling twine and bits of hay. Our children were (and continue to be) our constant companions as we milked the cow, renovated buildings, ran errands, planted the garden, worked cattle, and built businesses.

It was a rocky adjustment at first. I felt like a packhorse for baby paraphernalia. Everything took longer thanks to nonstop interruptions of diaper changes and snack distributions. It was tedious for a while. But ever so slowly, my capacity expanded. Bringing the kids along got a little easier, and I felt slightly less overwhelmed. And even on the days when there was a diaper blowout in the middle of the pasture or they ripped out the garden seedlings as fast as I could plant them, I could see a glimmer of what was to come.

As my children hit the usual milestones (first tooth, first step, first word), they passed homestead milestones, too (digging their first potato, carrying their first egg, bottle-feeding their first goat). They began to interpret animal behavior and learn which plants you can eat. They discovered that boredom isn't deadly, that nature is incredibly entertaining, that it's okay to be cold or hot, that if you fall down in the dirt, you get back up, and that if a goose chases you, you have to stand your ground. They soaked it up like little sponges: watching, listening, and noticing.

And then one day, the tables flipped. Suddenly, my littles weren't just along for the ride—they had become a crucial part of our team. They assumed responsibility for their domains. They solved problems on their own. They cared for small, helpless things. Their confidence and capability exploded. It was then that I realized those early years, as halting and frustrating as they were, were setting the stage for something priceless.

So that's how I stumbled across my parenting philosophy, if you can even call it that. I don't have it all figured out—I make mistakes daily. Honestly, I was hesitant to even write this chapter. Talking about gardening and cooking feels easy compared to potty training or navigating sibling rivalry.

But over the years, I've collected a handful of ideas that have helped my kids to thrive (and have made my life easier in the process). These ideas are best summed up by the next trait of an old-fashioned on purpose mindset: *We empower our children by offering them more autonomy.* There are myriad ways to do this. However, this path of child-rearing can feel foreign when compared to the modern parenting paradigm. So let's start by gleaning a bit of reassurance from the past.

My journey started with an observation. Whenever I would post photos of my kids' antics online, the response was electric. People were surprised, amused, and most of all, *nostalgic*. Curiosity got the best of me as I dissected the comments:

"This reminds me of my childhood!"

"Kids don't play like this anymore."

"It makes me so happy to see kids playing outside!"

As I dug in, I realized these responses went far beyond mere sentimental observations. Something *has* changed. By historical standards, my kids' exploits are hardly noteworthy. But compared to childhoods of even just sixty years ago, modern childhood is almost unrecognizable.

Part of the shift is the change in how we use our time. Before the advent of industrialization, parents had a lot more to do just to keep the family fed and functioning. Child-centered activities were rare because children were needed to help with household duties. As a result, the kids of yesteryear had a lot more responsibility, but also much more free time.

Fast-forward to today. It no longer takes an entire family to keep a household afloat. Parents are also now waiting longer to have kids, which means many families have more disposable income and more time to devote to helping their kids thrive. We all want to give our kids a leg up in the world, and the options are plentiful: sports, tutoring, music lessons, college prep, and the list goes on. We want to smooth the path for our kids, to lessen the sting of failure, to obliterate challenges, to protect them from all danger, to defeat any foes that dare cross their paths, and most of all, to make them as successful as possible. But what if our good intentions are having the opposite effect?

In our modern parenting paradigm, free play has all but vanished, and nature is no longer a regular part of childhood. Screens have taken the place of physical activity. Psychological disorders and suicide are on the rise. Children's core strength and balance are decreasing. "From the vantage point of history, contemporary children's lives are more regimented and constrained than ever before," writes Steven Mintz in *Huck's Raft*.

> **in our well-meaning quest to create the perfect childhood, we may have left some crucial things behind.**

It's a striking paradox: modern parents are more attentive, more protective, more aware, and more driven than previous generations. But in our well-meaning quest to create the perfect childhood, we may have left some crucial things behind.

However, we can still offer our kids independence and autonomy, even in this fast-paced world. For our family, that looks like a mix of old-fashioned freedom and real responsibility. And this formula is accessible to any parent—no farm required. In the following pages, I'll share my personal parenting approach and how you can implement these concepts in your own home. Please know that I don't follow any of these ideas perfectly. Like any family, we have really good days and really crummy ones. But after sticking with these ideas for over a decade now, I like the results I'm seeing. So, I'll share what we do, in hope that you can find some of your own inspiration in the process.

Encourage Curiosity

The easygoing mood of our summer evening was shattered when the toilet started gurgling. I braced myself for the worst as Christian headed outside to inspect the issue. But thirty minutes later, we'd completely forgotten about our septic stress. Instead, we had been transported to a different world—the planet of the *ants*.

Ant piles are a common sight in our pastures, but for some reason, our prairie ants decided to build a palace right next to our septic tank. When Christian removed the concrete cover to troubleshoot the unhappy toilet, the inhabitants of Ant Land were furious. Thankfully, these were black ants, and not the stinging red variety, but they shook their tiny insect fists at us as they raced to repair the damage to their city. The kids were intrigued. And so were we.

As we watched the ants swarm, we noticed a pattern. Distinct trails, like lanes of an interstate, led in and out of the septic tank metropolis. This wasn't any old anthill—this was an ant superhighway. Thousands of tiny beings carried out an imperceptible drama under our feet. My son shrieked with delight as he discovered the route stretched over fifty feet into the backyard. The organization was amazing. The ants moved in an orderly fashion as they transported rocks, sticks, and bodies of other ants up and down their road system. At one point, a disoriented beetle attempted to cross the lanes the wrong way and was promptly chastised. We lost ourselves in the world of the ants that night. As the sun dipped below the horizon, we finally awoke from our trance with a fresh appreciation for the miniature world around us.

Can you learn about ants by writing a five-page report? Sure. But my kids learn much better from real-life experience. And so do the rest of us.

"Today when most people think of education they think of school. In other words, they think of education as something done *to* children *by* adults. But education long predates schooling, and even today most education occurs outside of school," writes developmental psychologist Peter Gray in *Free to Learn*. Humans are born with an innate drive to educate themselves. But our job as parents is to keep that drive active as long as possible.

According to Gray, three instinctive human traits drive us toward self-education: curiosity, playfulness, and sociability.

All three of these concepts were at work during our evening with the ants.

Curiosity jump-started the process: Where were the ants going? What were they doing?

Then, a sense of **playfulness** took over as we ditched our waiting chores and enjoyed the show. "Look how far their trail goes! Ooooh, this ant has a giant pebble!" This sort of play-led learning manifests itself frequently on the homestead, as the kids test their balancing skills across fence rails, master new tricks on the trampoline, and mix different soils to create innovative mud pies.

And last, **sociability** came into action as the kids showed their friends the marvels of the ant superhighway in the days following the initial discovery.

Their personal experience has spurred countless questions that they've since researched on their own. How do ants make their hills? What do ants eat? What types of ants live in our yard? Why are some ants half black and half red? Now that they have a tangible connection to the topic, they've become self-motivated to seek out related information on their own. Even the best ant unit study in the world couldn't compete with that sort of excitement. This sort of innate curiosity is what drives children to engage with their world. On average, a preschooler at home asks seventy-six questions *per hour*. (If you've ever spent time around small kids, you know this number is conservative.) Asking questions is a fundamental part of being a child.

Yet when children enter the educational system, the number of questions they ask plummets. When rates of question-asking were measured in kindergarten classrooms, one researcher observed that there were only two to five questions asked in a two-hour period. These findings held true as she observed older grades, too. She concluded that "many children are spending hours a day in school without asking even one question or engaging in one sequence of behavior aimed at finding out something new."

These findings cause me to wonder if we're accidentally educating the curiosity out of our children. And if so, how can we bring it back? I try to steer clear of making sweeping recommendations when it comes to education, since it's such a nuanced topic. While homeschooling is a beautiful fit for our family, I realize it isn't right for everyone. Ultimately, you get to decide what works best for your family. But whether you choose public school, homeschool, or something in between, all kids can benefit from more wonder in their life.

As we work to bring curiosity to the surface in our children, it helps to consider how we learn, even as adults. Ask yourself: What motivates you to dig into a topic? What prompted you to pick up this book? Perhaps you're trying to solve a specific problem in your life. Or maybe you're feeling restless and wanting to make a change.

More than likely, you grabbed this book at the store or library because you were *curious*. If you had been required to read it, you probably would have done so begrudgingly, if at all. You're holding this book in your hands because you find these topics at least somewhat compelling, so you decided to follow that spark of intrigue. That's how the most valuable learning starts—for all of us.

Following sparks of curiosity has led me down incredible paths. Believe it or not, the impetus for this book started with one of my curiosities that began at the age of fifteen. That's when I started my first blog as a sophomore in high school. The internet was a fairly new place, and I was fascinated by the idea of having my own website. However, back then, there weren't fancy tools that allowed you to post your thoughts to the world with a single click. I had to do it the old-fashioned way. I taught myself HTML, downloaded an archaic precursor to Adobe Photoshop, and figured out how to use FTP to upload my website to the interwebs. (It was a website about horses, of course.) My mom has since admitted she was slightly concerned that the many hours I spent designing graphics and coding HTML would make me an antisocial hermit. But to her credit, she didn't protest.

When I left home to chase my real-life horse dreams, I assumed my website-building days were over. Little did I know that my computer nerd propensities would come in handy down the road. The knowledge I had collected a decade prior gave me the confidence to launch *The Prairie Homestead* website in 2010 and subsequently reach millions of people.

If not for the space my parents gave me to pursue my dorky fifteen-year-old interests, there's a good chance you wouldn't be reading this book today. Simple curiosity started it all. (By the way, thanks Mom and Dad.)

Children are far more prone to mimic our behavior than our words. It's one of the neatest and most horrifying parts of parenting. It also holds the key if you're wondering how to get your kids to start being more curious. *Curiosity starts with us.*

As parents, we can talk until we're blue in the face, but nothing sticks in those little brains like the moments when we lead the way. The more curious I am, the more curious my children become. But I can't encourage inquisitiveness in my children if I'm disinterested in the world around me and absorbed in my phone. They need someone to model wonder and to help them make connections. To show them the stretchy joy of bread dough, to lead the celebration of a basket of freshly dug carrots, to point out the storm clouds brewing in the distance, to marvel at the ingenuity of ants, to continue asking questions with unknown answers. When we awaken to the world around us, we give our children permission to do the same.

> **When we awaken to the world around us, we give our children permission to do the same.**

Some of the best moments of curiosity and wonder are kindled from the most random activities. Recently, my nine-year-old was using a dictionary to look up the meaning of several words for spelling practice. He prefers our antique dictionary since it has clearer definitions. As he flipped through the pages, a colorful page of flags caught his eye.

"Look! That's Hitler's flag!" he exclaimed, recognizing the symbol from a book about the Holocaust that he'd read earlier this year.

I was surprised to see a red-and-black flag emblazoned with a swastika listed as Germany's official banner. "Hmm, let's see what year this book was published," I said, as I showed him how to flip to the copyright page. Sure enough, the date was 1937, two years before World War II began. I explained that this flag was Germany's flag for just a short time.

His eyes lit up. Now he wanted to study the rest of the page. The questions came rapid-fire. "The American flag has a story. Do you think these other flags have stories, too? Have you been to any of these countries? Why do a lot of the flags include the color red? Soviet Russia...is this the same Russia that has invaded countries like Ukraine? Czech...o...slo...va...kia... How do you pronounce this one?"

I struggled to keep up with his rapid-fire questions. We took a thirty-minute detour from spelling that day, but in the process, we covered history, geography, and current events. Not every day is like this. Some are much more run-of-the-mill. But I've learned to watch for these rabbit trails and let them play out. While they may seem like a distraction to the work at hand, they often end up sparking more genuine learning than even the best textbooks.

Watching my own children chase their passions is one of the most fulfilling parts of parenting for me. I can't help but wonder which curiosities might open unexpected possibilities for them, just like blogging did for me. So far, their eclectic interests include show steers, rabbits, watercolors, welding, turtles, mechanics, archery, chickens, basketball, sketching, and braiding hair, just to name a few. Like my own parents, I give them space to explore what lights them up. They're most motivated when they get to lead the way, so I do my part by celebrating breakthroughs when they have them and providing help when requested. But the rest is up to them.

Foster Playtime

When our math and reading lessons are completed each day, school takes on a different appearance. As the kids shove their books back on the shelf, they race to pull on their shoes and coats. "Bye, Mom!" they yell as the door slams shut behind them. They think they're done with school for the day, but I know the real education is just beginning.

Outside, they run and scream. They ride bikes and kick balls. They poke sticks in the cattle's water tank and pretend they are fishing. (Recently, unbeknownst to me, they graduated to using a real fishing pole and a worm to catch one of the unsuspecting goldfish that live in the stock tank to help control algae. Ahem.) They climb on the hay bales and slide down the sides. They coerce the barn cats from their hiding spots and cuddle them until they melt in their arms. They "dig for treasure" in the driveway with their mini metal detector. They embark on grand adventures behind the house, weaving in and out of the tree rows. And they use their small collection of hand tools to build all sorts of things (just the other day they walked by with a handsaw and a hammer, declaring their intent to build a house for the goose).

If the weather isn't cooperating, the play moves inside. Board games are a favorite, followed by sword fighting, hide-and-seek in the dark basement, art projects, and turning cardboard boxes into cars, trains, wagons, and houses. My house is rarely clean,

I step on a lot of LEGO, and there are always bits of cardboard and construction paper littering the floor, but it's worth it.

"Play is nature's way of teaching children how to solve their own problems, control their impulses, modulate their emotions, see from others' perspectives, negotiate differences, and get along with others as equals," writes Peter Gray in *Free to Learn*. "There is no substitute for play as a means of learning these skills. They can't be taught at school."

The value of play is even evident in animals. Young animals engage in play to prepare themselves for the unexpected, established social hierarchies and promote healthy brain development. And we're no different. Yet free playtime is rapidly shrinking, thanks to decreasing recess time, more extracurricular activities, a bigger focus on academics, and a rise in parental fears. We live in a different world than our great-grandparents, but I still firmly hold to the belief that play is possible. And it's one of the most valuable things we could ever offer our kids.

I'm not against extracurricular activities. We participate in 4-H, occasional sports, and a handful of other events each year. But the antics they create in their own free time are where creativity and curiosity blossom.

So how do we facilitate healthy free play? There are a handful of tricks I use, but the most important is that *I do as little as possible.*

I've learned to fight the urge to micromanage their play or offer too many suggestions. And they prefer it that way. It's not my job to entertain them. Instead, I let them create, explore, and problem-solve. Sometimes I'll jump-start the process by offering a suggestion, but that's it. (Did you notice the big puddle in the back pasture is full of water? I think I heard some frogs!) The rest is up to them. If they need help, I'm available. But they usually don't.

If you're new to this idea and your child isn't immediately enamored by the concept of hours of screen-less free time, don't fret. When a child is used to a packed schedule, making a shift to hours of open space can feel intimidating. Expect there to be a transition period and stick with your plan. If they do complain about being bored, fight the urge to fix it for them. If complaints of boredom persist at our house, I may offer suggestions (coloring, bikes, Frisbee, LEGO), but I don't initiate the play. That's up to them. Most of the time, these protests quickly fade and, before long, I find them immersed in their next adventure. Remember, boredom is a vital ingredient in creativity. When we let it simmer, good ideas will float to the surface.

> ## boredom is a vital ingredient in creativity.

And no, it's not sunshine and butterflies all the time. Sometimes they fight. Sometimes they get frustrated. Sometimes they come to the house with scraped knees and snot running down their faces. But these bumps in the road are just as much a part of the learning experience as the fun times. So I troubleshoot, apply Band-Aids when needed, wipe noses, and send them on their way.

One of the hardest parts of old-fashioned parenting for me is letting my kids experience failure. As parents, it's incredibly tempting to protect our children from all mistakes. However, when we do this repeatedly, we rob them of valuable life lessons.

In *The Gift of Failure*, Jessica Lahey points out that protecting kids from failure in the short term prevents them from gaining a growth mindset (the belief that effort trumps talent), which is crucial for success and happiness later in life. "The setbacks, mistakes, miscalculations, and failures we have shoved out of our children's way are the very experiences that teach them how to be resourceful, persistent, innovative, and resilient citizens of this world," writes Lahey.

And so, we do our best to celebrate failure in our house. I let the kids see me try new things and fail spectacularly. I encourage them to tackle challenging tasks with a high rate of failure. And most of all, I do my best to let them experience the full range of their actions, even when it's easier for me to "fix it." This often looks like allowing natural consequences to do the heavy lifting. For example: In the past, I've spent a ridiculous amount of time begging my older kids to wear coats. But now? It's on them. When we're headed out the door, I might say, "I'm bringing my coat since it might get cool later," but I refrain from offering fifty-seven reminders to bring their own jackets or packing one for them. If they get chilly while we're out, it's a fantastic reminder to plan ahead next time.

Of course, dangers still exist. No part of life is risk-free, and times have changed. Unfortunately, we no longer live in a world where kids can ride their bikes across town unattended without someone calling the authorities. All kids are different, so it's up to us as parents to determine what they are ready to handle. Therefore, I weigh the risks with the understanding of my children's abilities and make judgments accordingly. That being said, I'm always surprised at how capable and careful children can be. Allowing our kids time to think, create, run, and roam doesn't require much from us as parents. But don't let the simplicity fool you—this precious blank space is powerful stuff.

Get to Know Nature

As a young mom, "nature time" felt oddly formidable. Maybe it was the not-so-helpful craft ideas in the parenting magazines (no thank you to pine cones and glitter) or the social media photos of families trekking through national parks with matching backpacks and toddler-sized hiking poles. Adorable? Yes. But that's just not how we roll. I love the idea of my kids running through the woods and climbing trees, but as you know from previous chapters, forests are rather scarce out here on the prairie.

And so, I carried mom guilt about our perceived lack of nature time for years. Until one day I realized how silly that was. While elaborate scavenger hunts and extended camping trips aren't a part of our regular routine, nature is actually a huge part of our life. *We just engage with it in our own way.* And you can, too.

For us, nature time looks like talking about the hawks sitting on the fence posts as we drive the back roads. It's noticing the flock of wild turkeys that live on the edges of our tiny town. It's the countless "special rocks" my kids collect and scatter all over the house. (So. Many. Rocks.) It's time spent in the garden looking at the plants and talking about germination, compost, soil, and stewardship. It's watching bees hover from flower to flower as we discuss dandelions and pollination and why we don't use pesticides. In the early years, it was placing wriggling earthworms in my toddlers' chubby hands as I explained how worms make the dirt happy.

My kids enjoy these sorts of activities just as much as glitter and construction paper crafts. And the best part is that it's doable for this busy mom. I don't have to bring the magic— nature does that for me.

> **There was nothing quite like the mystery and excitement of exploring untamed areas by ourselves.**

Much of my children's free play and self-led learning happens in nature as well. While I love spending time with them outdoors, I have a hunch that some of the most meaningful interactions happen when my kids are by themselves. It's a feeling

I distinctly remember from my childhood. There was nothing quite like the mystery and excitement of exploring untamed areas by ourselves. The thrill of the unknown and the whispers of risk engage all the senses and draw children into the natural world in a way we adults can't duplicate.

But as crucial as it is, nature is absent from most modern childhoods. In *How to Raise a Wild Child*, Scott Sampson writes that children spend only four to seven minutes outdoors per day, but a whopping seven hours per day on screens. Beyond the obvious benefits of physical exercise, nature offers opportunities for precious solitude, reduces anxiety, helps children process trauma, boosts social skills, and fosters creativity.

One study showed that children diagnosed with ADHD were able to better focus on mental tasks after getting a "dose of nature" during a walk in a park. Environmental psychologist Nancy Wells has a fascinating body of research that highlights the fact that nature "moderates or buffers the impact of life stress on children." In addition to reducing our stress, the natural world has a way of awakening our senses. This may be one of my favorite benefits, both for my children and for myself. Our society is structured in a way that the bulk of our day is spent processing information given to us by others. There are benefits to this, of course, but we desperately need the chance to still experience our world firsthand, to come to our own conclusions, and to make our own observations.

There's no better way to counteract this than through concentrated time spent in nature. While screens give us momentary flashes of excitement and quick hits of dopamine, they will never hold a candle to a three-dimensional universe we can see, hear, smell, touch, and taste for ourselves. Children desperately need the tangible connections they create when they gather their own information. When this happens, their surroundings come to life, and they have a reason to care for the world around them.

Remember, nature is already around you; all you must do

is start noticing it. As we do this, our children will follow our example. Let them see your curiosity awaken. Look at the sky, notice the clouds, and watch the patterns of the birds. Give them exposure to wild places, so they can learn there are things bigger and grander than our human scale. Use your unique location to your advantage, whether you live in a tree-studded state, near the beach, or in the midst of the desert. If you don't have a homestead or public land nearby, use whatever parks and open spaces you have in your neighborhood. Dig into the uniqueness of your landscape and bring it to life for your children.

If you can give your children access to untamed spaces, do it. More and more "unstructured parks" are popping up as some playground planners are realizing that kids don't always need fancy equipment. Dirt piles and scrap lumber are far more entertaining. (The best gift we ever gave our kids was the massive pile of dirt left over from remodeling our house. Six years later, they still talk about it.) But even if you don't have free-play park options in your area, you can create smaller versions in your backyard, or visit natural areas where kids can find their wild.

Animals are another valuable source of learning. Family pets (yes, even goldfish) teach kids mindfulness for other beings. My children quickly learned if you act like a maniac in the chicken coop, the chickens run away. Therefore, if you want to pet one, you must learn to control your body and your energy. (Trust me, this lesson means far more coming from a chicken than a mom.)

When it rains, the kids like to play "save the worms" by scooping up distressed earthworms in the driveway and transferring them to the garden. Even my rambunctious boy has learned how to watch fragile baby chicks for signs of illness, and he carefully cradles them in his hands when he needs to bring one to the house for aid. If you can't have animals, show them how to watch the wild creatures around them. Notice the birds in the park or the squirrels that scurry across your path. What cues are they giving?

I hope it's as reassuring for you as it was for me that engaging in nature with your kids doesn't have to be an overwhelming production or a yearlong road trip to all the national parks. A few weeks ago, the kids and I decided to go for a walk. I had no intention of turning our stroll into a lesson; we just wanted to get out of the house. As we made our way down the road, we talked about which way the wind was blowing. We looked for birds and talked about the time we found a hognose snake on the road. We stopped at a lone yucca plant growing in the ditch so they could touch its pointy leaves. The kids cracked open one of the dried seedpods and counted the flat black discs that were packed together like sardines. They filled their pockets with the seeds as they declared their intention to plant a crop of yucca at home. (Naturally, I ended up digging the seeds out of my washing machine a week later...)

> ## the very best lessons are the ones that happen by accident.

The next morning, they woke up asking if we could take another walk to visit the yucca plant. And once again, I was reminded that sometimes the very best lessons are the ones that happen by accident.

Cultivate Capability

When I left for town one afternoon, the sun was shining. But an hour later, the wind began to rage as it blew sheets of snow across the prairie. In response, the highway department closed the interstate, and I was stuck figuring out how to get back to the homestead.

Christian was at home with the kids but preoccupied with calving (babies are always born during a blizzard). As I slowly made my way north on the back roads, I called to check in on my eleven-year-old, who was in the house with her siblings. "Mom, we're fine," she replied matter-of-factly as I expressed my concern. "I just put a batch of biscuits in the oven, we added wood to the fire, and I'm keeping an eye on Ingrid (the very pregnant goat). It's no big deal."

Clearly, my savvy preteen was unfazed by the prairie drama that swirled around her.

Ninety minutes later, I arrived home to a cozy house and supper on the table. The kids stood in the doorway with Cheshire cat smiles. As they showed me the waiting biscuits and gravy and gave reports on the goats and calves, their pride was palpable. They walked a little taller, knowing they had stepped up to the plate and played a valuable role in our family operations that night.

"Our culture tells us our kids are fragile and weak, but in reality, they are so much more capable than most parents think," said Katie Kimball, TEDx speaker and creator of the *Kids Cook Real Food* program, in a recent conversation we had. Katie is the leading voice of healthy kids cooking and a passionate advocate for teaching children real-life skills. "This generation of parents asks too little of their kids because too little was asked of them. We try to make their lives easier, but on accident we make their adulthoods more difficult and strip from them the sense of security and confidence that knowing how to handle life skills would give them."

Like many researchers, Katie connects our culture's lack of confidence and self-esteem to the rise in depression and anxiety in teens. "They feel out of control," Katie stated. "They're depressed because they don't feel rooted to family and friends, and they don't feel like they control their environment at all. We know that, as human beings, when we have boundaries, we feel safe, but we also need to be able to be agents of our own destiny within those boundaries. When parents do everything

for their kids, they think they are keeping their children safe
and protected, when in fact, psychologically, they are doing the
exact opposite. Because kids don't feel like they can do anything
to improve their life or take care of themselves, they are infused
with a sense of insecurity."

Over the years, I've discovered that plenty of free play tem-
pered with healthy boundaries and a helping of age-appropriate
responsibility is the magic combination for our family. It helps
our home to run more smoothly and leaves my kids with no
doubt that they are an important part of our team.

Here are a few of the strategies we've used over the years—
maybe some of these ideas will work for your family, too.

- **Start small.** If your children are too little to have their
  own solo tasks, let them help you with yours. Toddlers love to help. (I do use this term loosely.) They
  can empty small wastebaskets, sweep the floor, or carry
  laundry to the washing machine. Yes, it will take longer, and sometimes they make a bigger mess in the process. But the time you invest during those early years
  pays off. Barn chores used to take us forever. We'd put
  on the snowsuits, hats, gloves, and boots, gather up the
  blankies, and finally head outside. They'd accidentally
  break the eggs and leave gates open. They'd fall down,
  take a million bathroom breaks, or forget things. It was
  a circus of chaos. But we survived. And the day your
  kids beam with confidence as they make supper for the
  family and do the dishes afterward is the day you'll realize it was all worth it.

- **Move up the ladder.** As they grow, kids can graduate
  to more challenging tasks. Around age four, our kids
  started feeding the dogs. Then they moved up to gathering eggs. Then it was on to feeding the chickens, before eventually graduating to the rest of the barn chores.

Fast-forward to today, my three kids handle the entire barnyard on a daily basis, including feeding hay, chopping ice, managing the milk cow, and moving animals from pen to pen. They rarely need my help, and they take a lot of pride in their ability to keep things running smoothly. Every family and every child is different, so you get to tailor responsibilities according to your children's ability. Just remember, they are almost always more capable than we think.

- **Let them mess up.** I know, it's hard. If it makes you feel any better, like most parents, I struggle with jumping in to "help" or fix problems for them. I must constantly remind myself to sit back and let them do it on their own. But I've noticed that nothing kills my kids' motivation faster than when I attempt to micromanage their tasks. ("Did you remember to add the salt to the recipe?" "Don't forget to wear your gloves!") Supervision is necessary at times, but as much as possible, allow your kids to make mistakes and find their own solutions. If they forget to set a timer and burn the cookies this time, it's a much more effective lesson than you nagging them every time to check the clock.

- **Let the loop do the work.** In my conversation with Katie Kimball, she referenced the confidence competence loop—a phenomenon well-documented by sociologists and psychologists. This loop is the secret sauce in raising self-motivated kids. As she shared with me, "When a human builds competence, it gives them confidence, which feels good. Therefore, they want to come back and learn more of that skill. And of course, as they learn more, their competence grows, which in turn creates more confidence." As a parent, I've noticed that if I can

provide that initial encouragement to try something new,
the loop takes over and does the heavy lifting.

- **Celebrate the uncomfortable.** No one likes to be
  uncomfortable. Many adults struggle with the ability to
  push outside of their comfort zones, which causes dissatisfaction and even heartache later in life. So, we try to
  address this early on with the kids. I want them to know
  that even if you're hot or cold or tired, you will survive.
  And you might even become tougher in the process.
  Naturally, they do complain sometimes—they're still
  kids. When those occasions arise, we talk about why
  the task we're working on is important ("We're stacking firewood so we have enough wood for the winter.")
  and discuss how good it'll feel when the job is done
  ("Think about how amazing it'll feel to sit next to the
  warm fire tonight and have a bowl of soup!"). Kids are
  tougher than you think, and they quickly learn how rewarding it can be to complete challenging or uncomfortable tasks. (Obviously, there is a difference between
  "uncomfortable" and harmful. We aren't forcing our
  kids to stay in truly dangerous conditions where frostbite or heatstroke could occur.)

Give Them Knives

When you become a parent, you're assaulted with safety warnings the moment your child exits the womb. Sorting through all
the books, magazines, checklists, blogs, warnings, documenta-
ries, and recalls devoted to keeping your child safe can feel like
a full-time job. I remember staring at my day-old newborn and
wondering how on earth I was going to keep her alive.

So my next sentence will likely come as a shock:

Kids *need* exposure to risk-filled situations. In fact, it's crucial for healthy development.

No, I'm not saying you should allow your kids to play in the middle of an intersection or give your eighteen-month-old a meat cleaver, but kids do need more exposure to healthy risk than they currently have in most of our modern culture.

When we treat children like breakable objects, we do them a great disservice. Like our immune systems, muscles, bones, and even the prairie ecosystems we talked about in the previous chapter, kids are *antifragile*. Nassim Nicholas Taleb first introduced this term in his book *Antifragile*. He defines antifragility as being "beyond resilience or robustness. The resilient resists shocks and stays the same; the antifragile gets better."

I love this concept, because it gives us permission to lean into the hard things without fear. Rather than being damaged by disorder, adventure, or chaos, antifragile things thrive in challenging conditions. The more they are exposed to hardships (whether those hardships are viruses, lifting heavy weights, or hordes of hungry bison), the stronger they become. This theory suggests that our antifragile children *need* elements of risk and challenge to thrive.

A paper by Dr. Ellen Sandseter caught my attention since it flies in the face of our hyper safety-obsessed culture. She's a professor of psychology at Queen Maud University College of Early Childhood Education in Norway, and her specialty is risky play. She's identified six different types:

1. Heights (climbing or balancing above the ground)

2. Speed (biking, skating, or running fast)

3. Hazardous Tools (playing with knives, ropes, or hammers)

4. Dangerous Locations (playing near cliffs or fire)

5. Roughhousing (wrestling or play-fighting)

6. Disappearing (exploring without supervision)

It reads like a list of every parent's worst nightmare, doesn't it? But contrary to popular belief, research has shown that allowing children to engage in these types of play (within reason) has major benefits.

When exposed to higher-risk situations, kids have the chance to develop important life skills that they'll need later. While it may make our parental hearts skip a beat, allowing our children to participate in activities with a reasonable element of risk (such as walking across a fallen log or using a handsaw) helps them to have better socialization, problem-solving, and self-regulation skills, as well as a *decreased* chance of injury. Yes, you read that right—the *more* your children engage in high-risk play, the *less* their chances of being hurt. This is because healthy exposure to challenging scenarios helps to create better judgment.

By exposing children to situations they may have previously feared, risky play shows them they have the power to overcome difficulties, while also helping them to decipher truly dangerous situations from everyday occurrences.

So the million-dollar question is, how can we give them appropriately dangerous situations but also keep them alive?

There's no denying this is a tricky balance, especially when it feels like we're *expected* to hover over our children. Even I have caved to the pressure at public playgrounds when I sensed the disapproval of other parents over my free-ranging ways. More than once I've "spotted" my child on the slide just to appease the other moms, even though I knew she was perfectly capable of handling the playground equipment on her own. As parents we're left trying to balance what is good for our kids and society's vision of "good parenting." It's a juggling act that can leave us feeling stuck.

But there is good news: kids are safer than they've ever been.

While the constant bombardment of news feeds, tweets, and social media posts may make it feel like the world is more dangerous than ever, most of our fear is unfounded. Child mortality rates and crimes against children have declined in recent years, as have deaths from car accidents and stranger abductions. While threats of human trafficking do remain a growing problem in our modern society, much of the "grooming" and "recruitment" is taking place online, adding yet another reason to get our children away from their screens and out into nature (while educating them about healthy versus unhealthy relationships and maintaining open communication with them about these contemporary issues).

So how do we help our kids navigate their world in a brave yet wise way? Much of it depends on the child's level of development. As the parent, you get to decide what they are ready for at each stage. Some kids can easily handle a pocketknife at age eight, while others might be better off waiting a while longer. Since children all mature at different rates, there aren't any formulas. But you'll know when they're ready for a greater challenge or thrill.

Over the years, we've granted our children access to pocketknives and BB guns. In the kitchen, they regularly use our gas stove and my collection of chef's knives. They have kid-sized toolboxes with real hammers and handsaws inside. They build fires in our fireplace, jump across the highest haystacks, and tiptoe along the top rail of the garden fence like a balance beam. Sometimes it takes my breath away. But as their freedom has expanded, they have risen to the occasion. They treat grown-up tools with respect, and their judgment calls in precarious situations are (usually) impressive. We don't thumb our noses at safety. They wear helmets when they ride horses, and we buckle our seat belts in the car. But I remind myself that when safety is our *only* goal, we hinder their development. And the same principle applies to emotionally challenging situations, too.

A lot of parents email me wondering how their children will handle the loss of animals when they move to a homestead. I don't have a polished, sound-bite-worthy answer. It's hard, every time. But I will share this: Witnessing the natural cycles of life and death hasn't permanently traumatized my children. In fact, the opposite has occurred.

My children have cradled tiny chicks as they left this world. They've witnessed orphaned calves lying in our mudroom taking their last rattly breaths. They've watched me unsuccessfully attempt to resuscitate newborn triplet goats after a difficult birth in the middle of the night. While death is often sanitized and hidden, on a homestead, it's on full display.

More than once I've found myself monitoring an animal that's dying in one barn while awaiting the birth of new life in another. It's a lot to take in. Even for an adult. But I can't hide it from them forever, nor do I want to.

Rather than hardening them, these experiences have helped my children become more resilient, kinder, and more aware. They fully grasp the fleetingness of life and honor it, while also realizing death is a natural process. When loss happens, it hurts. But we grieve together, and then we move on. It's another example of the antifragility that kids possess. To navigate this world, they'll need generous helpings of competence and resilience, and those life skills only come from being tested.

Let Them Eat Dirt

Have you ever seen goat poop? It bears an uncanny resemblance to a Milk Dud. The pellets are perfectly round, irresistibly soft, and the perfect size for popping into your mouth. As toddlers, all of my children have tasted it at least once. They also regularly eat dirt, although that isn't intentional. It just happens in the course of eating carrots straight from the soil, or plucking spinach leaves right from the plant. I suspect they also take licks from the cattle salt block on occasion, though they plead the Fifth when I ask them. Yet not once have their unorthodox snacking habits made them sick. Could it happen? Maybe. But the odds are very small. Studies show there's actually a greater long-term risk from living in a perfectly sterile world. In fact, all the unwashed carrots they've eaten may be making them healthier.

A study conducted in Austria, Germany, and Switzerland showed that early childhood exposure to farms, stables, and farm milk protected children against hay fever and asthma. Another fascinating study in *The New England Journal of Medicine* compared childhood asthma rates in the Amish and Hutterite societies. While both groups follow similar traditional practices, Amish children showed a remarkably low rate of asthma, while Hutterite children had above average occurrences of the respiratory disease. These findings are surprising considering both groups have the same genetic ancestry and similar lifestyles. So what was the difference?

It all came down to exposure. Amish communities practice more traditional farming methods, which exposes them to a more diverse set of microbes. However, the Hutterites follow the standard industrialized agriculture model. The paper concluded that "the Amish environment provides protection against asthma by engaging and shaping the innate immune response." In other words, the more microbes present, the healthier the kids.

Dangerous bacteria still exist, but friendly varieties are far more prevalent. And they are incredible assets to our environments and our bodies. Invisible microbes shape daily life on our homestead in the very best of ways. The microscopic organisms in the soil help us to grow healthy vegetables. The beneficial bacteria and enzymes in raw milk support our gut health. Colonies of yeast and bacteria help my sourdough loaves to rise.

And lactic acid bacteria ferment my homemade kombucha and sauerkraut.

> **The research is clear: our kids need exposure to natural environments to stay healthy.**

The research is clear: our kids need exposure to natural environments to stay healthy. So, think of bacteria as your partner—both in delicious kitchen pursuits and in raising healthy, resilient kids.

There are plenty of ways to exercise your family's immune systems, even if you don't live on a farm.

- **Get a pet.** Studies have shown that having a family dog not only boosts immune systems but may also reduce rates of allergies and asthma in children.

- **Play outside.** Not only does it give your kids a chance to engage with nature, it also gives them a chance to come into contact with healthy soil bacteria.

- **Visit farms.** Even if farm animals aren't a part of your daily routine, visit rural settings as much as possible.

- **Avoid antibacterial.** From wipes to cleaners to soaps, antibacterial is all the rage. However, these products haven't been shown to be much more effective than plain soap and water, plus they can contribute to resistant bacteria.

- **Add in probiotics.** Yogurt, kombucha, kefir (fermented milk), and fermented vegetables are old-fashioned ways to add beneficial bacteria to your diet and your gut.

Simple Wins Again

In a world of high expectations constantly placed on parents, it's reassuring to me (and hopefully to you, too) that old-fashioned parenting removes much of this burden. When we encourage curiosity, learning opportunities present themselves in the most surprising ways (without us having to force it to happen). When we allow our kids time to play, there's less pressure on us to entertain them. And when we foster responsibility, they become more capable, and our families run more smoothly overall. I love that each time I lean into these time-honored ideas, I end up with happier, more confident kids, and I don't have to run myself ragged in the process.

And remember—you get to decide what this looks like for your family. If you don't have a horse trailer or an ant pile for them to play with, that's okay. You can still take these principles and run with them. Cities have plenty of opportunities for your children to explore new surroundings, experiment with decision-making, and practice autonomy. You can encourage creativity and out-of-the-box thinking anywhere. You can peel your kids off the screens and point them toward nature, even if you live in an apartment. You can celebrate failures and experience adventure. And you can bring them along for the ride and show them they are a part of the team no matter where you live.

Old-Fashioned Action Steps

- Avoid overscheduling. Block out time each week for them to just be kids.

- Encourage free play as much as possible, both indoors and out.

- Allow your kids to partake in reasonably dangerous activities.

- Fight the urge to micromanage their play. Good things come from boredom.

- Be on the lookout for what passions your kids are developing, then give them space to chase them.

- Remember, dirt is your friend. Immune systems are *antifragile*—they need exposure.

- Remove stigma around failure. Share your own failures regularly with your children and allow them to see you model resilience and persistence, too.

- Model being a curious person. Let your children see you asking questions and learning new things.

- Resist the urge to segregate life into "adult" and "child." Sometimes this is appropriate, but whenever possible, bring your kids into your world.

CHAPTER 11

Cultivate Your Community

It was a Friday evening in late March. Our tiny Wyoming town had planned to have "community night" at the local school, complete with supper and an "anyone can play" volleyball game afterward. Unfortunately, at the very last minute we discovered we wouldn't be allowed access into the school due to a leaky roof, and no other venue options existed in our village of 175 people.

So we did what any self-respecting ranching community would do. Someone parked his feed truck front and center in the school parking lot, we plopped the pot of soup on the back next to the pitchforks and bundles of baling twine, and everyone dished up. There weren't any chairs or tables, so there we stood—bundled in our Wyoming winter wear, sipping soup on the asphalt, and enjoying several hours of impromptu fellowship while the sun sank low in the sky. I was struck by the specialness of it all.

These cherished times of human connection can happen anywhere, but I've never seen them more on display than when I moved to rural America. French sociologist Émile Durkheim coined the term "collective effervescence" to describe the synchronicity that occurs when people come together in a shared goal. That term has resonated deeply with me since the mo-

ment I first heard it. I've felt it many times, but I never knew
it had a name.

> **It's the electricity that settles over a
> group of people when real connec-
> tion and vulnerability exist.**

Collective effervescence reminds me a lot of the "flow" we
talked about in the previous chapters, except flow usually arises
during solo projects, and collective effervescence happens in
groups. It's the electricity that settles over a group of people when
real connection and vulnerability exist. It's the magic that takes
place each spring when local ranchers hold their annual brand-
ings, when dozens of people show up to rope, wrestle, and vac-
cinate calves before lingering to tell stories over a home-cooked
meal. It's the dynamic that occurs when someone needs a little
extra help with a project, and friends show up in droves to pitch
in. It recalls memories of the barn raisings of yesteryear, when
communities came together to share labor and break bread.

But this is changing. As the years march on, we're steadily
becoming *less* connected, not more. Although we can talk to
almost anyone in the world with the tap of a button, true community feels elusive. Despite being the most technologically
connected group of humans to ever walk this planet, we are
facing an epidemic of loneliness. Our typical societal connections have started to crumble in recent decades. Americans are
less likely to live with a romantic partner (married or otherwise) than in years past. We maintain fewer friendships and
don't entertain in our homes like we used to. Engagement in
civic organizations, churches, and volunteer organizations has
plummeted. And the majority of Americans report that they
don't know most of their neighbors.

It's a trend we can't afford to ignore. Chronic loneliness has the potential to be more damaging to our health than lack of physical activity or obesity. One researcher even noted that a lack of social connection could be more damaging than smoking fifteen cigarettes a day.

While we usually think of growing gardens or baking bread when we consider vintage pursuits, a desire for a thriving community is one of the most old-fashioned and healthy aspirations we can have, especially in today's disconnected world. And this brings us to the final trait of an old-fashioned on purpose person: *We cultivate community wherever we go.*

> **In reality, not one of us is sufficient in and of ourselves. We all need each other in some way.**

While I've used the term "self-sufficiency" several times throughout this book, it's a bit of a misnomer, regardless of whether we're talking about the past or the present. In reality, not one of us is sufficient in and of ourselves. We all need each other in some way. It's easy to assume that the homesteaders of yesteryear were independent, isolated hermits. But history shows us otherwise.

Of all the eras when one would assume community-building would be low priority, the homestead era would be at the top. The homesteaders and pioneers of old had every legitimate excuse to "just stay home." They had an endless list of chores (just to survive), and they usually lived miles from town with transportation that was unreliable and uncomfortable. Nothing about developing relationships was easy or automatic for them. Yet they did it anyway. In countless towns across America, old grange halls, schoolhouses, and churches stand as testaments to our ancestors' vibrant social networks.

As I've scoured through old writings, I've become intrigued at how often the topic of community comes up. In the July 1913 edition of *The Independent*, Mabel Lewis Stuart writes of the social life of claim communities and shares how single women homesteaders would often take claims near each other so they could stay in contact. She adds, "Aside from this pleasant social life with the nearer neighbors there is a great deal to take away any tendency of 'lonesomeness' on the claim in various social organizations." She goes on to list the many activities of her small South Dakota community, including church services, oratorical contests, receptions, and "a series of socials, parties and literary and musical entertainment [that] kept the community humming." Another single woman homesteader wrote, "The social side of life is not neglected, and many congenial friends can be found among the settlers."

Although many of these people didn't have running water or indoor plumbing, they enjoyed more robust social lives than many of us in our modern cocoons of convenience. Fascinating, isn't it? Even in the hardest times, they knew social gatherings were crucial to their survival.

Therefore, I can't think of a more old-fashioned practice than choosing to cultivate the communities around us. I realize this is a tall order—especially in our modern world. But if someone living in a tar paper shack twelve miles from town with no paved roads and a wagon as their only vehicle can do it, so can we. Oddly enough, it wasn't until I moved thirty-plus miles from civilization that I began to truly understand the importance of community. And our homestead lifestyle continues to teach me the ropes of creating vibrant connections, even in the unlikeliest of places.

How to Cultivate Community (No Matter Where You Live)

Bloom Where You're Planted

Several years before we purchased our homestead, I had a vision. No, not the kind with angelic beings or voices from the clouds. This was a vision of the more pedestrian variety. But it still got my attention.

As I stood in the kitchen chopping onions that day, a simple scene floated across the canvas of my mind. I saw our home filled with people. The door was always open, and the neighbors always felt comfortable stopping by, knowing there would be a cup of hot coffee or something good to eat. It was the kind of place that served as a respite for people carrying heavy burdens—a place where friends would feel safe and seen. As I mulled over the concepts that had popped into my mind, I felt a deep sense of satisfaction and joy. I knew this was exactly what I wanted to have someday.

There were just a couple problems.

At the time, we were renting a single-wide mobile home far off the beaten path. Reaching it required a thirty-minute drive on the interstate before following an old highway for several miles, and then zigzagging through grids of prairie land and farm fields. We were hardly on a main thoroughfare.

I also didn't know anyone in the area. So while I loved the idea of people "just swinging by," I had no earthly idea who that would be. Most of the locals didn't know we existed. I wasn't a very good cook at that point either, so the "delicious food" part of my vision would need some work.

While these goals were wholesome, they also felt ridiculously implausible. I ruminated on the idea for a while, then cataloged it in some filing cabinet in my brain before forgetting about it entirely.

And then…a decade later, while standing in a different kitchen (this time the one in our current homestead), the memories of that vision resurfaced. My long-ago desire tapped me on the shoulder to say, "Hey! Remember me?" And in that moment I realized my dream was coming to pass. Our little house, though still far from civilization, had, against all odds, become a hive of happy activity.

On many days, a steady stream of trucks files in and out of our driveway as neighbors stop by to chat or do business. Over the years, I've become much better at throwing together meals on the fly, and I no longer panic if my house isn't perfectly clean. We welcome people in, even if some dog hair coats the couch and half-finished art projects litter the table. Each year we host gatherings and get-togethers, and I've fed hundreds of people at our table over the last few years. We laugh until we cry, engage in hard conversations, and do our best to solve the world's problems over pie and coffee. Small talk is boring, so we get to the good stuff as quickly as we can. Nothing is off-limits—politics, religion, philosophy, business—we unpack it all.

In a stealthy, surprising way, my vision came to fruition. And it has served as a powerful reminder that setting intentions, even when they feel impossible, can go a long way. However, it took us a while to get to this point. It's not because the opportunities weren't there, but rather because *I wasn't willing to dig in.*

When we first moved to our homestead, we didn't engage in our local area much at all. Blame it on demanding jobs, pregnancies, babies, or building businesses, but the truth is, we were simply more inward-focused than outward. I suspect this mirrors the realities of many modern folks—sometimes it's all we can do to keep our own balls in the air and survive. I get it. But for us, there came a point when we began to crave deeper relationships. It's easy to place the blame elsewhere.

"There are no like-minded people."

"There's no one our age."

"It's too far to drive."

But these sorts of stories can prevent us from seeing the possibility right in front of our noses.

Christian and I realized our homestead had thrived only because we had invested energy there. So we began to ask ourselves, "What if we diverted some of that energy and passion in our community instead?" That's when it got exciting.

All too often, we give lip service to the idea of building connections, but spend our most valuable resources elsewhere. This hamstrings growth and connection because it strips YOU—your energy, your enthusiasm, your resources, and your time—from your local area. Making the conscious choice to dig in and bloom where we are planted (even if we're planted in less-than-ideal locations) is powerful. That moment of decision changes everything. And make no mistake, sometimes it'll feel like you're digging into solid bedrock. But I discovered the more time I spent in our local area, the more gems I found. I would have missed them all if I had continued focusing my energies on other towns and groups. So yes, it will take time, but there's gold just below the surface. Keep digging. If I can find community while living a million miles from civilization, you can do it, too.

Joining a Rural Community

For obvious reasons, I'm a huge fan of investing in rural America. While small-town populations have been on the decline for several decades in a row, the chaos of the COVID pandemic has sparked a renewed interest in less populated areas. That's good news for our struggling rural towns. It's no secret that small communities offer a different dynamic than urban or suburban lifestyles. This adds to their charm but also can make things a little challenging for newcomers. After living in one of the tiniest towns in Wyoming since 2005, here are a few tricks I've picked up along the way (and these work for making inroads into other communities, too!).

1. Always wave. If you're standing in your yard watering flowers and someone drives by—wave. If you pass someone as you're walking down the sidewalk—wave. If you're driving down a back road and meet an oncoming car—wave. It doesn't have to be a beauty-pageant-winner wave. Just lifting your fingers off the steering wheel will do. But it matters. And yes, people notice. I've heard more than one local resident express their concerns over a newcomer by stating, "They just don't seem friendly. They never wave when I drive by." Be the person who waves. Always.

2. Be humble. It's a favorite movie storyline for a reason: the know-it-all city slicker moves to the country and repeatedly makes a fool of himself in front of the seasoned farmers and ranchers. While it's amusing on the big screen, it's not exactly fun when you're the greenhorn. Thankfully, it's easy to avoid these embarrassing moments. I've found that most people are very happy to share their knowledge if you approach the subject from a place of humility. This especially applies if you're moving into an agricultural area. If you don't know how to build a fence or ride a horse, just say so. False bravado always ends poorly.

3. Honor their history. Residents of small towns are usually suspicious of anyone they suspect might want to change their town too much. While this can be challenging (sometimes even *good* change is met with resistance), I've found that taking a genuine interest in the history of the area goes a long way. As we've worked to improve several local properties, our most well-received results have come when we are able to fix things up while still honoring the place's original history. (Plus, I've gained a whole new appreciation for our town's past in the process.) If you want to strike up conversation in a small town, ask longtime residents about their stories, what their childhoods were like, and how the town has changed over the years. It's a great way to build bridges.

Cast a Vision

When people hear me waxing poetic about our small town, I think they assume it's the type of place you'd find in a Hallmark movie. Allow me to set the record straight. Chugwater, Wyoming, is a hardscrabble frontier town that arose from the middle of the windswept prairies at the end of the nineteenth century. It's been holding on by its fingernails ever since. In 2005, the town sold lots for $100 in an effort to convince folks to move to the area. In 2013, our only gas station burned down and wasn't rebuilt for four years. Tumbleweeds regularly blow across Main Street. We have vultures. Yes, real, actual vultures. They perch on the grain silos downtown and stare at us all summer long. (It's sort of disturbing, but also kind of hilarious.) I adore this town, but trust me—it's not beautiful in the classical sense.

Yet like anywhere else, there are hidden gems to be found. The Swan Land and Cattle Company, one of the largest ranching operations of the early twentieth century, was headquartered here. Steamboat, the iconic bucking horse on the Wyoming state license plate, was born on a Chugwater ranch. If you can picture the quintessential Western town, complete with stagecoaches, rodeos, and cowboys, that was us. But now, these iconic characteristics are mere shadows of the past—all except one: The Chugwater Soda Fountain. Throughout all the ups and downs of the last century, this vintage landmark still stands.

For years, I drove by the nondescript beige building, with its cluttered windows and leaning brick facade, and couldn't help but wonder, "What if?"

But then the rational side of my brain would kick in. Who in their right mind would buy a small-town restaurant that needed *so much* work? In the middle of a pandemic, no less.

Well, as it turns out, Christian and I would.

Sometimes a little gumption is exactly what it takes. When I interviewed entrepreneur and rural advocate Danna Larson of *Rural Revival*, a podcast focused on bringing life to rural communities, she echoed this sentiment. Fledgling communities need that "first person to take the jump," Danna shared. "The common denominator in towns that are successful in bringing revival to their communities is that there is always someone there casting vision." This mindset holds true whether you're cultivating community in rural Wyoming, a suburb, or a high-rise apartment complex.

> **Visionaries have an uncanny ability to see magic in the everyday things that others might miss.**

Oftentimes, casting that vision means you must stop being reasonable and rational, at least for a moment. Visionaries have an uncanny ability to see magic in the everyday things that others might miss. Where many others saw an ancient soda fountain whose heyday had long passed, I saw the tiniest glimmer of possibility. In an area where the wind tips over dumpsters and semitrucks, I saw a century's worth of rugged Wyomingites who had braved the blizzards and hailstorms to make a home here. And in a town that's the brunt of many jokes, I saw a quirky place with an unforgettable name that's worth preserving.

For you, casting a vision might mean pursuing the potential of transforming that empty corner lot into a community garden, or reaching out to a family that others tend to ignore, or turning that boarded-up storefront into a café, or being the one to initiate community softball games or a neighborhood potluck.

No matter what type of community you hope to create, action-takers and dreamers are the ones who do the bulk of the heavy lifting. While your investments into your community likely won't involve a hundred-year-old soda fountain, the principles remain the same.

Take Imperfect Action

"If only somebody would do something about..." I've heard those words more times than I can count. And unfortunately, while they're usually meant well, they are entirely unhelpful. If *somebody* has to give the snowball of community momentum the initial shove—it might as well be you. If you want to see something happen (a book club, a revived downtown, a community garden, a weekly card game, a neighborhood barbecue), don't wait for it to appear—*create it*. The world has enough spectators already. Be the leader and do the inviting. Is there greater risk for disappointment, rejection, and criticism if you're leading the charge? Absolutely. But it's worth it. Whenever I start to feel jittery about putting myself out there, I ask, "Which is worse? The discomfort I might feel if people don't like my idea, OR the disappointment I'll feel in myself for never trying?" Trust me, the latter is always worse. So onward I go.

I frequently draw encouragement from Theodore Roosevelt's "Citizenship in a Republic" speech, which he gave in 1910. The most famous portion is known as "The Man in the Arena." These words light a fire in me every time I read them. I'm including them here so you can also lean on them as you take those first nerve-racking steps into your own arena:

> *It is not the critic who counts; not the man who points out how the strong man stumbles, or where the doer of deeds could have done them better. The credit belongs to the man who is actually in the arena, whose face is marred by dust and sweat and blood; who strives valiantly; who errs, who comes short again and again, because there is no effort without error and shortcoming; but who does actually strive to do the deeds; who knows the great enthusiasms, the great devotions; who spends himself in a worthy cause; who at the best knows in the end the triumph of high achievement, and who at the worst, if he fails, at least fails while daring*

greatly, so that his place shall never be with those cold and timid
souls who neither know victory nor defeat.

No matter what you do, there will be critics. There's this frustrating aspect of human nature that causes us to poke at anyone who dares to step out from the confines of the pack. I call it "crabs in a bucket" syndrome. As the story goes, a bucket of crabs doesn't need a lid, because if one crab decides to make a break for the top, the other crabs will pull him down. While I don't know for certain if this is true (I've never had a bucket of crabs), I do know it's a very accurate depiction of how humans work. Action can make people uncomfortable because it shines a light on their own inaction. And if you're the one brave enough to take that first step, odds are, you're going to ruffle some feathers. But people will have opinions no matter what you do, so you might as well be doing something that lights you up. And at the end of the day, I want to be the woman in the arena, doing the things, making the mistakes, and daring greatly, even if it means I have to eat some dirt in the process.

> **people will have opinions no matter what you do, so you might as well be doing something that lights you up.**

If you can't lead the charge, you can still show your support for community growth by participating. Posting flyers, volunteering to help with setup, offering to bring cookies, or even just attending various events can go a long way. Trust me, when you're the one planning the event, having even just a handful of people in your corner showing up as cheerleaders instead of cynics means *a lot*. In the hardest moments of our soda fountain remodel, local friends came by with bits of encouragement that kept us going. You'll never know how much a simple pat on the back or an "I believe in what you're doing—it's gonna be great!" means to someone.

Hold a Barn Raising

In the rural communities of yesteryear, a barn raising or "raising bee" was when a group of neighbors came together to complete a big project, such as building a barn. Many Amish communities still practice barn raisings, and it's not uncommon for them to erect massive structures in a single day. These events make quick work of what could be long, tedious projects and provide important social connection, too. While you might not have an actual barn to build, you can replicate the vibe in many other ways. This also happens to be one of my favorite tricks for getting to know new people. We all have those friends with whom we are most comfortable, but what about the people on the margins? What connections might we be missing by only ever hanging out with our existing friend groups? Having a task to focus on reduces awkward small talk and provides a healthy dose of collective effervescence, too. (By the way, this works for dating as well as friendship-building. My second date with Christian involved trenching in electrical lines for a friend. Very romantic.)

This act of cocreation helps to elevate community above individuals and provides a dose of magic that's almost impossible to replicate in other ways. The next time you have a big project to complete, bring your friends along for the ride. Some of my favorite group activities have been gathering with neighbors to work cattle, chop firewood, or tackle cleanup or construction projects. The bonds that come from shared experience are hard to beat (even if that experience is painting a shed or cleaning up trash alongside a roadway). In the process, you'll complete large projects much faster than you could have doing it alone, hone new skills, meet new friends or strengthen existing connections, and most of all, *have fun*.

Modern-Day Barn-Raising Activities

The best projects have components for many hands, bring people together in a shared objective, and are followed by a meal. Projects can be personal ("I need help renovating my chicken coop!") or working toward a shared community goal ("Let's clean up this abandoned lot!").

A few ideas:

- Painting (buildings, fences, rooms, etc.)
- Cleaning up trash in shared spaces
- Working on charity projects (making quilts for the homeless, food drives)
- Building small construction projects
- Planting a garden
- Preserving food (pressing cider, canning tomatoes)
- Repairing fences
- Stacking hay
- Laying sod
- Stacking or splitting firewood
- Organizing a fundraising activity
- Helping to restore a public place
- Volunteering to landscape or plant flowers in a park or shared area
- Assisting elderly neighbors with yard work

Add the Secret Ingredient (Food!)

Eating is an intimate act. And there's nothing better at creating connection than food. I have a (probably irrational) belief that I can fix almost anything by bringing people around my table and feeding them well. Coming together to break bread doesn't to be a fancy affair. Even the humblest meals can connect and bond us.

Cooking for larger groups used to intimidate me, but over the years, I've built a collection of standby meals. These options allow me to do the prep work ahead of time so I can be a part of the crew that day, whether we're working cattle, cleaning up a community space, or just watching the kids play. (Because no one wants to be stuck in the kitchen while everyone else is having fun.) Here are my go-to meals for groups:

- **Shredded pork or beef sandwiches.** Slow-cook several roasts the day before, then shred and season the meat. Reheat it when it's time to eat and serve with buns, coleslaw, or potato salad.

- **Tacos.** You'll never go wrong with tacos. Taco meat can be prepared a day ahead and kept warm in a slow cooker. The other toppings (shredded lettuce, tomatoes, guacamole) store well in the fridge if you want to prep them ahead of time.

- **Baked potato bar.** Similar to tacos, most of the prep for a baked potato bar can happen ahead of time. I like to cook up the meat the day before (sausage, bacon bits, ground beef, or shredded chicken or pork are all solid options). An hour or two before we plan to eat, I wash and prick whole potatoes, rub them with olive oil and salt and pepper, and bake them until tender. As mealtime approaches, I set out the other toppings (chili, tomatoes, lettuce, sautéed broccoli, onions, shredded cheese, sour cream, and butter), and then people assemble their own loaded potatoes. This is also a fantastic option for a group that has food allergies, since the toppings can be tailored to fit a variety of dietary needs.

- **Burgers and hot dogs.** Burger patties can be made ahead, as can any sides (potato or pasta salad, green salad, watermelon slices). Plus, grilling outside tends to act as a bit of an icebreaker.

- **Chili.** A giant pot of chili is an economical way to feed a crowd. It's easy to scale up or down and can simmer in a slow cooker while everyone is working. Here in Wyoming, chili is commonly served with cinnamon rolls, although I grew up eating it accompanied by chunks of corn bread.

- **Sloppy joes.** The filling lends itself well to reheating in a slow cooker and is always a crowd-pleaser.

- **Enchiladas or burritos.** These require a little more prep up front but are low-maintenance on the day of serving. Fill tortillas with meat/beans/cheese (or whatever you like), roll them up, and refrigerate or freeze until you need them. Reheat the day of the gathering and serve with salsa, sour cream, and guacamole.

- **Lasagna or pasta bakes.** Like enchiladas, pasta dishes require more hands-on time the day before, but once the dish is assembled, all you have to do is bake and serve.

- **Soup.** You can't beat soup after a chilly day working together outside. The options are limitless (chicken noodle, vegetable, beef stew, potato and sausage, minestrone, tomato, etc.). If you want to get extra fancy, pair your soup selection with biscuits or crusty bread. (Homemade rolls can be frozen and quickly reheated for the times you need bread in a hurry.)

- **Charcuterie spreads.** These sound fancy, but are a last-minute lifesaver. Simply set out a variety of cheeses, meats, and crackers and let your guests serve themselves buffet-style. You can also add in olives, pickles, hummus, chips, salsa, sliced fruits, or random veggies from the fridge or garden. Try displaying the spread on a variety of wooden cutting boards if you're so inclined. Otherwise, just stick it on a platter and call it good.

Stone Soup Suppers

One of my favorite stories as a kid was "Stone Soup." It's a classic European folktale of hungry travelers who arrive in a village looking for a meal. Since the villagers' food supply is running low, they are hesitant to offer anything to the strangers. So the travelers come up with a clever idea: they'll make stone soup. They offer to provide the stones if each villager can spare a meager ingredient from their pantry. One by one, the people offer a handful of carrots, a few potatoes, a head of cabbage, and a sprinkling of salt. In the end, the meager contributions come together to form the most magnificent stew. And it all started with a pot of stones.

This old story has an important lesson in our modern world—humble contributions can add up in impressive ways. Gatherings don't have to be major productions, nor does one single person always need to carry the load.

Since my local friends and I all live far from the grocery store, we regularly practice stone-soup-style meals. "Anyone want to get together for taco night? I have tortillas!" the text thread often begins. A few minutes later, someone will respond, "I have a pound of ground beef thawing in the fridge," followed by someone else offering shredded lettuce, a bag of cheese, or a tub of sour cream. It's rare that one of us has all the ingredients for a taco feast or spaghetti night, but when we come together, we can usually pull off some impressive spreads. Even if you live close to the store, try this idea with your own group of friends. It removes the pressure of "entertaining" and instead makes get-togethers an impromptu, stress-free, collaborative affair.

Don't Shy Away from Uncomfortable

When groups of humans come together, there will be rifts. It's a problem as old as time. However, what's not as old as time is our modern ability to silo ourselves into ultrahomogenous groups. This is a symptom of social media culture that's creating division at a dizzying pace.

You eat a different diet than me? UNFRIEND! You voted for a different candidate? BLOCKED! And of course, algorithms only make it worse by showing us the things with which we agree. Before long, we find ourselves in echo chambers of ideas and opinions that never challenge our perceptions. And we don't even know it's happening.

But in a real-life community, escaping from uncomfortable viewpoints isn't as easy. And that's a *good* thing. Being confronted with those different from us offers the opportunity to compromise, negotiate, and problem-solve. This makes us better humans.

One of the most seductive aspects of social media is its ability to eliminate the risky parts of relationships. Communicating through texting and apps quells our fears of saying the wrong thing or finding ourselves in the middle of an awkward moment. When we type instead of talk, we can avoid uncomfortable open-ended conversations and edit our words until they are just right. I'm as guilty of this as anyone. More than once I've opted to text a response instead of saying it in person because the former felt less scary. But it's this very feature that is contributing to the death of meaningful connection and is ultimately leaving us lonely. In *Reclaiming Conversation*, Sherry Turkle writes that the most endangered kind of conversation is "the kind in which you listen intently to another person and expect that he or she is listening to you; where a discussion can go off on a tangent and circle back; where something unexpected can be discovered about a person or an idea."

When we hypercurate our words and our responses, we miss out on the chance to make discoveries about each other. While several of my friendships have begun on social media, none of them truly blossomed until we had a chance to sit eyeball to eyeball and talk. When I'm sitting across the table from someone, I can read their body language. I can feel their energy. I can tell if what I'm saying *really* resonates with them, or if they're just being polite. And try as we might, it's impossible to communicate those nuances with emojis, comments, and thumbs-ups.

We *need* these imperfect conversational interactions to unclutter our minds, even when we might say the wrong thing. We need the chance to sit in the awkward pauses, to explore topics in rambling, uncurated, and unedited discussions, to look each other in the eye, to build empathy, and to forge bonds in the imperfect moments. And it all starts with making space for these messy moments of connection.

And nope. Regardless of what type of community you hope to develop, you won't like everyone. Nor will everyone like you. You're bound to rub someone the wrong way, and vice versa. But when we can sit with this discomfort and resolve conflict, instead of running away, it strengthens both our groups and us. There's enough division out there already. Therefore, I can't think of anything more old-fashioned than *not* siloing ourselves with perfectly like-minded people. Cultivate relationships with people different than you and see what happens. You don't have to be twins to be friends.

Host an Old-Fashioned Dinner Party

We're used to making our own fun out here on the homestead. Living in a place with nothing has been the ultimate gift in teaching us to think outside of the box when it comes to entertainment. Here are a few of my favorite ideas that you can use no matter where you live.

- **Start soup night.** Invite each attendee to bring a different variety of soup. You provide bowls, rolls, and corn bread. This works especially well for autumn-themed get-togethers.

- **Host Friendsgiving.** Sometimes family isn't available for holiday celebrations, so host "Friendsgiving" or "Friendsmas" instead. Gather up any friends that may be spending the holiday alone and make a new set of traditions.

- **Build a bonfire.** The primal nature of a burning flame draws us in, relaxes us, and gives us something to focus on. So, plan your evening around a firepit or bonfire. Cook hot dogs (or other campfire food) over the open flame, then finish with marshmallows and s'mores.

- **Get fancy.** There aren't a lot of fancy restaurants in our area, so occasionally we host "fancy supper night" with our friends. We find childcare for the evening, and one person is elected to host. We work together to come up with a fancier-than-usual meal plan (filled with things we'd never bring to a gathering with children), dress in our nicest clothes, and gather for a classy, candlelit supper.

- **Host a home concert.** Have friends with musical talent? String up lights in your backyard or garage, set up chairs, whip up some hors d'oeuvres, and host an intimate concert for your friend circle.

- **Hold a workout party.** This has only happened once

so far, but it was such a blast, I have to include it. One frigid evening in February, we hosted a glow-in-the-dark Zumba night here on our homestead. We asked a good friend who is a certified instructor to come teach the class in our shop, which we outfitted with disco balls and music speakers. Our entire friend group—men, women, children, and babies—completed the routine (well, mostly—some of us spent the bulk of the workout laughing hysterically). Afterward, we all collapsed in a pile and ate tacos. It was glorious.

- **Go with a theme.** Themes make planning get-togethers even easier. Focus on a certain decade (the 1920s or 1970s are always popular) and fill your evening with period-appropriate food and activities. If you have homestead-minded friends, host "home-grown" night when each person brings a dish featuring an ingredient they grew themselves. Or focus on a particular style of cuisine, such as Italian or Mexican. The sky's the limit.

Let Go of Perfect

My social life became much more fulfilling when I stopped waiting for my house to be clean and my menu plan to be dialed in before inviting people over. Your house doesn't need to be polished and you don't need a five-star meal to start fostering connection with those around you. Keep staples on hand that allow you to throw together quick meals, or use the stone soup approach. The kinds of friendships where no one bats an eye when you show up wearing workout clothes with messy hair are the best kind, anyway. The purpose of get-togethers like these is to foster connection and relationship—not to impress the neighbors. If you burn the lasagna or the campfire gets rained out, it's okay. Sometimes, these snafus end up being even more memorable than an event that turns out perfectly. Laugh and move on. And nothing says you must always host in your home. Parks or other community spaces make great meeting areas that require zero housecleaning beforehand. The more you're willing to let yourself be seen as you truly are, the faster you'll build real, lasting community.

Homespun Gift-Giving

Whether you need an idea for a housewarming present or a holiday or birthday gift, try one of these homemade options rather than reaching for something from the store.

- Homemade candles in a unique jar wrapped in ribbon (see the tutorial on page 153).

- Packets of heirloom seeds (or seeds you saved from your garden) paired with growing instructions and cute garden tools.

- A jar of sourdough starter. Print out instructions for using it and tie them to the jar with a ribbon and a wooden spoon.

- Homemade lip balms (page 156), salves (page 167), or bath scrubs.

- From-scratch mixes. Food is always a welcome gift. Make homemade hot cocoa or chai mixes, DIY cookie or brownie mix, or a collection of spice mixes packaged in attractive jars.

Lessons from a Steer

It was a summer night in late July. We were at our town's weekly family softball game. These informal games are a new tradition started by a handful of people who saw the need for family activities and made it happen. The games are quaint and imperfect, with frequent interruptions by small children—and they've been a massive success. Everyone gets a chance to play, regardless of age or experience level, while the rest of us snack on concessions served out of the red-and-white shed on the side of the field.

That night, I was perched on the edge of a picnic table, working on a plate of nachos as I shared my concern over my daughter Mesa's 4-H project with the people sitting next to me. Our county fair was only two weeks away, and her steer was still underweight. If he didn't gain quickly, she wouldn't be able to sell him at the annual sale, which is the culmination of a year's worth of hard work. A few friends offered suggestions, which I gladly took, before loading my tired, sweaty kids into the car and heading home.

Early the next morning, I got a text message. A friend offered to bring over some special feed to boost the steer's weight. "No charge," she said. "Just take it!" A few hours later, my phone rang. A rancher friend had overheard our conversation and had taken it upon himself to call up the superintendent of beef projects at the fair and gather some ideas. He shared what he had learned and offered his own advice gleaned from decades of feeding cattle. Over the next few weeks, various people checked up on the steer's progress and offered their well-wishes. In the end, her steer sailed past the weight minimum, and Mesa had a successful sale.

In those moments, in something as silly as a steer's weight, I was once again reminded of the sacredness of building connection. Make no mistake—it's messy sometimes. There will be hurt feelings and misunderstandings, gossip will circulate, and discouragement may feel formidable when certain challenges arise. But it's still worth it—I promise. Even when it feels like your efforts are in vain, and even when it takes longer than you had hoped. You're creating something meaningful that can never be achieved by merely clicking "like" on a Facebook post. Although my experience has been in our quirky Wyoming town, the community waiting for *your* gifts and passions might be your neighborhood, your apartment complex, your church community, your PTA, or your homeschool group. Building community will require all the intention and grit you can muster, but it's an old-fashioned practice that always pays off.

Old-Fashioned Action Steps

- Keep your phone off the table during meals.

- Start noticing the times when you pick up your phone to avoid awkward silences. Practice creating conversation during those moments instead.

- Schedule time each month when you can engage with your community in new ways. This might be attending town council meetings, joining various clubs, participating in community service activities, or just inviting someone new to lunch or coffee.

- Practice the art of true listening.

- The next time you have a big project on the to-do list, invite friends over to help.

- Plan a bonfire, get ingredients for s'mores, and tell your friends to come over.

- Create a list of meals you can make on the fly with standard pantry ingredients. These will reduce your stress level on the occasions someone unexpectedly drops by for supper.

- Initiate a stone soup meal with a group of friends.

- Designate "TV nights" and leave the rest of the evenings open for community-building activities.

- Wave and smile. Always.

- If there's something you've been wishing your community offered, take the steps to get the ball rolling.

CHAPTER 12

The Next Frontier

A turn-of-the-century church and cemetery can still be seen nestling in the fields east of our town. They stand as a remnant from Iowa Flats, one of many satellite communities that formed near Chugwater back in the day. Built in 1910, this humble white chapel appears out of nowhere as you drive across a patchwork of wheat fields and native prairie grass. After passing several abandoned homesteads and wondering if you might have taken the wrong turn, there it is. The steeple pierces the horizon, a silent testament to the vibrant, resolute people who lived on this prairie long before asphalt roads and power poles conquered the land.

One minister wrote of the rural families he served here, including one family that traveled eleven miles each way by wagon to attend the Sunday services. They packed a lunch, loaded up their eight children, and left right after morning chores to ensure they would arrive in time. But while the little church once formed the epicenter of life for this community, it now stands empty, except for a handful of holiday celebrations and the occasional funeral.

The thermometer registered well below zero the day I drove to the church. As I walked inside the unheated sanctuary, my foggy breath mixed with the golden light streaming through wavy glass windows. Old places like these carry a special sort of energy, almost as if the people who were here before left a bit of themselves behind. Proof of their existence is evident in the scratched floor planks, the railings worn smooth by decades of hands, the patinaed metal shaped by long-ago craftsmen, and the nostalgic scents that linger in the air. The veil of time feels thinner in these places, as history beckons us to reach out and touch it.

As I walked across the creaky wooden floors and sat in one of the cast-iron pews, I thought about the century's worth of people who have crossed that same threshold. While they might have arrived by wagon and I came by SUV, we're more alike than we are different. They were homesteaders, townspeople, cowboys, and farmers—some of whom still have descendants living in this area. They had dreams, and goals, and a desire to scratch a life from this unforgiving landscape, just like we do today.

They sat in those same church chairs and balanced plates of potluck food on their knees while they hollered at their children running up and down the aisles, just like we do today.

They gathered in that little sanctuary to sing songs of worship and to grieve their lost loved ones, just like we do today.

They filled the walls of that place with laughter, sadness, lively debate, and whispers of fear and struggle, just like we do today.

They discussed wars and pandemics, calving woes and droughts, just like we do today.

I think this is why I love old things and old places so much. They remind me that I'm not the first, and that I won't be the last. Thinking of that little church standing on the prairie through the Spanish flu epidemic, the Great Depression, two World Wars, the Blizzard of '49, the cyclical droughts, and the swirling tornadoes is strangely reassuring. This sacred space has seen it all, and yet it remains—strong and steady.

the real things haven't changed.

We're not the first generation to face uncertainty and upheaval in our lifetime. It's an inescapable part of this beautiful yet messy human experience. But I wholeheartedly agree with Laura Ingalls Wilder who wrote, "...so many changes have made living and learning easier. But the real things haven't changed. It is still best to be honest and truthful; to make the most of what we have; to be happy with simple pleasures; and have courage when things go wrong." Good things always last.

Throughout each of these chapters, we've explored a different way that our rush for progress has led us to places we never intended to go. Time and time again, a desire for ease has led us astray. And our next challenge looms on the horizon. Wendell Berry imagined that the "next great division of the world will be between people who wish to live as creatures and people who wish to live as machines." And the age of the human machine is rapidly approaching.

As our society becomes increasingly obsessed with the artificial, I can't shake the sense that we're standing on the edge of another precipice. Will we soon choose to spend more time in virtual reality than the real world? Will corporations convince us that food developed in test tubes or 3D printers is better than food grown in soil? Will artificial intelligence shake the foundations of life as we know it?

Only time will tell.

At the turn of the century, it was fashionable for women homesteaders to share reflections from life on the Plains with newspapers and magazines. I seem to be falling into their ranks. Yet while my predecessors often wrote to convince their eastern counterparts to move west, I'm advocating for a different kind of move—a move toward time-honored ideas that will keep us grounded in a world that spins ever faster. I champion a shift from synthetic, to real; from artificial, to alive; from sedated, to aware; from consumer, to producer; and from mindless, to meaningful.

Because no matter how sophisticated we may become, we're still flesh and blood. We are biological beings with ancient compositions. We're not mere impostors in this natural world, *we're a part of it*. And when we sink into those truths, everything aligns. The very fibers of our being awaken, and we can then experience what it means to be fully alive.

This book is a rallying cry. In my mind's eye, I picture people like you and me carefully packing these timeless principles in our suitcases and gripping them tightly while we charge headfirst into the unknown. I don't know what the future holds or how the world will change in the coming decades. But I do know these old-fashioned principles will hold true, just like they always have.

But before our time together ends, I have a few more ideas to pack into your suitcase. As you implement the principles from this book, you are bound to face challenges. Although struggles vary, there are several that seem to arise for almost all of us. I want to leave you with my best tools for overcoming these inevitable roadblocks.

Beware the Stories

Sometimes our opposition will come from the outside, but more often, it comes from within. As you embark on your old-fashioned on purpose journey, all the best excuses will be waiting right under the surface. The words *"I can't because…"* will erupt from your lips. And whatever roadblock you're facing at that moment will do its best to convince you that it is unscalable. So we must be ready to go into battle, sometimes with ourselves.

One of my favorite questions to ask at this point of the process is, "What is the story I'm telling myself right now?" We all have stories, many of which we have created to protect ourselves over the years. However, these very stories often prevent us from moving toward the things we really want. And they almost always lead us back to an external, passive state in which we see ourselves as helpless. I've told myself many self-limiting stories over the years:

"We bought a homestead in the wrong place."

"I have nothing to contribute to this town."

"I can't exercise because it's too cold outside."

"Our income is stuck where it is."

"People like me don't do things like *that*."

None of those stories were true, but they sure felt like it at the time. When we expose these stories to light, it gives us the opportunity to reframe them into statements of power, instead of helplessness. Such as:

"This location is challenging, but I'm going to learn so much by growing food in this climate."

"There isn't an obvious place I fit in this town, which means I have an opportunity to create something new."

"If I can't exercise outside, I'll try a new workout in the living room."

"Money will flow as I provide value in new ways."

"Why *not* me?"

Remember—don't believe everything you think. At least not without testing it first.

Don't Wait for Permission

Another phenomenon that arises at the cusp of a new adventure is that we start looking for other people to eliminate obstacles and give us permission to move forward. We hope that maybe, just maybe, if we wait long enough, someone will show up and save the day. But that's not how it works. A truth I've learned the hard way: No one cares about your life and your results as much as you. Not your politicians, or your family, or your pastor, or your boss, or your friends, or your coworkers. They might all be wonderful people, but your results are ultimately up to you.

your results are ultimately up to you.

When we wait for someone else to make the first move or give us permission, our growth comes to a screeching halt. And it allows outside voices to influence us in negative ways. One of my biggest disappointments of adulthood is that it's almost always easier to find people who will encourage you to play small than people who will cheer you on to greatness. Anytime Christian and I have decided to do something big in our life, there are plenty of well-meaning people ready to encourage us to *not* take action. *("Oh dear...that's going to be a lot of work." "You have a nice job. Are you sure you want to start your own business?" "You know you can buy that at the grocery store, right?" "Do you know how much easier your life would be if your kids were in public school?")*

When you're fighting your own internal stories, these comments can be disorienting. Often, people don't realize they're being discouraging. Sometimes they're simply projecting their own fears onto you, or perhaps your action could be making them uncomfortable because they know they aren't taking action in their own lives. But regardless—be ready. You can nod and smile, and then follow your gut and keep on trucking.

Be Ready for the Resistance

For as long as I can remember, I've struggled with inner opposition. I thought I was the only one, but it turns out we all share this internal critic. Author Steven Pressfield calls this struggle the Resistance. It's sure to show up whenever we choose "any act that rejects immediate gratification in favor of long-term growth, health, or integrity." It's that little voice that tells you to dial it back, to not risk it, to stay in your lane, and to avoid making waves. It hates risk, formulates world-class excuses, and will sabotage you at every turn.

Resistance is the antithesis of creativity.

Resistance is the thing standing between you and what you've always wanted.

Resistance is hell-bent on keeping you in your comfort zone.

And Resistance is keeping you from trying some of the ideas in this book.

But as formidable as it may seem, Resistance is part of all of us. It's normal, but no less damaging. And once you can recognize it for what it is, you can beat it.

With all the over-the-top projects Christian and I have undertaken over the years, it might seem like we're immune to the fear bombs Resistance likes to toss our way. But I promise, we're not. I'm scared to death every single time we embark on a new adventure. The fear of the unknown never goes away. We've just learned how to deal with it.

Whether you're speaking onstage to thousands of people, starting a new job, or busting out the pressure canner for the first time, you can push through the fear. "The amateur believes he must first overcome his fear; then he can do his work," writes Pressfield. "The professional knows that fear can never be overcome. He knows there is no such thing as a fearless warrior or a dread-free artist."

The key is sorting through those fear signals. Sometimes, fear keeps us safe. If you're walking down a dark street at night and feel uneasy, it's wise to pay attention to those feelings. The problem is that our brain's fear response can't tell the difference between real danger and made-up danger. It shoots out the same chemicals whether we're being chased by wild dogs or starting up a new business venture. The former is justified. The latter? Probably not.

So how do we tell the difference?

The answer lies in our gut.

Our intuition is one of the most powerful tools we have. But in our comfortable, modern habitats, its still, small voice is easily drowned out. Thankfully, the more we tune in, the louder it becomes.

The fear I feel when I'm standing next to a coiled rattlesnake is different than the fear I feel when I'm on the verge of something amazing. Paying attention to those small differences is crucial. Yes, the fear is still there with the latter, but there's also a feeling of excitement, a sense of knowing that I'm on the cusp of something good.

To help sort through all the nerves, I always ask myself this question:

"Jill, if you DON'T do this, how will you feel?"

Then I listen.

If I feel a true sense of relief at the thought of opting out, this often means the venture isn't meant for me, or that I was feeling pushed toward it based on other people's expectations.

But if I feel a *little* relief (because I don't have to do the scary thing) but mostly sadness at the thought of letting myself down, I have my answer.

It's go time.

Putting the World Back in Order

I believe the greatest thing I can do for someone is to show them something is possible. Sometimes that means teaching people how to pressure-can beef stew, and sometimes it means helping them break through their self-imposed beliefs.

Thoreau famously wrote, "The mass of men lead lives of quiet desperation." I believe adopting an old-fashioned on purpose life is the first step in waking up from this state. The most meaningful, heart-pounding moments of knowing have come when I'm chasing these retro skills. It's never easy, but it's always worth it.

Perhaps some of the topics in this book have helped to shine a light on areas you'd like to address in your life. Maybe you've felt disconcerted by the research about kids no longer playing outside, or the mind-boggling amount of plastic we throw away each year, or the artificial environments we live in, or the realization of how many chemicals are hiding in our food.

Whatever you're feeling, consider these stirrings your call to adventure. (And yes, for our purposes, digging up a piece of your backyard so you can plant some carrots or making a piecrust for the first time qualifies as adventure.)

Taking action doesn't have to be monumental or drastic. Often those first steps are tiny and halting. But action is always the key. It is the path to responsibility, the antidote for fear, and the answer to dissatisfaction. And while some of the problems you may identify might seem overwhelming or even impossible, let their magnitude spur you onward. As Viktor Frankl wrote, "When we are no longer able to change a situation [...] we are challenged to change ourselves."

If we want to change anything—our planet, our society, or ourselves—it starts with us. I can't promise your results will be grand or sweeping, but they will be something. And even if no one else notices, *you'll know*, and that's all that matters.

And this is why I write these words with optimism. People are waking up. They want *more*. And not more in terms of shiny possessions and more stuff. They're hunting for more meaning, more purpose, and more fulfillment. *And it's time*. While there is certainly work to be done, it is *good work*. Despite some of the gloomy statistics I've uncovered in my research, hope remains. Because while this book doesn't contain all the answers, I do know this: the person who is cooking in their kitchen, growing a little herb garden, spending time in nature, feeding the soil in their backyard, taking ownership of their life, choosing to do hard things, raising resilient kids, cultivating their communities, or relishing in the creative process is bound to be more happy, whole, and balanced. And that is no small thing.

So dear reader, as you forge ahead into these old-fashioned ways,
May your garden be bountiful,
Your kitchen alive with scrumptious foods,
Your days filled with meaningful challenges,
Your hands covered in happy calluses,
Your intuition guiding loud and clear,
Your resolve strong and steady,
And most of all, may you feel more alive than ever before.

Peace, Love, and Mason Jars,
Jill

Quick-Start Garden Guide

When starting a garden, it's easy to get caught up in endless re-search. And sooner versus later, you'll find yourself growing a crop of stress instead of squash. I've found that action is the very best cure for overwhelm (in both gardening and life), so consider this your gardening action guide. Start with the basics, get those seeds in the ground, and the rest will fall in place.

The first step in launching a garden is determining your frost dates. A simple Google search (try "frost dates for [your zip code]") should yield the information you need. Take note of your last spring frost date as well as your first fall frost date. This will give you an idea of the length of your growing season. Next, use the seed-starting information in this guide to map out when you'll plant each of your seeds and whether they'll be started indoors or directly sown.

Direct sowing means you'll plant the seed directly in your garden soil. This method is best for veggies that don't trans-plant well. Starting seeds indoors means you'll plant the seeds in small containers and keep them inside under lights for four to ten weeks before your last frost date. This is the best method for plants that take longer to reach maturity, since it gives them a head start before they move to the great outdoors.

Temp It!

Along with knowing your frost dates, it's wise to watch soil temperatures when sowing seeds or transplanting seedlings into your garden. If it's a particularly cold year, it may take longer than normal for your seeds to germinate. Ideal temperatures vary according to the variety of plant, but a soil temperature of 60–65°F is a safe bet for the most varieties.

How and When to Plant Vegetable Seeds

Beans
Best Planting Method: Direct sow.
Time Frame: Anytime after the last frost date, when the soil is at least 50°F.
Notes: Beans do not transplant well, which is why they thrive with direct sowing. Consider soaking the bean seeds in warm water for a few hours before planting to speed germination.

Beets
Best Planting Method: Direct sow.
Time Frame: Two weeks before the last frost date.
Notes: One beet "seed" is multiple seeds, so expect to thin the plants as they mature. Thankfully, beet roots and beet greens are both delicious and can be eaten many ways.

Broccoli
Best Planting Method: Start indoors or direct sow.
Time Frame: Start inside six to eight weeks before the last frost date or direct sow in early spring as soon as the soil is workable.
Notes: Set broccoli seedlings outside when the plants are five to six inches tall, or approximately two to three weeks before

the last frost date. Broccoli is cold-hardy and handles light frost with no issue.

Brussels Sprouts
Best Planting Method: Start indoors or direct sow.
Time Frame: Start seeds inside six to eight weeks before your last spring frost date. You can also direct sow seeds four months before your first fall frost date.
Notes: Plant seedlings in the garden after the danger of spring frost has passed and the seedlings have their first true leaves. Brussels sprouts take a long time to mature, so expect a late fall or early winter harvest.

Cabbage
Best Planting Method: Start indoors or direct sow.
Time Frame: Start seeds inside six to eight weeks before your last spring frost date or direct sow in early spring when the soil is workable.
Notes: Transplant cabbage seedlings when they are three to four inches tall, or two to three weeks before the last spring frost date. Like broccoli, cabbage prefers cooler temps and doesn't mind a bit of frost.

Carrots
Best Planting Method: Direct sow.
Time Frame: Sow carrot seeds three to four weeks before the last spring frost date. You can also stagger plantings throughout the spring and early summer for a longer-lasting harvest.
Notes: Carrots can take up to two weeks to germinate, so be sure to keep their soil moist after planting.

Cauliflower
Best Planting Method: Start indoors.
Time Frame: Start seeds four to six weeks before your last frost date.

Notes: Transplant seedlings outside when the seedlings are five to six inches tall. Cauliflower can handle light frosts without damage to the plants.

Corn
Best Planting Method: Direct sow.
Time Frame: Plant seeds directly in the soil one to two weeks after the last spring frost date, when the soil temperature is at least 60°F.
Notes: Corn is a heavy feeder and requires rich soil, so be sure to amend with plenty of compost.

Cucumbers
Best Planting Method: Direct sow.
Time Frame: Sow cucumbers in the garden one to two weeks after the last frost date.
Notes: Cucumbers are sensitive to cold, so if you're having a cooler spring, wait to plant them until the soil temperature reaches 65–70°F. Cucumbers also like to climb, so giving them a trellis to grip while they grow makes harvesting easier.

Lettuce and Greens
Best Planting Method: Direct sow or start inside.
Time Frame: I prefer to direct sow lettuce seeds since they grow so quickly (wait until soil temps are at least 45°F). However, if you'd like a jump-start on your harvest, lettuce can be started indoors. You can start indoor seeds up to ten weeks before the last frost date in spring. Transplant the seedlings as soon as the soil can be worked in the early spring.
Notes: Lettuce bolts (goes to seed) in warm weather, so it grows best in the early spring or early fall.

Peas
Best Planting Method: Direct sow.

Time Frame: Sow seeds outside four to five weeks before the last frost date, when soil temperatures are at least 45°F.

Notes: To extend your harvest, stagger plantings so you can have a continual harvest of peas throughout the growing season.

Peppers

Best Planting Method: Start indoors.

Time Frame: Start seeds inside eight to ten weeks before the last frost date.

Notes: Peppers are slow to sprout, so don't be concerned if they take a week or two to pop from the soil. Peppers also prefer to be warm, so keep seed trays at least 70–75°F during germination. Wait to transplant peppers outside until your outdoor temperatures are averaging 65°F during the day and 55°F at night.

Potatoes

Best Planting Method: Direct sow.

Time Frame: Plant seed potatoes two to three weeks before the last frost date. Hard frosts will damage potato foliage but not the underground portions.

Notes: You can purchase seed potatoes from your local garden store. To stretch your seed, cut larger potatoes into two to three chunks, ensuring there is at least two "eyes" per piece. Allow the cut edges to dry overnight at room temperature before planting.

Pumpkins

Best Planting method: Start indoors or direct sow.

Time Frame: Start pumpkins indoors two to four weeks before your last frost date. Transplant the seedlings outdoors after all frost danger has passed and soil temperatures are at least 65°F. If direct sowing pumpkin seeds, plant them outdoors one to two weeks after your last frost date.

Notes: Pumpkins love rich soil that's amended with lots of compost.

Radishes
Best Planting Method: Direct sow.
Time Frame: Sow seeds as soon as the soil is workable in the spring, which is usually two to four weeks before your last frost date.
Notes: Depending on the variety, some radish plantings are ready to harvest in as little as twenty-two days. Since they will become bitter and often bolt in hot weather, you may want to consider succession planting. Direct sow some radish seeds as early as you can in the spring, and then continue planting groups of seeds up to the last frost date in the fall.

Winter or Summer Squash
Best Planting Method: Direct sow.
Time Frame: Direct sow seeds outdoors one to two weeks after your last frost date, or when the soil temperature is around 60°F.
Notes: Squash is another heavy feeder that appreciates soil that is well amended with compost or well-aged manure.

Tomatoes
Best Planting Method: Start indoors.
Time Frame: Start seeds indoors six to eight weeks before your last spring frost date.
Notes: Do not transplant outdoors until all danger of frost has passed and soil temperatures are at least 60°F. Tomatoes are very sensitive to transplanting. Minimize transplant shock by slowly acclimating tomatoes to the outside world. To do this, place the seedlings outside for increasing amounts of time each day over a weeklong period, starting with a few hours in a sheltered spot and gradually increasing the exposure to include full sun and wind.

The Top Five Biggest Seed-Starting Mistakes

1. *Choosing the Wrong Potting Mix*
While some gardeners prefer the finer texture of seed-starting

mixes, I usually start seeds in a regular potting mix. However, there's one caveat: be sure to invest in a quality potting mix. In recent years, lower-quality potting soils have caused major issues for gardeners since they don't contain enough nitrogen to sustain plant life. You can avoid this by spending a little more on a reputable brand. Trust me—it's worth the investment!

2. Chilly Seeds

Seeds crave warmth to germinate effectively. In the past, I've used a small space heater in my chilly basement storage room where I start my seedlings. However, I recently switched to inexpensive seed mats, and the speedier germination times and increased growth have been well worth the investment. Shoot for a temp of 75–90°F for optimal germination. *(Some seeds will sprout at cooler temps, but for the majority, warmer is better.)*

3. Not Enough Water

While mature plants can handle occasionally dry soil, it's the kiss of death for germinating seeds and baby plants. Make sure you're checking the soil in your seed trays every day for moisture. I place pans under my seedlings that allow me to water from the bottom. This helps the seedlings absorb just the right amount of water and develops stronger root systems in the process.

4. Skimping on Light

Starting seedlings in a south-facing window is a lovely idea, but it rarely provides enough light to grow healthy seedlings. Full-spectrum LED lights are a worthy investment that will pay dividends year after year. I hang LED shop lights from metal baker's racks. I can drop the lights close to the seedlings (about four to six inches from the tops of the plants) when they are first sprouting, then raise the lights as the plants grow (if plants have to stretch for light, they'll become spindly and weak). Aim for sixteen to eighteen hours of light per day for seedlings (more mature plants only need about twelve hours).

5. Skip the Egg Cartons and Yogurt Cups
I know… I'm breaking some hearts here. While I appreciate the desire to recycle and reuse, seed-starting trays are one area where it makes sense to invest a little cash. I've tried many different containers over the years, but my favorites are sturdy, plastic forty-cell trays that can be reused year after year.

One of the best parts of gardening is how it's so customizable according to your space and goals. For those who aspire to grow enough produce to sustain their household, here are my best recommendations for kicking your gardening up a notch.

Your Perfect Planting Planner

You have the seeds, you've mapped out your garden plot, and you find yourself wrestling with that familiar question: How *much* should I plant?

This question can feel daunting, especially when you're first starting out. There is no golden formula for planting the perfect number of veggies, but I can help point you in the right direction with this easy guide.

With a little forethought and some simple math, you can feel confident in knowing exactly how much to plant this year.

A Few Considerations Before You Start:

- Do your best to guess how many pounds of each food your family consumes in a week. It won't be exact, but close counts.

- Use the equations to give yourself a starting point.

- If you plan to preserve food (canning, drying, freezing, fermenting), plant extra.

- If your garden space is limited, focus on the foods you eat the most and don't sweat the rest.

The Formula:

How Much to Plant

Pounds we eat weekly x Number of weeks = Pounds needed

Number of pounds needed ÷ Pounds per plant* = Number of plants I need

*A quick Google search should help you estimate the amount of harvest you can expect from each type of food you plant.

Here's a specific example so you can see how this works.

Each year, I aim to grow and can enough tomato sauce for an entire year. I know we consume around one quart of sauce each week and that there are roughly five pounds of tomatoes in each quart of sauce.

So, my tomato equation looks like this:

Five pounds eaten weekly x fifty-two weeks in a year = two hundred and sixty pounds.

Two hundred and sixty pounds divided by twelve pounds (on average) produced by each plant = I know I need to plant roughly twenty-two plants (and I always plant a few extra to account for bugs, weather, or other issues).

Keep in mind that this process doesn't have to be exact, but it's an excellent way to begin to map out your growing spaces.

And if you're brand-new to growing and still unsure how much to plant, this list is a solid place to start:

How Many Plants Do I Need?

Asparagus: 10–15 per person
Beans (bush): 10–15 per person
Beans (pole): 2–5 per person
Beets: 10–20 per person
Broccoli: 3–5 per person
Brussels Sprouts: 3–5 per person
Cabbage: 2–4 per person
Carrots: 20–30 per person
Cauliflower: 3–5 per person
Celery: 3–5 per person
Chard: 3–5 per person
Collards: 5 per person
Corn: 15–25 per person
Cucumbers: 3–5 per person
Eggplant: 1–3 per person
Garlic: 10–15 per person
Greens/Lettuce: 5–6 per person
Melons: 2–3 per person
Onions: 15–20 per person
Peas: 10–20 per person
Peppers: 3–5 per person
Potatoes: 15–20 per person
Radishes: 20–30 per person
Squashes: 2–3 per person
Sweet Potatoes: 5–10 per person
Tomatoes: 3–5 per person
Turnips: 10–20 per person

No-Stress Sourdough Guide

Flour and water. That's all it takes to make your own sour-dough starter.

How hard could it be?

Well, it depends on whom you ask. And unfortunately, the more you research the more confusing it gets. There are levains and bigas, grams versus cups, high hydration versus low hydration, not to mention the whole flour conversation: Should you use all-purpose flour, bread flour, whole-wheat flour, rye, spelt, or heritage grains?

Suddenly you find yourself with a Google-induced headache. So which is the right way? Well, they all are. It just depends on what you want. Sourdough can be a highly skilled artisanal hobby, or it can be a simple kitchen pursuit. Neither option is better than the other—it just depends on YOU.

My Sourdough Journey

Like many of you, sourdough captured my imagination at the beginning of my quest for a more old-fashioned life.

I started my first sourdough culture on October 11, 2010. (For some unknown reason, I made a note of it in one of my kitchen binders.)

It felt wholesome, quaint, and exciting to swirl flour and water in a jar and dream of what it could become.

But the romance faded when I pulled my first loaf from the oven. It was a brick. *A crumbly, inedible brick.*

And the more I tried, the worse it got.

I made loaves that were too sour to eat. Loaves that refused to rise. Loaves so dry you choked when you ate them. I also killed sourdough starters in spectacular ways—I accidentally cooked them, neglected them for so long in the fridge they gave up, and left them on the counter unattended for months (pro tip: when it has maggots, it's too far gone).

I became so frustrated that I stopped sourdough completely for several years. I felt like a homesteading failure.

Until one day I decided to give it one last try. I'm so glad I did.

Because I finally cracked the "code," and we've been eating the most amazing sourdough loaves ever since.

In this guide, I'll share my no-stress method for sourdough, as well as the mistakes I made in those early years that sabotaged me.

Remember: my way isn't the only way, but it's taught hundreds of thousands of people to successfully bake sourdough loaves, so it's a great place to start.

The Benefits of Real Sourdough Bread

Why bother capturing wild yeast when you can buy commercial baker's yeast at the grocery store? I'm so glad you asked.

- Sourdough is a fermented food. As sourdough bread dough ferments, proteins are broken down into amino acids, so your digestive systems job becomes much easier.

- As a result, your body can snag more nutrients out of the bread since its easier to digest. Sometimes folks who have issues with regular bread can tolerate sourdough since it's "predigested" in a sense.

- This fermentation process also breaks down the phytates, or antinutrients, present in wheat. This allows your body to absorb more of the vitamins and minerals in the flour.

- It's really rewarding. Like I write about in *Old-Fashioned on Purpose*, retro skills like making sourdough are good for our brains and help us become more confident, capable humans.

What is a Sourdough Starter?

Sourdough is naturally leavened bread made with wild yeast captured from the air. It's the way people have made bread since the beginning of time. The commercial yeast that is so common today is a relatively recent invention.

Using a sourdough starter does not mean your bread has to be sour. In fact, many people who dislike sourdough bread from the grocery store find they prefer homemade sourdough since it's easier to control the flavor. (Also, much of the sourdough bread you find at the store isn't true sourdough. It's often made with regular yeast and has other ingredients like vinegar added to make it sour.)

A true sourdough starter does not require commercially bought yeast. It is made by combining flour and water and letting it sit for several days to either capture wild yeast in the air or to activate the wild yeast already in the flour.

Okay, enough of the pregame warm-up. Let's get started!

How to Make Your Own Starter

There are a million and one ways to make a sourdough starter. Though I've tried many techniques through the years, I always come back to this solid, dependable method.

You Will Need:
- All-purpose flour
- Non-chlorinated water (see note below)

Instructions

Step one: Mix ½ cup flour with ½ cup water in a quart-sized glass jar. Stir vigorously, loosely cover, and then let sit for twenty-four hours.

Step two: Add an additional ½ cup flour and ¼ cup water to the jar and stir vigorously. You want the starter to have the consistency of thick pancake batter. If it is too thick, add more water. If it's too thin, add more flour. Loosely cover and let sit for another twenty-four hours. You should begin to see bubbles in your starter at this point. If not, don't give up yet.

Step three: Discard half of the starter (regardless of whether you see bubbles), then feed again with ½ cup flour and ¼ cup water. Stir, loosely cover, and let sit twenty-four hours.

Keep repeating step three until the starter doubles within four to six hours of you feeding it. If you still aren't seeing any bubbles after several days of this process, it's probably best to dump it out and start over.

Once the starter is bubbly, active, and doubling consistently after each daily feeding, it's ready to use in recipes.

Sourdough Starter Notes:
- I usually start this process in a quart-sized mason jar and move to a half-gallon jar later if I need a lot of starter for making pancakes or lots of bread. Stick with glass or ceramic containers since plastic can give your starter off-flavors.

- If you like, other flours can be used to create your starter. Whole-wheat flours (especially freshly ground) often provide a jump-start since they contain more micro-organisms and nutrients.

- Chlorinated water can kill your starter. If you have chlorinated tap water, run it through a filter first. Or try boiling the water and letting it cool before proceeding with the recipe. (Boiling speeds up the evaporation of chlorine.) Bottled water is another option, although some varieties still contain chlorine, and there's no easy way to determine that.

How to Care for a Sourdough Starter

Storage for Frequent Use:
If you plan to use your starter every day (or every other day), it's probably best to keep it on the counter and feed it daily. To do this, discard half of the starter each day, then feed it a 1:1:1 ratio—1 part starter to 1 part water to 1 part flour (in weight).

You can get super technical and weigh this out with a scale, but I prefer to keep it simple. I usually discard all but about ½ cup of the starter and then feed it with 4 ounces flour (a scant 1 cup) and 4 ounces water (½ cup).

Storage for Intermittent Use:
If you'll only be using your sourdough once or twice a week (or less), you can keep it in the refrigerator. This will prevent you from having to feed it daily (and ultimately using a lot of flour!).

To transfer a starter to the fridge, first feed it as you normally would. Let it sit out for one hour, then pop it in the fridge (covered). It's best to continue to feed it weekly in the fridge if you aren't using it much. However, I will confess I've sorely neglected my starter for many weeks and even months and I was still able to salvage it.

To Wake Up a Cold Sourdough Starter:
To prepare a dormant sourdough starter for baking, bring it out of the refrigerator at least twenty-four hours before you need to use it. Discard half of the starter and feed it the 1:1:1 ratio explained above—1 part starter to 1 part water to 1 part flour (in weight).

Repeat this every twelve hours or until the sourdough starter is active and bubbles within four to six hours of feeding (this likely will take two to three rounds). If you need a larger quantity of starter for baking, or you're planning on a big baking day, bulk it up by skipping the discard step in each feeding.

Starter FAQs:

Why do I discard part of the sourdough starter?
At step three of the sourdough process, you will discard half of the starter when you feed it. This can seem weird and wasteful. However, if we don't discard some, we'll end up having to add more and more flour to make the ratio correct. Since we don't want to waste flour, it's less wasteful to discard part of the early sourdough starter. At this point in the process, the starter isn't super sour and it's not very fermented.

However, you don't have to throw your discard in the trash. Try using it for pancakes or waffles, feeding it to your chickens, or putting it in your compost pile. Once your starter is more active, you may not have to discard any since you'll be using it regularly.

When Can I Start Baking with My Starter?
There's nothing harder than waiting for a brand-new starter to

mature enough for baking. But the timing depends on what you want to make.

If you want to use the starter to make pancakes, quick breads, or other recipes that use another sort of leavening agent (like baking soda), you can use it right away (see the end of this guide for some of my favorite recipes).

If you want to use your starter to rise loaves of bread (or other recipes where the starter is the only leavening agent), you'll know it's ready when:

- It doubles in size within four to six hours of a feeding.

- There are lots of bubbles.

- The texture is fluffy and foamy.

- It has a pleasant, tangy aroma.

- If you place a teaspoon of starter in a cup of cool water, it floats on top.

Why isn't my starter bubbly yet?

You may feel panicky if you're not seeing bubbles by day four or five, but don't give up yet. Wait at least seven to ten days before you decide if your sourdough starter isn't active. (I've noticed there's often a lull in activity on days four through six.) Sometimes it just takes time.

Also consider the following factors:

- *Warmth.* If your kitchen is drafty or cool, move your starter to a warmer location.

- *Flour.* If you're not seeing bubbles after a week, try using a different variety or brand of flour.

- *Water.* If your water contains chlorine, it may be harming the organisms that give sourdough its bubbles.

If you're still not sure if your starter is active enough for baking, place 1 teaspoon of the starter in a cup of water. If it floats, you're good to go! If it sinks, it needs more time.

Should I buy a sourdough starter?

Generally, I just use the simple method mentioned above and skip the commercial sourdough starter packets. That said, there's nothing wrong with purchasing a starter culture if you like.

If you have a friend with a starter, you can grab a little bit of culture from them and use that instead of starting from scratch.

My sourdough starter is too watery or too thick. What do I do?

If your starter is too watery, add more flour at the next feeding. If it's too thick, add more water at your next feeding. I find a starter with the consistency of pancake batter works the best for me.

Why is my sourdough starter separating? Why does it have black liquid on top and/or clear liquid on bottom?

The black liquid on top of your starter is the waste product of the yeast in your starter. It's called hooch. When your starter has eaten up all of its food and wants more, it separates and hooch will appear.

When this happens, you can either discard the hooch or stir it back in, then feed as usual.

If you see clear liquid pooling underneath the flour layer of your starter, this simply means you need to change your starter feeding habits. Try feeding it more often, using different water, or using different flour.

Why is my sourdough starter pink or orange?

While sourdough starters can vary in color, pink or orange coloration isn't a good sign. This usually means the starter is starving and an undesirable bacterium (*Serratia marcescens*) is multiplying at a fast rate. *Serratia marcescens* exists in most sourdough cultures (starters are a colony of many types of yeast and bacteria) but when a starter isn't fed enough, *Serratia marcescens* will jump at the opportunity to take over.

If your starter has a *slight* pink tinge, try scraping the pink layer from the top, transferring the starter to a new jar, and feeding twice per day until it looks and smells normal again. However, if the starter is very pink (or very smelly), it's best to toss it and start over.

Gray or brownish hues are normal and not a cause for concern.

Why does my starter smell like alcohol or nail polish remover?

Like a pink or orange starter, an alcohol/nail polish remover aroma can indicate your starter needs more food. Try feeding it more frequently until it smells better.

Is it better to measure or weigh the sourdough ingredients?

Weighing the ingredients is best, but you can use either method. Personally, I've learned what my measuring cups look like when there's 4 ounces of flour and 4 ounces of water in them, so I usually just eyeball it.

However, if you are unsure, weighing each component offers more precision and peace of mind.

Is it normal to see a skin on your starter prior to feeding?

Sometimes. When my house is extra hot, the top layer of liquid evaporates more quickly, and my starter tends to dry out. If that happens, I just stir the skin back in. If it keeps happening and it's bothering you, cover your sourdough with a lid (instead of a cloth or paper towel) to lock in more moisture.

Why is my sourdough starter moldy?

Mold is generally caused from contamination in the flour or in the jar.

To avoid this, make sure you start with a very clean jar. If that doesn't help, try switching out your flour. It's possible that you are buying flour from a store where it is not properly stored, or something is wrong with that particular brand. Unfortunately, it's hard to salvage a moldy starter. If there's only a small amount of mold on top, you may be able to scoop out several tablespoons from the bottom of the jar. But in most cases, it's best to toss it and start over.

Do I have to feed my sourdough starter twice a day?

There are a million different ways to care for a sourdough starter, and some sourdough connoisseurs will recommend two or even three feedings a day. If you notice that your starter prefers more frequent feedings, that's perfectly fine.

If I need my starter to be very active, I will feed it twice a day. Other times if I'm not baking as much, I stick with one feeding every twenty-four hours.

What if my kitchen is too cold for my sourdough starter?

Sourdough prefers a warm environment. If your house is chilly, you may need to get creative to figure out how to keep it happy. If you have a woodstove, place the starter in the vicinity of the stove. The top of a refrigerator is another warm place in a kitchen.

You can also keep your starter next to your oven in the kitchen, as the radiant heat will help keep your starter happy. Leaving it inside the oven with a light on is another option.

However, that one scares me a little bit because you might accidentally turn on your oven and kill your starter (which I have done...).

Can I make a gluten-free starter?

Yes! It's possible, although I must admit I don't have much expertise in this area. However, a quick Google search will yield dozens of recipes.

Can I use freshly ground flour in my starter?

Absolutely! If you have a grain mill, this is a fantastic option. Many people report that their sourdough starters love freshly ground flour, while other people say that freshly ground flour needs to age about five days before using it for best results. I'd try both and see which your starter prefers.

How do you switch from one flour to another for your starter?

You can switch at any time—no special steps needed. However, if you are concerned about switching flours, divide your starter in half, and stash one portion in the refrigerator—just in case.

Leave the other half of the starter on the counter and switch out the flour the next time you feed it. You do not have to slowly transition, just switch out the flours. Wait a few days (with continual daily feedings) before you try to make bread; however, starters are pretty resilient, and switching flours shouldn't cause any problems.

The Best Beginner Sourdough Bread Recipe

Just like making starters, there are dozens of ways to make a sourdough loaf. This recipe is perfect for people (like me) who like a simple, hearty loaf that doesn't require tons of effort and time. Start here, and then you can branch out to more complicated options in the future.

First, let's run through the simple equipment you'll need. You do NOT need a bakery full of fancy tools, but there are a few things that will make the process easier:

- **A five- or six-quart Dutch oven.** A Dutch oven does the very best job of baking sourdough loaves through mimicking the environment of a brick oven. This helps your homemade bread end up with a crusty outside and a soft center. If you don't want to use a Dutch oven, bake your loaf on a cookie sheet or baking stone instead. However, the crust of your finished sourdough will be different.

- **A large bowl.** Since this recipe rises overnight, use a bowl that's tall enough to avoid overflowing and the subsequent mess.

- **Bench scraper.** This little tool scrapes the dough out of the bowl and off the countertops without deflating it and ruining precious air bubbles. If you don't have a dough scraper, you can use a stiff spatula instead.

- **Proofing basket.** A proofing basket helps support the shape of the sourdough loaf during the final rise before baking. If you don't want to get proofing baskets, simply line a nine-inch bowl or colander with a linen tea towel that you've generously dusted with flour.

Ingredients

- ½ cup active sourdough starter *(see previous tips to determine if your starter is ready)*

- 1 ¼ cups lukewarm water

- 3 cups all-purpose flour

- 1 ½ teaspoons fine sea salt

Instructions

1. In a large bowl, combine the starter and water.

2. Stir in the flour, then sprinkle the salt on top.

3. Use a fork to mix everything together until it becomes stiff—then switch to your hands to bring the dough together in a rough ball. *Remember: don't overmix! This is supposed to be a no-knead-style wet dough.*

4. Keep the rough dough in the bowl, cover it, and let sit for thirty minutes.

5. After this resting time is complete, stretch and fold the dough a few times to form it into a ball. To do this, pick up one side of the dough (use wet hands so it doesn't stick to you). Let the weight of the dough stretch itself. Fold the dough over itself, then turn the dough ball a quarter turn and repeat. Allow the dough to rest for ten minutes. Repeat this process three more times.

6. Cover the dough with a clean dish towel and let it rise in a warm place overnight or until doubled in size (or about eight hours). I like to make the dough before bed and leave it in my turned-off oven (with the oven light on) to rise overnight.

7. The next morning (or after eight hours), turn the dough out onto your counter. Fold it over a couple of times to tighten it into a ball, then let sit for fifteen minutes.

8. After this resting period is complete, gently tighten the dough into a ball once more and place into a well-floured proof-

ing basket or a bowl lined with a well-floured dish towel. *Remember: don't add too much flour and do not knead the dough!*

9. Cover and rise for two to three hours, or until almost doubled.

10. Preheat the oven to 450°F.

11. Optional: sprinkle a thin layer of cornmeal in the bottom of a Dutch oven to prevent scorching on the bottom.

12. Tip the loaf out of the proofing basket onto a sheet of parchment. Lower the parchment into the Dutch oven.

13. Place the lid on the pot and bake for twenty minutes.

14. Remove the lid and bake for an additional thirty minutes, or until the loaf is deeply browned and crispy on top. (For a less crusty finish, bake for the entire time with the lid on.)

15. Move to a cooling rack and allow the loaf to cool completely before slicing it.

Common Bread Questions:

Why are my loaves dense and not rising?
Don't worry—it happens to the best of us. When sourdough bread dough doesn't rise, it's usually because the starter wasn't active enough. To remedy this problem, use a recently fed, active starter with lots of bubbles. Also, try using warm (not hot) water when you mix up the dough. If your bread doesn't rise properly, you can always use the loaf to make breadcrumbs.

Why did my loaf spread out flat?
Doughs that contain a lot of moisture tend to spread more than dryer doughs, so that could be the culprit. Try a few more

rounds of stretching and folding next time to help develop the tension in the dough a bit more.

How do you get a loaf with that lovely open crumb (aka big holes)?

If you want the loaves with the big open crumb and the bubbles that look like French bakery bread, the dough must be higher hydration (i.e., a wetter dough). The downfall to this is that wetter doughs are trickier to handle and take a little more finesse.

The first time I tried to make a high-hydration dough, it was a sticky MESS. Therefore, if you are a beginner, I highly recommend starting with a more standard dough texture like the recipe above. Once you get more comfortable with the process, start increasing the water in the dough and play around with different techniques for folding it.

Do I have to use all-purpose flour for this bread?

You can make sourdough bread with many different types of flour. However, if you're brand-new to sourdough, I recommend using all-purpose flour. It's far less finicky than heritage or whole-wheat flours, and it will rise more consistently for your first attempts. Bread flour is another great option since it has a higher protein content and lends itself well to springy loaves. All-purpose flour can vary greatly according to manufacturer, so if you have trouble with one brand, it's worth switching to see if another type is easier to handle.

How can I better handle my super-sticky dough?

If you're struggling with sticky, difficult dough, try dipping your hands into a bowl of cool water before you work it. It's tempting to keep adding more flour to the dough but fight the urge. A wetter, stickier dough, while more difficult to handle, produces a lighter, more pleasant loaf.

How can I make my sourdough loaves MORE sour?

I love the tangy taste of super-sour sourdough, too. There are a few ways to create a stronger-tasting sourdough loaf:

1. Use a higher ratio of flour to water when you feed your starter.

2. Use whole-grain flours to feed your starter (sour-producing bacteria seem to love them).

3. If your sourdough starter produces a brown liquid layer (aka the hooch), mix it back into the starter instead of pouring it off.

4. Use cool water and allow your dough to rise in a cooler location. This will extend the rise time and produce a sourer loaf.

How do I make my sourdough bread LESS sour?

Do the opposite of what's mentioned above. Feed your starter more often—at least twice per day. You can also help the loaves rise faster by putting them in an extra-warm location or by using extra starter in the bread recipe to help it rise faster.

Do I really have to cool the bread before eating it?

I know...it's cruel, isn't it?

Even though your kitchen now smells divine, resist cutting into your new bread until it completely cools to room temperature.

The reason? The loaf is still baking and developing texture as it cools. If you cut the bread open while it's hot, you'll crush the crumb. Plus, it'll dry out faster in storage.

How can I store my homemade sourdough bread?

Homemade sourdough is best eaten within forty-eight hours. I store mine at room temperature in a ziplock bag.

If you don't think you can eat the sourdough loaf within forty-eight hours, you can freeze the leftovers. Simply wrap it in plastic wrap or place it in a bag and it will keep in the freezer for up to two months.

★ ★ ★ ★ ★

RESOURCES

Online Resources

The Prairie Homestead: My personal blog with hundreds of recipes, tutorials, and how-tos for every part of your homesteading journey. *http://theprairiehomestead.com*

The Heritage Cooking Crash Course: Learn how to cook nourishing, homestead-style foods without spending your life in the kitchen (taught by yours truly). *http://homestead cookingclass.com*

Canning Made Easy: Learn how to safely and confidently preserve foods for later (also taught by me). *http://learnhow tocan.com*

The Old-Fashioned on Purpose Planner: Keep your old-fashioned life on track with this planner for homesteaders, by homesteaders. *http://prairieplanner.com*

Kids Cook Real Food: Online cooking class for kids that focuses on life skills. *https://theprairiehomestead.com/kidscook*

Rural Revival: Inspiration and mentorship for building rural communities. *https://www.ruralrevival.co*

Kitchen and Home

Genuine Beef Company: Our sustainably raised, grass-finished beef. Raised on the Wyoming prairie and shipped to your doorstep. *http://genuinebeefco.com*

Redmond Salt: My favorite unrefined sea salt. It's mined in the USA and is full of naturally occurring minerals. Use code HOMESTEAD for 15 percent off. *http://theprairiehomestead.com/salt*

Azure Standard: A bulk food buying co-op that delivers monthly. Go here to see if they deliver where you live: *https://theprairiehomestead.com/azure*

New England Cheesemaking Supply Company: A one-stop source for cheesemaking cultures, kits, and equipment. *http://theprairiehomestead.com/cheesemaking*

Toups & Co Organics: My favorite source for beef tallow balms and nontoxic makeup. *https://theprairiehomestead.com/makeup*

Harvest Guard Reusable Canning Lids: Conventional canning lids are designed for single-use, but these innovative lids can be used repeatedly, which saves money and reduces waste. *https://theprairiehomestead.com/canninglids*

NutriMill Grain Mills: My home grain mill of choice for freshly ground flour. *https://theprairiehomestead.com/mill*

Bite Toothpaste Bits: Zero-waste toothpaste and floss. *https://bitetoothpastebits.com*

Barnyard and Garden

Redmond Agriculture: At-home kits for testing your garden soil. Use code HOMESTEAD for 15 percent off every order. *https://theprairiehomestead.com/soiltest*

True Leaf Market: My preferred choice for organic, heirloom seeds. *https://theprairiehomestead.com/seeds*

St. Lawrence Nurseries: An excellent source of very cold-hardy fruit trees and bushes. *https://www.slngrow.com*

ENDNOTES

Chapter 2

"U.S. Agricultural Statistics—A History—and New Historical Timeline," U.S. Department of Agriculture, last modified February 21, 2017, *https://www.usda.gov/media/blog/2012/05/23/us-agricultural-statistics-history-and-new-historical-timeline*.

John Claudius Loudon, *A Treatise on Forming, Improving and Managing Country Residences* (Longman, Hurst, Rees, and Orme, 1806), 4.

Horace Smith and Paul Chatfield, *The Tin Trumpet*, 1859.

Mary Isabel Brush, "Woman on the Prairies: Pioneers Who Win Independence and Freedom in Their One-Room Homes" (*Colliers*, January 28, 1911).

Richard White, *Railroaded: The Transcontinentals and the Making of Modern America* (W. W. Norton & Company, 2011), Chapter 11.

Christine Frederick, *Selling Mrs. Consumer* (New York: The Business Bourse, 1929), 4.

Fatma Al-Maskari, "LIFESTYLE DISEASES: An Economic Burden on the Health Services," United Nations *UN Chronicle*, accessed August 20, 2022, *https://www.un.org/en/chronicle/article/lifestyle-diseases-economic-burden-health-services*.

Jean M. Twenge, "The Sad State of Happiness in the United States and the Role of Digital Media," *World Happiness Report*, last modified

March 20, 2019, *https://worldhappiness.report/ed/2019/the-sad-state-of-happiness-in-the-united-states-and-the-role-of-digital-media/.*

G.K. Chesterton, "The Drift from Domesticity," *The Thing* (S&W; First Edition, January 1, 1929), Chapter 4.

Chapter 3

Alfred Rehwinkhel, *Dr. Bessie: The Life Story and Romance of a Pioneer Lady Doctor on Our Western and the Canadian Frontier as Told by Herself and Here Presented in a Running Narrative by Her Husband* (St. Louis: Concordia Publishing House, 1963).

Maria Cohut, "How Can Our Health Benefit from Colder Temperatures?" *Medical News Today*, last modified December 1, 2017, *https://www.medicalnewstoday.com/articles/320214.*

Alice Park, "Tip for Insomniacs: Cool Your Head to Fall Asleep," *Time Magazine*, last modified June 17, 2011, *https://healthland.time.com/2011/06/17/tip-for-insomniacs-cool-your-head-to-fall-asleep/.*

Véronique Ouellet, Sébastien M. Labbé, Denis P. Blondin, Serge Phoenix, Brigitte Guérin, François Haman, Eric E. Turcotte, Denis Richard, and André C. Carpentier, "Brown Adipose Tissue Oxidative Metabolism Contributes to Energy Expenditure during Acute Cold Exposure in Humans," *The Journal of Clinical Investigation* 122, no. 2 (February 2012): 545–552, *https://www.jci.org/articles/view/60433?key=5e3684aee3d55b74adc8.*

David E. Levari, Daniel T. Gilbert, Timothy D. Wilson, Beau Sievers, David M. Amodio, and Thalia Wheatley, "Prevalence-Induced Concept Change in Human Judgment," *Science* 360, no. 6396 (June 29, 2018), *https://www.science.org/doi/10.1126/science.aap8731.*

Chapter 4

Lars T. Fadnes, Jan-Magnus Økland, Øystein A. Haaland, and Kjell Arne Johansson, "Estimating Impact of Food Choices on Life Expectancy: A Modeling Study," *PLOS Medicine Journal*, last modified February 8, 2022, *https://journals.plos.org/plosmedicine/article?id=10.1371/journal.pmed.1003889.*

Robert N. Spengler III, "The Silk Road Origins of the Foods We Eat,"

University of California Press, last modified January 5, 2022, *https:// www.ucpress.edu/blog/45550/the-silk-road-origins-of-the-foods-we-eat/*.

"Scotland to China and Back Again…10,000-Mile Trip to Your Table," *The Herald*, last modified August 21, 2009, *https://www.heraldscotland.com/ default_content/12765981.scotland-china-back-cods-10-000-mile-trip-table/*.

Jane Black, "What's in a Number? How the Press Got the Idea that Food Travels 1,500 Miles from Farm to Plate." *Slate Magazine*, last modified September 17, 2008, *https://slate.com/human-interest/2008/09/how-the-press-got-the-idea-that-food-travels-1500-miles-from-farm-to-plate.html*.

Mengyu Li, Nanfei Jia, Manfred Lenzen, Arunima Malik, Liyuan Wei, Yu-tong Jin, and David Raubenheimer, "Global Food-Miles Account for Nearly 20% of Total Food-Systems Emissions," *Nature Food* 3 (June 2022): 445–453, *https://doi.org/10.1038/s43016-022-00531-w*.

Dan Charles, "Why Lots of Grass-Fed Beef Sold in U.S. Comes from Down Under," NPR, last modified October 3, 2013, *https://www. npr.org/sections/thesalt/2013/10/04/228659915/why-most-grass-fed-beef-sold-in-u-s-comes-from-down-under*.

"Victory Gardens," U.S. Department of Agriculture. Miscellaneous Publication: Number 483, 1943, *https://www.nal.usda.gov/exhibits/ipd/small/ exhibits/show/victory-gardens/victory-garden-aids*.

Shannon J. Conk and Christine M. Porter, "Food Gardeners' Productivity in Laramie, Wyoming: More than a Hobby," *American Journal of Public Health* 106, no. 5 (May 1, 2016): 854–856, *https://doi.org/10.2105/ AJPH.2016.303108*.

C. Milesi, C. Elvidge, J. Dietz, B. Tuttle, R. Nemani, and S. Running, "A Strategy for Mapping and Modelling the Ecological Effects of U.S. Lawns," *Semantic Scholar*, published 2005, *https://www.semanticscholar. org/paper/A-STRATEGY-FOR-MAPPING-AND-MODELING-THE-ECOLOGICAL-Milesi-Elvidge/e351112504b670c36a7790b 1beba2d949ee2a516*.

Sharanbir S. Grewal and Parwinder S. Grewal, "Can Cities Become Self-Reliant in Food?" *Cities* 29, no. 1 (February 2012): 1-11, *https://doi. org/10.1016/j.cities.2011.06.003*.

Ann Wright, "Interactive Web Tool Maps Food Deserts, Provides Key

Data," U.S. Department of Agriculture, last modified April 30, 2021, *https://www.usda.gov/media/blog/2011/05/03/interactive-web-tool-maps-food-deserts-provides-key-data.*

Chapter 5

Carolyn Wyman, *Better Than Homemade: Amazing Food That Changed the Way We Eat* (Philadelphia: Quirk Books, 2004), 23.

"1950's Food TV Commercials," BlueLotusFilms, Footage from Prelinger Archives, last modified March 2, 2020, *https://www.youtube.com/watch?v=nU4ChEhKqiA.*

Karen Hamrick, "Americans Spend an Average of 37 Minutes a Day Preparing and Serving Food and Cleaning Up," Economic Research Service: United States Department of Agriculture, last modified November 7, 2016, *https://www.ers.usda.gov/amber-waves/2016/november/americans-spend-an-average-of-37-minutes-a-day-preparing-and-serving-food-and-cleaning-up/.*

Priceonomics, "Here's How Much Money You Save By Cooking At Home," *Forbes,* last modified July 10, 2018, *https://www.forbes.com/sites/priceonomics/2018/07/10/heres-how-much-money-do-you-save-by-cooking-at-home/?sh=7041931935e5.*

Eliana Zeballos and Brandon Restrepo, "Adult Eating and Health Patterns: Evidence from the 2014-16 Eating & Health Module of the American Time Use Survey," Economic Research Service: United States Department of Agriculture, last modified October 2018, *https://www.ers.usda.gov/webdocs/publications/90466/eib-198.pdf?v=2280.7.*

Michael Pollan, *The Omnivore's Dilemma: A Natural History of Four Meals* (New York: Penguin Press, 2006), 403-404.

"Benefits of Family Dinners," The Family Dinner Project, accessed May 10, 2022, *https://thefamilydinnerproject.org/about-us/benefits-of-family-dinners/.*

Chapter 6

Kelly Lambert, *Lifting Depression: A Neuroscientist's Hands-On Approach to Activating Your Brain's Healing Power* (New York: Basic Books, 2010).

Girija Kaimal, Kendra Ray, and Juan Muniz, "Reduction of Cortisol Levels and Participants' Responses following Art Making," *Journal of the American Art Therapy Association* 33, no. 2 (May 2016): 74-80, *https://doi.org/10.1080/07421656.2016.1166832.*

Nicholas A. Turiano, Avron Spiro, and Daniel K. Mroczek, "Openness to Experience and Mortality in Men: Analysis of Trait and Facets," *Journal of Aging and Health* 24, no. 4 (January 2012): 654–672, *https://doi.org/10.1177/0898264311431303.*

Matthew B. Crawford, *Shop Class as Soulcraft: An Inquiry into the Value of Work* (New York: Penguin Books, 2010), 155.

Benjamin Franklin, *The Autobiography of Benjamin Franklin* (Barnes & Noble Inc., 2005), 135.

Wendell Berry, *The Unsettling of America: Culture and Agriculture* (Berkeley: Counterpoint Press, 2004), 22-27.

Adam Smith, *The Wealth of Nations* (United Kingdom: Collier, 1902), 45.

Shannon Hayes, "Pushing Back against Consumer Culture," interview by Jill Winger, *Old-Fashioned on Purpose Podcast*, last modified August 15, 2022, *https://www.theprairiehomestead.com/tph_podcasts/season-10-episode-4-pushing-back-against-consumer-culture-with-shannon-hayes.*

Cal Newport, *Digital Minimalism: Choosing a Focused Life in a Noisy World* (London: Portfolio Publishing, 2019), 166.

Amy Dacyczyn, *The Complete Tightwad Gazette: Promoting Thrift as a Viable Alternative Lifestyle* (New York: Villard, 1998).

Mihaly Csikszentmihalyi, *Flow: The Psychology of Optimal Experience* (New York: Harper Perennial Modern Classics, 2008), 4.

Chapter 7

Michael Wolf, "Cana Unveils Molecular Beverage Printer, a 'Netflix for Drinks' That Can Make Nearly Any Type of Beverage," *The Spoon*, last modified January 24, 2022, *https://thespoon.tech/cana-unveils-molecular-beverage-printer-a-netflix-for-drinks-that-can-make-nearly-any-type-of-beverage/.*

Brandon H. Hidaka, "Depression as a Disease of Modernity: Explanations for Increasing Prevalence," *Journal of Affective Disorders* 140, no. 3 (November 2012): 205-214, *https://doi.org/10.1016/j.jad.2011.12.036.*

William Osler, "Lectures on Angina Pectoris and Allied States," Volume 64 of the *New York Medical Journal*, 1896, located in National Library of Medicine (U.S.), History of Medicine Division, *https://profiles.nlm.nih.gov/spotlight/gf/catalog/nlm:nlmuid-101743406X308-doc.*

World Health Organization, "Cardiovascular Diseases (CVDs)," last modified June 11, 2021, *https://www.who.int/en/news-room/fact-sheets/detail/cardiovascular-diseases-(cvds).*

Roundtable on Population Health Improvement; Board on Population Health and Public Health Practice; Institute of Medicine, "Business Engagement in Building Healthy Communities: Workshop Summary," *National Academies Press (US)*, (May 8, 2015), *https://doi.org/10.17226/19003.*

Alan Mozes, "Strength Training May Give Boost to Seniors' Brains," *U.S. News*, last modified April 23, 2012, *https://health.usnews.com/health-news/news/articles/2012/04/23/strength-training-may-give-boost-to-seniors-brains.*

Moira Lawler, "What Is Blue Light? A Complete Scientific Guide," *Everyday Health*, last modified June 21, 2021, *https://www.everydayhealth.com/wellness/what-is-blue-light-a-complete-scientific-guide/.*

Anne-Marie Chang, Daniel Aeschbach, Jeanne F. Duffy, and Charles A. Czeisler, "Research Progress about the Effect and Prevention of Blue Light on Eyes," *International Journal of Ophthalmology* 11, no. 12 (August 2018): 1999-2003, *https://doi.org/10.18240/ijo.2018.12.20.*

U.S. Department of Health and Human Services, "1 in 3 Adults Don't Get Enough Sleep," Centers for Disease Control and Prevention, last modified February 16, 2016, *https://www.cdc.gov/media/releases/2016/p0215-enough-sleep.html.*

Harvard Medical School, "Blue Light Has a Dark Side," Harvard Health Publishing, last modified July 7, 2020, *https://www.health.harvard.edu/staying-healthy/blue-light-has-a-dark-side.*

Laura Paddison, "The Argument for Switching Off Lights at Night," BBC, last modified July 19, 2021, *https://www.bbc.com/future/article/20210719-why-light-pollution-is-harming-our-wildlife.*

Lisa Marshall, "Why Dirt May Be Nature's Original Stress-Buster," University of Colorado-Boulder: *CU Boulder Today*, last modified May 5, 2019, *https://www.colorado.edu/today/2019/05/09/natures-original-stress-buster*.

Maja Vujcic, Jelena Tomicevic-Dubljevic, Mihailo Grbic, Dusica Lecic-Tosevski, Olivera Vukovic, and Oliver Toskovic, "Nature Based Solution for Improving Mental Health and Well-Being in Urban Areas," *Environmental Research* 128 (October 2017): 385-392, *https://doi.org/10.1016/j.envres.2017.06.030*.

Richard Thompson, "Gardening for Health: A Regular Dose of Gardening," *Clinical Medicine Journal* 18, no. 3 (June 2018): 201-205, *https://doi.org/10.7861/clinmedicine.18-3-201*.

David G. Smith, Roberta Martinelli, Gurdyal S. Besra, Petr A. Illarionov, Istvan Szatmari, Peter Brazda, Mary A. Allen, Wenqing Xu, Xiang Wang, László Nagy, Robin D. Dowell, Graham A. W. Rook, Laura Rosa Brunet, and Christopher A. Lowry, "Identification and Characterization of a Novel Anti-Inflammatory Lipid Isolated from Mycobacterium vaccae, a Soil-Derived Bacterium with Immunoregulatory and Stress Resilience Properties," *Psychopharmacology* 236, no. 5 (May 2019): 1653-1670, *https://doi.org/10.1007/s00213-019-05253-9*.

Kara Rodgers, "Biophilia Hypothesis," entry in *Britannica*, accessed March 5, 2022, *https://www.britannica.com/science/biophilia-hypothesis*.

N.E. Klepeis, W.C. Nelson, W.R. Ott, J.P. Robinson, A.M. Tsang, P. Switzer, J.V. Behar, S.C. Hern, and W.H. Engelmann, "The National Human Activity Pattern Survey (NHAPS): A Resource for Assessing Exposure to Environmental Pollutants," *Journal of Exposure Science & Environmental Epidemiology* 11 (July 2001): 231–252, *https://doi.org/10.1038/sj.jea.7500165*.

Gaétan Chevalier, Stephen T. Sinatra, James L. Oschman, Karol Sokal, and Pawel Sokal, "Earthing: Health Implications of Reconnecting the Human Body to the Earth's Surface Electrons," *Journal of Environmental and Public Health* 2012 (January 2012), *https://doi.org/10.1155/2012/291541*.

Richard Louv, *Last Child in the Woods: Saving Our Children from Nature-Deficit Disorder* (New York: Algonquin Books, 2008), 58.

Chapter 8

Trevor Wheelwright, "2022 Cell Phone Usage Statistics: How Obsessed Are We?" *Reviews.org*, last modified January 24, 2022, *https://www.reviews.org/mobile/cell-phone-addiction/*.

Drew Wilkinson, "Screen Time Trends in the Age of COVID-19," *Beyond Texting*, last modified June 8, 2021, *https://simpletexting.com/screen-time-survey/*.

Tristan Harris, "How Technology is Hijacking Your Mind—from a Magician and Google Design Ethicist," *Thrive Global*, last modified May 18, 2016, *https://medium.com/thrive-global/how-technology-hijacks-peoples-minds-from-a-magician-and-google-s-design-ethicist-56d62ef5edf3*.

Rachael Pells, "Giving Your Child a Smartphone Is Like Giving Them a Gram of Cocaine, Says Top Addiction Expert," *Independent*, last modified June 7, 2017, *https://www.independent.co.uk/news/education/education-news/child-smart-phones-cocaine-addiction-expert-mandy-saligari-harley-street-charter-clinic-technology-teenagers-a7777941.html*.

Gary Small and Gigi Vorgan, *iBrain: Surviving the Technological Alteration of the Modern Mind* (William Morrow Paperbacks, 2009), Chapter 1.

Joseph Firth, John Torous, Brendon Stubbs, Josh A. Firth, Genevieve Z. Steiner, Lee Smith, Mario Alvarez-Jimenez, John Gleeson, Davy Vancampfort, Christopher J. Armitage, and Jerome Sarris, "The 'Online Brain': How the Internet May Be Changing Our Cognition," *World Psychiatry: Official Journal of the World Psychiatric Association* 18, no. 2 (June 2019): 119–129, *https://doi.org/10.1002/wps.20617*.

Sherrie Bourg Carter, "6 Reasons You Should Spend More Time Alone," *Psychology Today*, last modified January 31, 2012, *https://www.psychology today.com/us/blog/high-octane-women/201201/6-reasons-you-should-spend-more-time-alone*.

Health Essentials, "An Ode to Silence: Why You Need It in Your Life," Cleveland Clinic, last modified August 7, 2020, *https://health.clevelandclinic.org/why-you-need-more-silence-in-your-life/*.

Nikola Tesla, "An Inventor's Seasoned Ideas: Nikola Tesla, Pointing to 'Grievous Errors' of the Past," interview by Orrin E. Dunlap Jr., *New York Times*, April 8, 1934.

Moira Burke and Robert E. Kraut, "The Relationship between Facebook Use and Well-Being Depends on Communication Type and Tie Strength," *Journal of Computer-Mediated Communication* 21, no. 4 (July 1, 2016): 265–281, *https://academic.oup.com/jcmc/article/21/4/265/4161784*.

Robert Putnam, *Bowling Alone: The Collapse and Revival of American Community* (New York: Simon & Schuster, 2020), 399.

Ryan J. Dwyer, Kostadin Kushlev, and Elizabeth W. Dunn, "Smartphone Use Undermines Enjoyment of Face-to-Face Social Interactions," *Journal of Experimental Social Psychology* 78 (September 2018): 233-239, *https://doi.org/10.1016/j.jesp.2017.10.007.*

Chapter 9

Sierra Dawn Stoneberg Holt, "Reinterpreting the 1882 Bison Population Collapse," *Rangelands* 40, no. 4 (August 2018): 106-114, *https://doi.org/10.1016/j.rala.2018.05.004.*

Dan Flores, *American Serengeti: The Last Big Animals of the Great Plains* (Kansas: University Press of Kansas, 2017), 3.

Kathy Weiser-Alexander, "Kiowa—Nomadic Warriors of the Plains," Legends of America, last modified November 2021, *https://www.legendsofamerica.com/na-kiowa/.*

Leo Horrigan, Robert S. Lawrence, and Polly Walker, "How Sustainable Agriculture Can Address the Environmental and Human Health Harms of Industrial Agriculture," *Environmental Health Perspectives* 110, no. 5 (May 2002): 445–456, *https://www.ncbi.nlm.nih.gov/pmc/articles/PMC1240832/pdf/ehp0110-000445.pdf.*

"Prairies and Grasslands," National Park Service, last modified October 27, 2021, *https://www.nps.gov/tapr/learn/nature/prairies-and-grasslands.htm.*

Kat Kerlin, "Grasslands More Reliable Carbon Sink than Trees," UC Davis, last modified July 9, 2018, *https://climatechange.ucdavis.edu/climate/news/grasslands-more-reliable-carbon-sink-than-trees.*

Wayne A. White, "Pasture Management and Carbon Sequestration: Healthy, Diverse Pastures Are Natural 'Carbon Sinks,'" *Mother Earth News*, last modified May 9, 2014, *https://www.motherearthnews.com/homesteading-and-livestock/livestock/pasture-management-zmgz14jjzsto/.*

Roadsides for Wildlife, "Put Down Some Roots, Plant Prairie," State of Minnesota, Department of Natural Resources, 2008, *https://files.dnr.state.mn.us/assistance/nrplanning/community/roadsidesforwildlife/putdownroots_poster.pdf.*

Tallgrass Ontario, "Tallgrass Prairie and Carbon Sequestration," accessed
    April 2, 2022, *https://tallgrassontario.org/wpsite/carbon-sequestration/#:*:text=
    Photosynthesis%20is%20the%20biochemical%20process,as%20a%20
    %E2%80%9Ccarbon%20sink%E2%80%9D.*

Meriwether Lewis, *History of the Expedition under the Command of Captains
    Lewis and Clark, to the Sources of the Missouri, Thence across the Rocky
    Mountains and down the River Columbia to the Pacific Ocean: Performed dur-
    ing the Years 1804-5-6. By Order of the Government of the United States,*
    Volume 2 (New York: Bradford and Inskeep, 1814), 420.

Albert Howard, *An Agricultural Testament* (Oxford: Benediction Classics,
    2010)

Mariko Thorbecke and Jon Dettling, "Carbon Footprint Evaluation of
    Regenerative Grazing at White Oak Pastures," *Quantis*, last modified
    February 25, 2019, *https://blog.whiteoakpastures.com/hubfs/WOP-LCA-
    Quantis-2019.pdf.*

"Food Waste in America in 2022," *RTS*, accessed April 2, 2022, *https://www.
    rts.com/resources/guides/food-waste-america/#:*:text=Here's%20some%20
    %E2%80%9Cfood%E2%80%9D%20for%20thought,80%20billion%20
    pounds%20%E2%80%94%20every%20year.*

Frank Mitloehner, "The Carbon Impact of Food Waste: The Problem with
    What We're NOT Eating," Clarity and Leadership for Environmen-
    tal Awareness and Research at UC Davis, last modified November 13,
    2020, *https://clear.ucdavis.edu/blog/carbon-impact-food-waste-problem-what-
    were-not-eating.*

Maureen Breen, "The Value of Backyard Chickens in Reducing Municipal
    Solid Waste," West Chester University Doctoral Projects, last modified
    Spring 2019, *https://digitalcommons.wcupa.edu/all_doctoral/33/.*

Christina Troitino, "Americans Waste about a Pound of Food a Day, USDA
    Study Finds," *Forbes*, last modified April 23, 2018, *https://www.forbes.
    com/sites/christinatroitino/2018/04/23/americans-waste-about-a-pound-of-
    food-a-day-usda-study-finds/?sh=5bd7712c4ec3.*

Liza Gross, "More than 90 Percent of Americans Have Pesticides or Their
    Byproducts in Their Bodies," *The Nation*, last modified March 21, 2019,
    https://www.thenation.com/article/archive/pesticides-farmworkers-agriculture/.

"PAN International List of Highly Hazardous Pesticides," last modified March 2021, *https://pan-international.org/wp-content/uploads/PAN_HHP_List.pdf.*

Bee Informed Partnership, "Loss & Management Survey," *Bee Informed*, accessed August 30, 2022, *https://beeinformed.org/citizen-science/loss-and-management-survey/.*

Juliana McDonald, "Curbing America's Trash Production: Statistics and Solutions," *Dumpsters.com*, last modified July 13, 2022, *https://www.dumpsters.com/blog/us-trash-production#:*:text=As%20Americans%2C%20we%20create%20an,re%20on%20the%20high%20end.*

Heather A. Leslie, Martin J.M. van Velzen, Sicco H. Brandsma, A. Dick Vethaak, Juan J. Garcia-Vallejo, and Marja H. Lamoree, "Discovery and Quantification of Plastic Particle Pollution in Human Blood," *Environment International* 163 (May 2022), *https://doi.org/10.1016/j.envint.2022.107199.*

Andrew Krosofsky, "What Percentage of Recycling Actually Gets Recycled?" *GreenMatters*, last modified March 16, 2021, *https://www.greenmatters.com/p/what-percent-recycling-actually-gets-recycled.*

Valentina Portela, "The Fashion Industry Waste Is Drastically Contributing to Climate Change," *CALPIRG*, last modified March 9, 2021, *https://pirg.org/california/articles/the-fashion-industry-waste-is-drastically-contributing-to-climate-change/#:*:text=85%25%20Of%20Our%20Clothes%20End%20Up%20In%20Landfills%20Or%20Burned&text=Furthermore%2C%20it%20is%20estimated%20that,11%2Dyear%2Dold%20child!.*

Chapter 10

Steven Mintz, *Huck's Raft: A History of American Childhood* (Cambridge: Belknap Press, 2006).

Peter Gray, *Free to Learn: Why Unleashing the Instinct to Play Will Make Our Children Happier, More Self-Reliant, and Better Students for Life* (New York: Basic Books, 2013), 113-128.

Michael M. Chouinard, "Children's Questions: A Mechanism for Cognitive Development," Monograph for *Society for Research in Child Development* 72, no. 1 (June 2008): vii-ix, 1-126. *https://doi.org/10.1111/j.1540-5834.2007.00412.x.*

Susan Engel, "Children's Need to Know: Curiosity in Schools," *Harvard Educational Review* 81, no. 4 (Winter 2011): 625-645, *https://doi.org/10.17763/haer.81.4.h054131316473115*.

Gray, *Free to Learn*, 175.

Lee Alan Dugatkin and Sarina Rodrigues, "Games Animals Play," *Greater Good Magazine*, last modified March 1, 2008, *https://greatergood.berkeley.edu/article/item/games_animals_play*.

Jessica Lahey, *The Gift of Failure: How the Best Parents Learn to Let Go So Their Children Can Succeed* (New York: Harper Press, 2015), xii.

Scott Sampson, *How to Raise a Wild Child: The Art and Science of Falling in Love with Nature* (Boston: Mariner Books, 2016), 5.

Andrea Faber Taylor and Frances E Kuo, "Children with Attention Deficits Concentrate Better after Walk in the Park," *Journal of Attention Disorders* 12, no.5 (March 2009): 402-409, *https://doi.org/10.1177/1087054708323000*.

Nancy M. Wells and Gary W. Evans, "Nearby Nature: A Buffer of Life Stress among Rural Children," *Sage Journals: Environmental & Behavior* 25, no. 3 (May 2003): 311-330, *https://doi.org/10.1177/0013916503035003001*.

Nassim Nicholas Taleb, *Antifragile: Things that Gain from Disorder* (New York: Random House Publishing Group, 2014), 3.

Ellen Sandseter, "Children's Risky Play from an Evolutionary Perspective," *Evolutionary Psychology* 9 (2011): 257-284, *https://doi.org/10.1177/147470491100900212*.

Mariana Brussoni, Takuro Ishikawa, Sara Brunelle, and Susan Herrington, "Landscapes for Play: Effects of an Intervention to Promote Nature-Based Risky Play in Early Childhood Centres," *Journal of Environment Psychology* 54 (December 2017): 139-150. *https://doi.org/10.1016/j.jenvp.2017.11.001*.

David Finkelhor, "Trends in Adverse Childhood Experiences (ACEs) in the United States," *Child Abuse & Neglect* 108 (July 2020), *https://doi.org/10.1016/j.chiabu.2020.104641*.

Josef Riedler, Charlotte Braun-Fahrländer, Waltraud Eder, Mynda Schreuer,

Marco Waser, Soyoun Maisch, David Carr, Rudi Schierl, Dennis Nowak, Erika von Mutius, and the ALEX Study Team, "Exposure to Farming in Early Life and Development of Asthma and Allergy: A Cross-Sectional Survey," *The Lancet* 358, no. 9288 (October 2001): 1129-1133, https://doi.org/10.1016/S0140-6736(01)06252-3.

Michelle M. Stein, Cara L. Hrusch, Justyna Gozdz, Catherine Igartua, Vadim Pivniouk, Sean E. Murray, Julie G. Ledford, Mauricius Marques dos Santos, Rebecca L. Anderson, Nervana Metwali, Julia W. Neilson, and Raina M. Maier, "Innate Immunity and Asthma Risk in Amish and Hutterite Farm Children," *The New England Journal of Medicine* 375 (August 2016): 411-421, https://doi.org/10.1056/NEJMoa1508749.

Caterina Almqvist, A.C. Egmar, G. Hedlin, M. Lundqvist, S.L. Nordvall, G. Pershagen, M. Svartengren, M. van Hage-Hamsten, M. Wickman, "Direct and Indirect Exposure to Pets—Risk of Sensitization and Asthma at 4 Years in a Birth Cohort" *Clinical and Experimental Allergy: Journal of the British Society for Allergy and Clinical Immunology* 33 (October 2003): 1190-1197, https://doi.org/10.1046/j.1365-2222.2003.01764.x.

FDA, "Antibacterial Soap? You Can Skip It, Use Plain Soap and Water," U.S. Food & Drug Administration, last modified May 16, 2019, https://www.fda.gov/consumers/consumer-updates/antibacterial-soap-you-can-skip-it-use-plain-soap-and-water.

Chapter 11

Emilie Durkheim, *The Elementary Forms of Religious Life* (Library of Alexandria, 1954).

Richard Fry and Kim Parker, "Rising Share of U.S. Adults Are Living without a Spouse or Partner," Pew Research Center, last modified October 5, 2021, https://www.pewresearch.org/social-trends/2021/10/05/rising-share-of-u-s-adults-are-living-without-a-spouse-or-partner/.

Daniel A. Cox, "The State of American Friendship: Change, Challenges, and Loss," Survey Center on American Life, last modified June 8, 2021, https://www.americansurveycenter.org/research/the-state-of-american-friendship-change-challenges-and-loss/.

Leslie Davis and Kim Parker, "A Half-Century after 'Mister Rogers' Debut, 5 Facts about Neighbors in U.S.," Pew Research Center, last modified August 15, 2019, *https://www.pewresearch.org/fact-tank/2019/08/15/ facts-about-neighbors-in-u-s/.*

Julianne Holt-Lunstad, Timothy B. Smith, J. Bradley Layton, "Social Re- lationships and Mortality Risk: A Meta-Analytic Review," *PLOS Medicine* 7, no. 7 (July 2010), *https://journals.plos.org/plosmedicine/ article?id=10.1371/journal.pmed.1000316#abstract1.*

Julianne Holt-Lunstad, *Testimony before the US Senate Aging Committee* (April 27, 2017), *https://www.aging.senate.gov/imo/media/doc/SCA_Holt_04_27_17. pdf.*

Mabel Lewis Stuart, "The Lady Honyocker: How Girls Take Up Claims of Their Own on the Prairie," *The Independent* (July 1913): 133-137.

Amy Armstrong, "Homesteading with a Chaperon," *Sunset Magazine* (June 1916), 25-26.

Danna Larson, "How to Grow a Thriving Business in a Small Town," in- terview by Jill Winger, *Old-Fashioned on Purpose Podcast*, last modi- fied August 31, 2022, *https://www.theprairiehomestead.com/tph_podcasts/ s5-e12-how-to-grow-a-thriving-business-in-a-small-town-with-dana-larson- of-rural-revival-2.*

Theodore Roosevelt, "The Man in the Arena," *Citizenship in a Republic* (April 23, 1910).

Sherry Turkle, *Reclaiming Conversation: The Power of Talk in a Digital Age* (London: Penguin Books, 2016), 23.

Chapter 12

Rev. L.P. Fagan, *The Wave Length of God, Memorable Experiences during Fifty Years as a Methodist Minister* (1958), information shared by Don Hodg- son in *Chugwater Prairie Press* (2013), *https://www.chugwater.com/_pdfs/ PrairiePress/2013/December%202013.pdf.*

Laura Ingalls Wilder letter to children, February 1947.

Wendell Berry, *Life is a Miracle: An Essay against Modern Superstition* (Berke- ley: Counterpoint Press, 2001), 54. Kindle.

Henry David Thoreau, *Walden* (NGN Books, 2022), 7. Kindle.

Steven Pressfield, *The War of Art: Break Through the Blocks and Win Your Inner Creative Battles* (New York: Black Irish Entertainment LLC, 2012), 6.

Pressfield, *The War of Art*, 79.

Viktor E. Frankl, *Man's Search for Meaning* (New York: Washington Square Press, 1984), 135.

ACKNOWLEDGMENTS

While writing is often a solitary endeavor, publishing a book is not. I'm continually amazed at how many people come together to birth a book. I'm convinced my crew is one of the best.

My husband, Christian, remains my number one cheerleader, counselor, and behind-the-scenes support. He kept our complicated life flowing while I was in creative mode and knows exactly when to tell me to step away from the computer and go ride my horse. He's a good man.

My children—Mesa, Bridger, and Sage—were patient throughout the long process and never complained when Mom had to go write "just a little bit more." Their continual questions, wonder, and curiosity for this old-fashioned life inspire me every day.

My agent, Sarah Passick, and the team at Park & Fine, championed the vision and message of this book from the very earliest conversations. I'm so honored to have this second book represented by them.

Julie Cantrell came along at the perfect time and was invaluable in shaping and refining my ideas, as well as faithfully encouraging me along the way. I can't imagine anyone better to have had as a collaborator.

I'm grateful to Park Row for so enthusiastically taking a chance on a cookbook author turned nonfiction writer. Erika Imranyi, my editor, was instrumental in streamlining the manuscript and taking my message to a whole new level (all while growing tomatoes and making pickles in the process!).

Rory Feek not only agreed to author the foreword, but also provided gentle words of encouragement along the way. Dr. Caitlin Youngquist generously reviewed and amended my information about sustainable agriculture to make sure I was on the right track. Rex Lockman and Justin Derner offered their expertise regarding Wyoming's grasslands. Don Hodgson provided extensive knowledge of Chugwater's history. And Katie Kimball kindly allowed me to interview her and glean insights into raising autonomous kids.

And finally, our incredible team of employees picked up the slack across our multiple businesses so I could focus on this massive undertaking. Cris Daining, my right-hand woman, kept my blog and inbox functioning, in addition to organizing my research and endnotes. Taran Whelchel and Kayla Visser stepped up to aid with countless homestead projects, Michelle Visser kept the podcast and other projects trucking along behind the scenes, and Kayce Lovett and the entire soda fountain crew faithfully ran the restaurant while I disappeared into book-land.

A million thanks to all of you. I cannot fully express how honored I am to have you as a part of my village.

INDEX

cardiovascular disease and, 176

convenience and ease from, 43–44

costs of, 44–46

early revolution of, 40–41

of farming, 204–6, 207

food and, 75, 79–81, 209

relief of stress and, 145–46

specialization and, 148

insects

ants, 237-38

barrier cloths in gardens, 223

homemade sprays and, 223–24

pesticides and, 222

plants for, 219

intentionality, 24–25

J

journey to old-fashioned on purpose

excuses not to embark on, 291–92

inner opposition to, 293–94

intuition and, 295

permission to embark upon, 292–93

stages of, 26–27

step-by-step guidelines for, 66–67

Wingers' early homesteading days, 28–33

K

Kids Cook Real Food (Kimball), 251

Kids Cook Real Food (website), 299

Kimball, Katie, 251, 253

L

Lahey, Jessica, 245–46

Lambert, Kelly, 144

Larson, Danna, 271–72

Last Child in the Woods (Louv), 184

laundry, 169–70

lawns, 94

leadership, 273–74

learning

curiosity and, 238, 239, 240–42

homeschooling, 240

play and, 238, 239, 244

questions and, 239, 242

from real-life experiences, 238

self-education, 238

sociability and, 238, 239

Lifting Depression (Lambert), 144

light, exposure to, 179–82, 186

lip balm recipe, 156–57

livestock

advantages of holistic approach to meat production, 102, 208–9

manure from, 215–16

methane emissions from, 212

skin moisturizer from beef tallow, 165–66

using every part, 102

Logsdon, Gene, 215

Louv, Richard, 184

M

"The Man in the Arena" (Roosevelt), 273–74

manual tasks, 143–47

S

Sacred Cow: The Case for (Better) Meat (Rodgers and Wolf), 210–11

Salmon-Safe, 210

Sampson, Scott, 248

Sandseter, Ellen, 255–56

scraps
    composting, 213–16
    repurposing, 103, 108–9, 163, 213
    using as skin moisturizer, 165–66

screen usage, 190–91
    See also cell phones

Second Nature (Pollan), 86

"seed libraries," 96

seed saving, 96–97

self-esteem, developing in children, 251–55

self-regulation, risky play and, 256

serotonin, 144

Shop Class as Soulcraft (Crawford), 145

skin care, 165–66

sleep and blue light, 179–80

slow cooker candles recipe, 153–54

Small, Gary, 191

Smith, Adam, 148

sociability and learning, 239

socialization and risky play, 256

social media
    controlling, 200–201
    Facebook, 196
    mindless scrolling of, 196
    personalized, intentional use of, 198

retro homesteading movement and, 198

risky parts of relationships and, 280–81

soil
    compost and, 214–16
    cover crops and, 217–19
    health of, 108
    mulch and, 95

solitude
    cell phones and, 189, 192
    importance of, 192–93
    scheduling time for, 193

sourdough starter recipe, 126–28

specialization, 147–49

sprouts, growing, 93

St. Lawrence Nurseries, 301

Steamboat (horse), 271

stewardship of Earth
    barriers to producers and, 206
    industrial farming and, 204–6
    starting steps, 204

stone soup suppers, 279–80

Stout, Ruth, 220

stress
    gardening as relieving, 98–100
    nature as moderating childhood, 248
    working with hands to reduce, 143–47

Stuart, Mabel Lewis, 266

Swan Land and Cattle Company, 271

T

Taleb, Nassim Nicholas, 255

technology
    attention spans and, 191